TALKING CHIPS

 **NATIONAL'S SEMICONDUCTOR TECHNOLOGY SERIES**

Books in the Series:

Thomas M. Frederiksen   INTUITIVE IC ELECTRONICS
Nelson Morgan   TALKING CHIPS

TALKING CHIPS

Nelson Morgan

With special contributions from Jake Buurma and Lloyd Rice

Cartoons by Beatrice Benjamin

McGraw-Hill Book Company

New York St. Louis San Francisco Auckland
Bogotá Hamburg Johannesburg London Madrid Mexico
Montreal New Delhi Panama Paris São Paulo
Singapore Sydney Tokyo Toronto

Library of Congress Cataloging in Publication Data

Morgan, Nelson.
  Talking chips.

  (National's semiconductor technology series)
  Bibliography: p.
  Includes index.
  1. Speech synthesis.   I. Buurma, Jake.   II. Rice,
Lloyd.   III. Benjamin, Beatrice.   IV. Title.
V. Series.
TK7882.S65M67   1984   621.3819   83-14914
ISBN 0-07-043107-8

Copyright © 1984 by McGraw-Hill, Inc. Cartoons copyright © by Beatrice Benjamin. All rights reserved. Printed in the United States of America. Except as permitted under the United States Copyright Act of 1976, no part of this publication may be reproduced or distributed in any form or by any means, or stored in a data base or retrieval system, without the prior written permission of the publisher.

1234567890   DOCDOC   89210987654

ISBN 0-07-043107-8

The editors for this book were Harry Helms and Susan Thomas, the designer was Jules Perlmutter, and the production supervisor was Thomas G. Kowalczyk. It was set in Primer by Santype-Byrd.

Printed and bound by R. R. Donnelley & Sons Company.

CONTENTS

FOREWORD	vii
PREFACE	ix
ACKNOWLEDGMENTS	xi
INTRODUCTION	1

Chapter 1 SPEECH SYNTHESIS — 7
1.1 Introduction — 7
1.2 Speech Perception and Production — 9
1.3 Time-Domain Synthesis — 17
1.4 Frequency-Domain Synthesis — 25

Chapter 2 SPEECH HARDWARE CONSIDERATIONS — 35
2.1 Introduction — 35
2.2 Analog vs. Digital Hardware — 35
2.3 Hardware for Discrete Time Processing of Signals — 39
2.4 Automated Design Tools — 53
2.5 The Berkeley Vocoder — 55

Chapter 3 SOME REAL CHIPS — 59
3.1 Introduction — 59
3.2 General-Purpose DSPs — 60
3.3 Dedicated Digital Synthesizers — 65
3.4 Analog Speech Synthesizers — 84

Chapter 4 ANALYSIS FOR SYNTHESIS — 89
4.1 Introduction — 89
4.2 Speech Spectrum Estimation — 89
4.3 Classification and Pitch Tracking — 99

Chapter 5 SYNTHESIS BY RULE   105

5.1 Introduction   105
5.2 Major Considerations for Formant Rules   106
5.3 A Phonetic Rule in Action   108
5.4 Generating Parameters by Rule   110
5.5 Duration and Intonation   112
5.6 Applications for Synthesis by Rule   113

Chapter 6 AUDIO FOR SPEECH ANALYSIS   115

6.1 Introduction   115
6.2 Original Recordings for Speech Analysis   116
6.3 Evaluation of Synthetic Speech   139

Chapter 7 WHAT'S NEXT?   145

7.1 Introduction   145
7.2 Make Your Own Speech   145
7.3 Residual-Driven Synthetic Speech   148
7.4 Music and Effects   149
7.5 Speech Recognition   152
7.6 Finale   155

Appendix A THE SHORT-TERM SPECTRUM   157

A.1 Introduction   157
A.2 Fourier Analysis   157
A.3 Windowing   158

Appendix B DISCRETE TIME SIGNAL PROCESSING   161

B.1 Sampled Signals   161
B.2 Filtering of Discrete Time Signals   165

Appendix C VOCABULARY GENERATION—DIGITALKER® II   167

C.1 Nuts and Bolts   167

MORE ADVANCED READING   168
GLOSSARY OF TERMS AND ABBREVIATIONS   169
INDEX   175

FOREWORD

The development of algorithms that can be used in computers to simulate human speech has been a research topic for a number of years. Until recently, these algorithms could only be implemented with the fastest special-purpose computers. This restricted their use to demonstrations performed in research laboratories. The advances of integrated circuit technology have now made it possible to implement the high-speed calculations on a single chip and have therefore dramatically opened up the number of potential applications for which speech can be used. In this book, Morgan has demystified the technology that makes it possible for integrated circuits to talk. I am sure he hopes, as I do, that a number of the readers of this book will take the next step of determining which speech applications will really be useful.

In the near future, the same technology that makes speech synthesis possible will be applied to speech recognition, which will give the computers the capability of listening. We can only hope that Morgan will unravel the complexities of these "listening chips" in the same humorous way as he has done it for the "talking chips."

R. W. Brodersen
Professor, U. C. Berkeley

For Sharon

PREFACE

Synthetic speech has been discussed at length in a number of excellent texts, some of which are listed at the end of Appendix C. It is only recently, however, that high-density integrated circuit (IC) techniques have brought speech technology to the consumer. The inquisitive user of speech products will want to understand the basics of these gadgets. This book is an attempt to bridge the gap between graduate-level texts and marketing hype.

Talking chips have developed from a fusion of disciplines including mathematical signal processing, microcomputers, electronics design, and acoustics. It is unlikely that many readers will have a strong background in more than one of these areas. Consequently, I have attempted to emphasize concepts and examples over theory and rigor.

The Introduction and Chapters 1 through 3 cover the topic of speech synthesis systems. The Introduction suggests some whys and wherefores for the technology. Chapter 1 provides a basis for the speech theory. Chapter 2 shows the range of hardware options to implement these theoretical notions. Chapter 3 is a collection of case histories of real speech chips.

Chapters 4 through 6 describe the process of parameter generation for speech synthesis systems. Chapter 4 discusses techniques for analysis of natural speech. Chapter 5 introduces phonetic rules for automatic synthesis from text or phonetic symbols. Chapter 6 covers the commonly ignored audio and acoustic considerations for recording and playback of speech.

Chapter 7 is a brief overview of the projected future for this technology.

Appendixes A and B are provided to explain a few background points about signal processing. Appendix C outlines the creative process of vocabulary generation for fixed-vocabulary synthetic speech.

Jargon has been deemphasized where possible, but there were certainly places where it had to be used. For example, Chapter 3 assumes some familiarity with the more common IC and microprocessor terms. The intrepid reader without appropriate background can make use of the glossary at the back of this book.

I had a lot of fun writing this book. I hope you enjoy reading it.

Nelson Morgan

ACKNOWLEDGMENTS

There are several people who were major forces toward the completion of this book. First and foremost was Bryan Costales, who contributed countless hours reading and correcting my scribbles in an attempt to make them intelligible. Lloyd Rice and Jake Buurma contributed the raw material for Chapters 3 and 5. Artist-at-large Beatrice Benjamin provided the drawings that may have saved this from being just another technical book. Finally, Harry Helms must be congratulated for pushing me into writing the book.

Many others assisted as well. Excuse me if I miss some of you, but here goes. Thanks to:

Juniper
Max Hauser
Hy Murveit
Steve Pope
Joe Santos
David Isenberg
Tom Frederiksen

Bob Brodersen
Joe Costello
R. F. Morgan
D. Thrall of the Telephone Museum
B. J. Morgan
Geri, Ben, and Soma
My ex-wives

and to the myriad researchers who have shared their experience so freely in casual conversations.

TALKING CHIPS

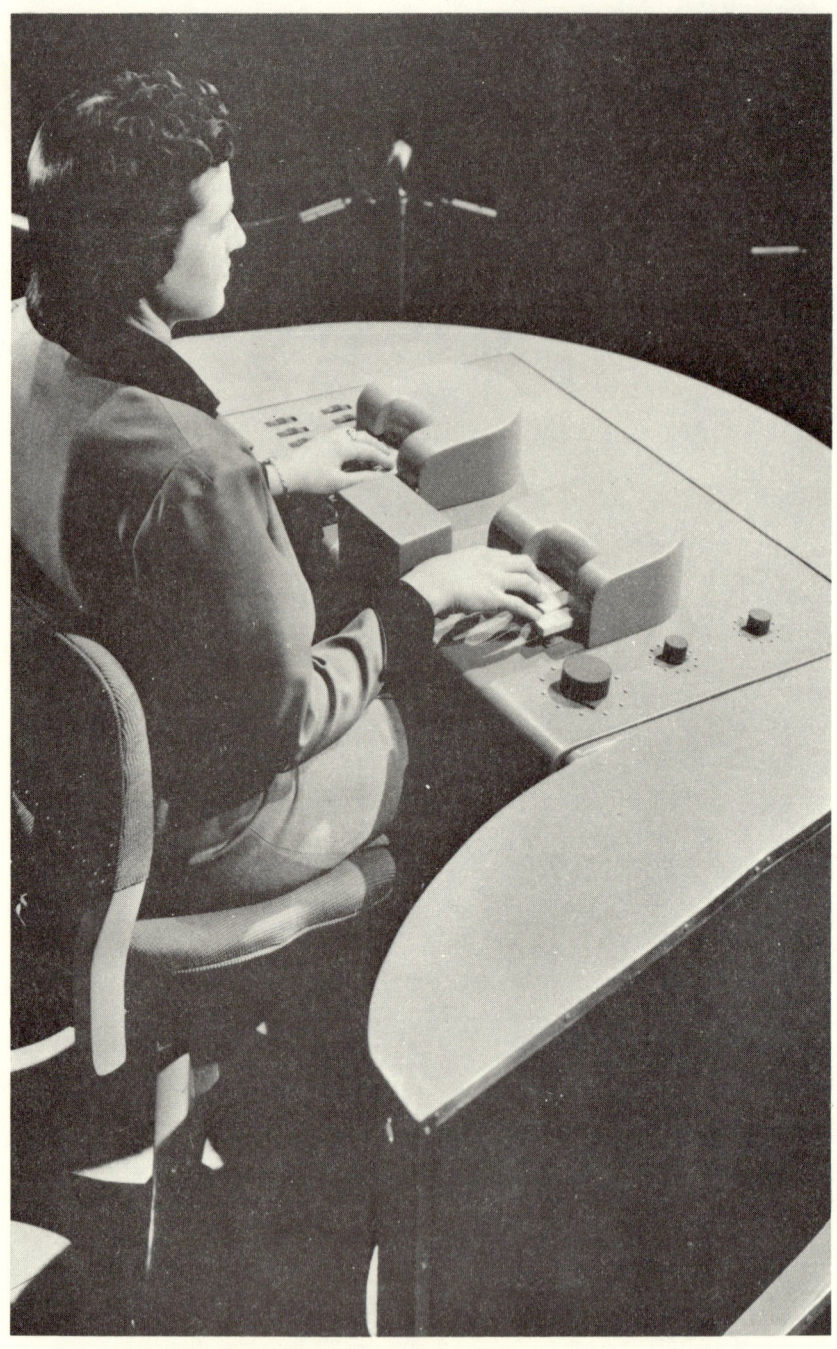

INTRODUCTION

FOR RELEASE
in Morning Papers
January 6, 1939

THE VODER

An electrical device which, under control of an operator at a keyboard, actually talks was demonstrated on January 5 at the Franklin Institute, Philadelphia. Known as the VODER, it is a development of Bell Telephone Laboratories as a scientific novelty to make an interesting educational exhibit for the Bell System's displays at the San Francisco Exposition and at the World's Fair in New York. It is built, except for its keys, entirely of apparatus used in everyday telephone service.

The VODER creates speech.

The VODER[1] (Voice Operation DEmonstratoR) was not a standalone talking machine. It was played like an instrument by a trained operator. The resulting acoustic output, however, bore a striking resemblance to the human voice. Someone would say, "How are you today, VODER?" The operator would manipulate keys and pedals and VODER would respond, "Fine. How are you?" This was entertaining and intellectually enticing as it showed how far the science of that time had come in its understanding of the production of speech.

The principal architect of this electrical marvel was a Bell Laboratories researcher named Homer Dudley. He did not, of course, create his VODER in a conceptual vacuum. Thinkers as far back as the Greeks have been intrigued with the idea of talking automata. Actual mechanical talking machines were built as long ago as 1779 by innovators like Kratzenstein and Von Kempelen. Vibrating reeds meant to simulate our vocal cords were connected to resonant chambers analogous to our vocal tract. While the speech quality must have been quite poor, these machines reputedly did work for discrete sounds.

It was not until Homer Dudley's VODER, however, that a machine was able to produce connected speech. Today, purely electronic and automatic devices, some of them contained on a single integrated circuit, can produce speech. Surprisingly, the fundamental theories involved in speech synthesis have not changed greatly from those used at the time of the VODER.

There has been an incredible upsurge in speech-synthesis design activity over the last few years. As of this writing, over one dozen speech-synthesis IC's have appeared. Virtually every electronics company of any size now employs a speech group of some sort. Why has this happened now? The high density and speed of modern *very large-scale integrated* (VLSI) circuits have given us the ability to build complex systems on a single chip of monolithic silicon. Manufacturers have been looking for something to do with all of that capability.[2]

Prior to this development, speech research was relatively mature, with impetus having come largely from two directions:

1. *Telephony needs.* Lower bit rates would greatly increase the capabilities of the telephone network.

---

[1] The full name for the VODER was "Pedro the VODER," named after Dom Pedro, the Emperor of Brazil. He evidently said "My God, it talks!" after listening to Bell's telephone at the Philadelphia Centennial Exposition in 1876. This was enough for the Bell people to name the VODER after him. Perhaps it helps to be royalty.

[2] "If the semiconductor industry had today a commercial million-transistor technology like VLSI, I'm not so sure it would know what to do with it."—Intel President Gordon Moore, 1979.

Introduction

2. *Military applications*. Lower bit rates would permit more bits to be used for error correction, thus making communication more reliable.

Result: A plenitude of algorithms, just waiting for the hardware to apply them. Not to say that the major theoretical speech problems are all solved—far from it!—but simply that the algorithms are certainly ahead of the hardware capability to implement them.

Speech seemed like a fruitful application for VLSI capability. And so it was. Speech products are beginning to proliferate. We will soon be seeing in common use talking toasters,[3] microwave ovens, scales, and toys. Synthetic speech will soon be available in most cars. These may seem to be mundane applications, but with the extension of information processing into the consumer domain, even these familiar devices might become unworkable without speech.

Speech can be another dimension in the operation of our tools. For example, as auto manufacturers begin to add sensors to determine different conditions, hazard monitoring by only visual means will become difficult if not dangerous.

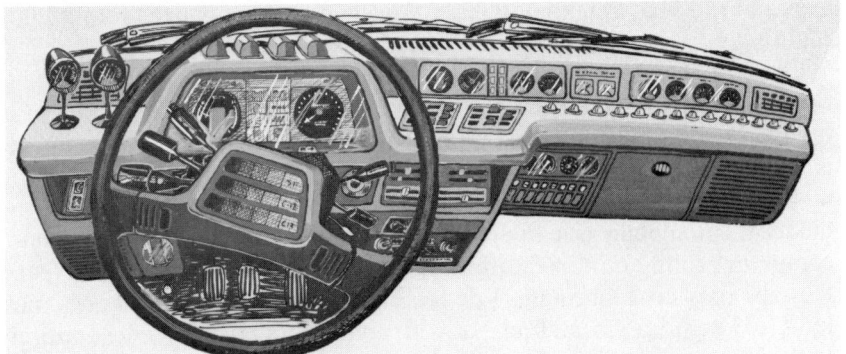

[3] The talking toaster is a little joke of mine. I hope.

If there are too many lights and buzzers, we will be unable to take advantage of them quickly or without taking our eyes off the road. Instead, the car can simply *tell* us what is wrong.

New products are also aiding the handicapped: talking calculators, typewriters for the blind, and phonetic speech synthesizers for the vocally handicapped (such as cerebral palsy victims). These are applications for electronic speech synthesis that really have no substitute.

All of these products are becoming endowed with a small degree of intelligence. The advent of the inexpensive microprocessor has enabled manufacturers to put computers into our daily world. Synthetic speech will simply alter the way these computers communicate with us. This communication is critical to our relations with the modern world.

The nature of the man-machine interface has been characterized as dehumanizing. Consider the reputation of the talking (much less, intelligent) computer. Asimov speaks of the "Frankenstein complex," or the tendency to consider artificial entities as threats to our humanity. There is the fear that they will take over, turning our lives into a 2001 nightmare.

Like fire, modern technological advances are morally and ethically neutral. Perhaps some strange artificial intelligence (AI) development of the future will have an "evil" intent. In practice, however, the computer is largely our friend. It reduces the necessity for much physical and mental drudgery. We accept routinely the complicated mechanism of the modern automobile but approach with trepidation the idea of distant computers ruling our credit life. I don't wish to make fun of those fears. Perhaps they are legitimate. I do feel that the negative experiences men have had with fire, fossil fuels, or with computers are due almost entirely to the improper use of those technologies by fallible humans.

Introduction 5

Recall Chaplin in the film *Modern Times*. For the sake of "efficiency," his employer fed Chaplin (a factory worker in the story), by means of an automatic worker-feeder. He was strapped in, and of course the machine malfunctioned, with comically messy results. In our modern times, we associate computers with the plethora of identification numbers with which we communicate to our corporate creditors. In this case, in fact in all cases, we perceive the computer through its input/output (I/O) interface. The current interfaces tend to be mildly annoying for some people. Yet this is enough to support the notion that computers are malevolent and dehumanizing. It *is* certainly dehumanizing to be addressed as a number rather than by name. However, these problems can be handled without rejecting the computers.

Speech I/O will go a long way toward a more humanly comfortable interaction with the ever-increasing number of computers around us. Up to now, men have struggled to bring themselves down to the level of the machine to communicate with it. The computer, along with the special-purpose hardware and software that are being developed, will inevitably bring the machine up to the human level of communication.

Speech processing can make the man-machine interaction natural and humanly based. Unless we destroy our own society with the violent technology that we have also developed, these machines will not be going away. Whatever one may think, it is clearly to our advantage to teach them our language.

6 Talking Chips

Mechanical speech has a long and fascinating history. This century saw the introduction of the first connected speech synthesizer, the VODER. Recent advances in IC technology have permitted complicated systems similar to the VODER to be placed on a single piece of silicon, truly a "talking chip."

The VODER has come of age.

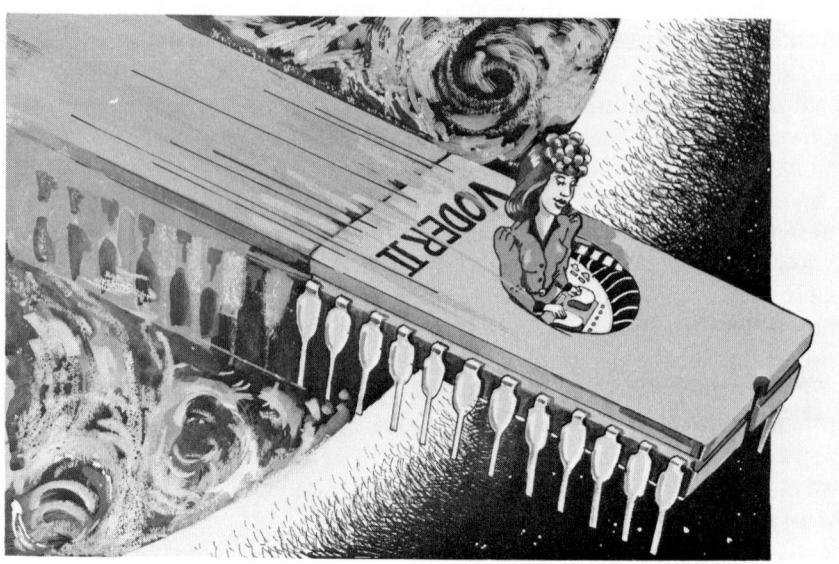

CHAPTER 1

SPEECH SYNTHESIS

1.1. INTRODUCTION

As the marvelous Electronic VODER Lady sails off into the sunset, we find ourselves poised on the doorstep of that mystifying world of modern talking machines. Swing open the door and enter. It won't be so bad. Really! There will be some concepts to be learned, a few stories to be told.

"Sure," you say, "talking machines would be fun to have around. They might even be useful. But why all the to-do? Why not just hook up some tape recorders and be done with it?"

There's a better answer than "because we need to keep speech engineers and scientists employed." That better answer *is* in fact money, but not just for speech professionals.

How much does it cost to make something talk? Tape recorders have increased in quality and decreased in cost over recent years. Yet they remain electromechanical beasts which wear down, break down, cost over $100, and are expensive to keep in good repair. In contrast, a fully electronic system composed of a few *chips* or integrated circuits can usually be marketed for under $20 in high volume, and is inexpensive to maintain. These prices will change, of course, but the ratio between the two should stay about the same. Electronic speech will remain cheaper than tape. This low cost makes electronic speech the obvious choice for high-volume applications, such as talking cars and computers.[1]

---

[1] Let's not forget the talking toaster. (On second thought, let's.)

8 Talking Chips

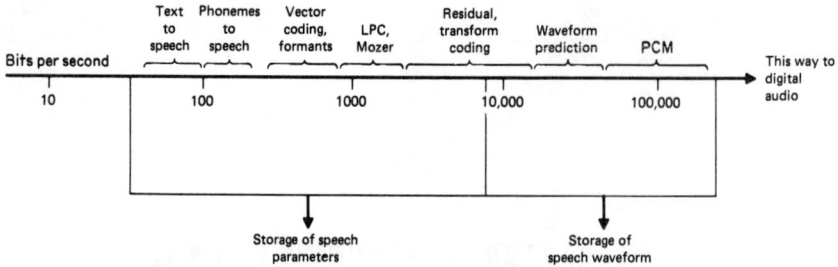

FIG. 1.1. Bit-rate chart.

A tape recorder can't translate text to speech. Nor can it easily access recorded sounds in an arbitrary order.[2] Many mathematical techniques have, however, been invented to translate from speech recordings to numbers. These numbers can then be used to create synthetic speech.

Numbers are usually stored in computer memory as binary digits (*bits*).[3] These binary numbers can represent a variety of the aspects of speech, ranging from a list of speech sounds used to a complete characterization of the speech wave over time. Different speech representations can be characterized by their storage requirements, as measured in bits per second (*bit rate*). These range from 70 bits per second, for speech storage as characters of corresponding text, to 64,000 bits per second for telephone speech. Peruse Figure 1.1. I will be referring to this bit-rate chart often.

Lower bit rates mean less storage, which costs less money. On the other hand, it takes a lot of calculation to achieve those low bit rates. A complex system is required to translate low bit-rate representations into something that sounds like speech. Formerly, this meant a heavy hardware investment to reduce memory. Now, the amazing integrated circuit has come to the rescue. It has done this in two ways:

1. Storage hardware has itself become inexpensive. Circuits called *read-only memories* (ROMs) have become mass-produced items. They currently permit storage of up to 128,000 bits and cost a mere few dollars.
2. Playback hardware is also inexpensive. Complete systems can be photographically produced on a single chip.

---

[2] Devices, such as the Mellotron, have been built with large numbers of independent tape loops for different sounds. They are nightmares to maintain, and they are very expensive.

[3] A bit is the simplest unit of information. A choice between one of two possible values, it can be used to represent a number in a system based on powers of 2 (much as the decimal number system is based on powers of 10.)

1.2. SPEECH PERCEPTION AND PRODUCTION

We commonly say that tape recorders "record sound." No way! Sound is a change of pressure over time that moves in the form of a wave.[4] Tape recorders store changes of magnetic flux along the surface of tape. They never store sounds.

We mean, of course, that some *representation* of the sound is stored on the tape. In the case of a tape recorder, the magnetic flux stored at any given moment is (ideally) proportional to the electrical voltage at the input.[5] Given an ideal microphone (and perhaps a preamp), this voltage will be proportional to the pressure in the air at that moment. Changes in the sound pressure will correspondingly be tracked by magnetic changes on the tape. Another way of saying this is that the tape recording is an *analog* of the variations of pressure at the microphone.

There is a very important sense in which our naive intuition is correct, a sense in which the same "thing" is stored on tape as is happening in the air. That "thing" is called a *signal*, and it can be defined as some *information-bearing* variation of a physical quantity. If one were to draw a graph of sound pressure at a microphone during the utterance of a vowel, for instance, one might get something like what is shown in Figure 1.2.

Note that the vertical axis is unlabeled. That's not a typo. By changing only the name of that axis, we could also show the ideal microphone output voltage, or the ideal preamp output, or the magnetic flux on the tape. The abstract entity that is transmitted and stored in this little system is the signal, and the function of time that is plotted is called the *waveform*.

If you say *ahhh* into a microphone, you are creating a pattern of pressure changes in the air. This speech *signal* is intercepted and converted into electrical variations by the microphone. These electrical variations are converted to magnetic flux changes by the tape recorder

---

[4] Some philosophical types have alternatively suggested that such a wave is only sound if someone hears it. It is often asked, "If a tree falls in the forest with no one there, does it make a sound?" I can't answer that question. I wasn't in the forest.

[5] Ignoring the equalization that is actually done in recorders and the nonlinearities of the whole process.

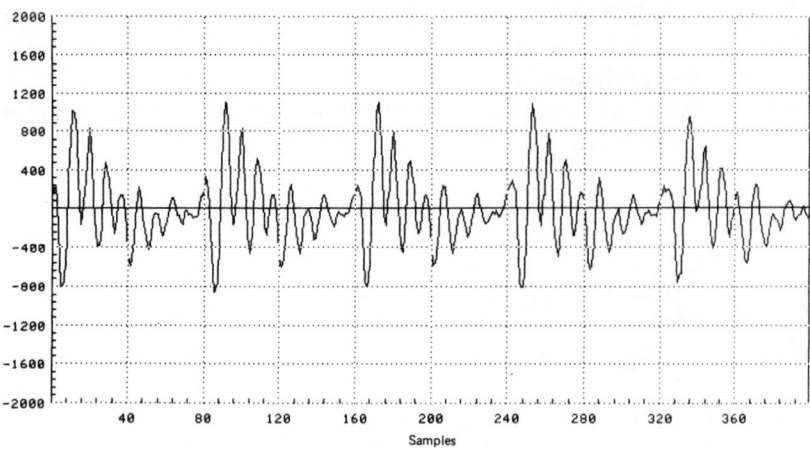

FIG. 1.2. Signal waveform.

and impressed upon the iron oxide of the tape. We have now stored the signal waveform, which can be converted back to sound by a similar (reverse) process.

All techniques which use a lot of storage for speech, such as tape recorders or high bit-rate computer techniques, represent the signal waveform in some manner. Tape recorders store an analog of the speech, while digital systems store a bunch of numbers which *represent* the waveform of the speech. These techniques are shown at the right end of the bit-rate chart. Speech storage of this type typically uses 16,000 to 64,000 bits for every second of speech. Digital audio systems can use up to a million bits per channel (left and right for stereo). These systems are definitely of interest to the world at large. However, the popularization of talking machinery requires low-cost hardware, including the memory chips. We must view speech in a different light in order to represent it more succinctly.

I referred to someone saying *ahhh*. This is a four-character description of the speech signal.[6] It is similar to the storage of musical scores as a sequence of notes on a staff. In both cases, low storage has been achieved. The trade-off is that a complex system (text-to-speech interpreter in the first case, trained orchestra in the second) is required for translation of these descriptions into sound.

Text-to-speech systems require the fewest bits for storage. Unfortunately, they are dependent on software that is limited by our understanding of both linguistics and acoustic phonetics. Because of both our

---

[6] I wondered if they'd let me use four-letter words in this book.

incomplete knowledge in these areas and the software complexity required to do a really good job, text-to-speech systems tend to sound distinctly artificial. They do, however, offer a potentially unlimited vocabulary (Chapter 5).

Systems using other speech representations, with bit rates from 600 to 16,000 bits per second, do not suffer from these problems but can only be used for storage of fixed vocabularies. These synthesizers all use stored numbers that represent important features of the speech and not the complete waveform. The best parameters for these methods are those which specify *perceptually significant* aspects of the speech. If some feature of the speech can be ignored without much effect on what you hear, why store it?

What we really want to do is create a waveform which sounds very much like the original speech, or at least sounds like the same words. Since we are not storing the waveform itself, it must be created. To do this, synthesizers must *convert* critical stored speech parameters into this new waveform. The real trick lies in determination of these perceptually significant parameters.

Over a century ago, scientists such as Ohm and Helmholtz suggested that speech could be completely represented by its *short-term spectrum*, or the frequency content of a short segment [typically 10–20 ms (milliseconds)] of speech. This implies a class of approaches to speech synthesis. First, speech can be chopped up into distinct sounds. Second, the amount of energy at each frequency, for each sound, can be specified. Synthesizers can then create waveforms that have roughly the same energy at each frequency (frequency content or spectrum) as the original segments.

The idea of using the frequency content to describe speech is backed up by the observation that human hearing uses this very kind of description. Consider this simplified functional picture of the auditory mechanism shown in Figure 1.3.

The outer and middle ears convert sound vibrations in the air to a traveling wave in the fluid of the inner ear. Nerve cells (neurons) in the inner ear send messages to the brain in the form of bursts, or "firings."

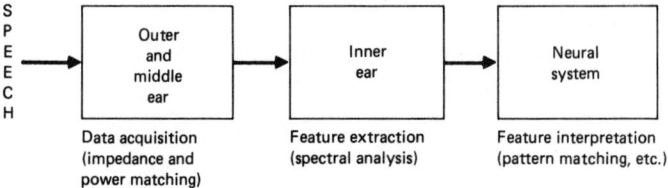

FIG. 1.3. A simple model of hearing.

The neurons fire when certain local cells are sufficiently displaced. The sound wave in the inner ear causes maximum displacement in a different physical place for each frequency. Thus, the nerves in the inner ear transmit a pattern to the brain that is very much like our idea of a spectrum.

The brain evaluates this spectrum over a period of milliseconds. Coincidentally, the neurons usually take several milliseconds to "charge up" between firings. Probably as a result of these latencies, small timing deviations (the phase) of the different frequency components are relatively unimportant for our perception of speech.[7] The *magnitude* of the speech spectrum (the amount of energy at each frequency) is therefore an important characterization of a sound.

All low bit-rate synthesis methods are based on the reproduction of the frequency content of natural speech. Storage is also reduced by isolating important speech features which change slowly and thus can be specified infrequently. One way of choosing such features is to have them correspond to the slowly varying characteristics of natural speech production. The speech synthesizer can then be an implementation of a speech production *model*. This is an approximation to the full speaking mechanism. By analyzing the original speech in the context of this model, we can evaluate those synthesizer control parameters which will result in speech segments with a frequency content close to that of the original speech.

The Simplified Speech Model (Figure 1.4) is the most common model for the production of human speech. Again, it is something I will be referring to often. In the Simplified Speech Model, an UP switch position indicates what is called *voiced* speech. Voiced refers to sounds produced by the vibration of the vocal cords. All of the vowels and many consonants fall into this category. Try saying *ee* and feel your throat. The "buzzing" you feel is the oscillation of your vocal cords. This vibration is caused by air pressure from the lungs forcing the vocal folds to open and close repeatedly. The rate of this oscillation is called the *pitch frequency*, and one cycle is called the *pitch period*. Note that:

Pitch frequency = 1/pitch period

Neighboring cycles of this buzzing sound source are usually of similar length and character. Therefore, a repetitive or *periodic* waveform of the proper shape is a good approximation for a model. The *spectrum* of a

---

[7] Ohm thought that the phase of the incoming speech was *completely* inaudible. This was known as Ohm's law of acoustics. You remember Ohm's other law. At least he had one that was right.

Speech Synthesis 13

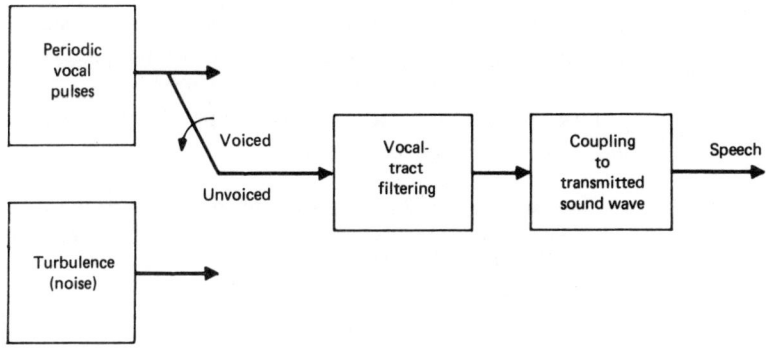

FIG. 1.4. A simple model of speech production.

periodic signal consists of components at the repetition frequency and its harmonics.

A DOWN switch position indicates what is called *unvoiced* speech. Unvoiced refers to sounds produced by turbulence at constrictions in the vocal mechanism. Many consonants fall into this category. Try saying *sh* and feel your throat. You will notice the vocal cords don't vibrate for this sound. Also notice that the sound is produced by pushing air past the obstruction of your teeth. These sounds are random, or noiselike, and so have no repetitive character. This sound source can be modeled as a random noise generator. The spectrum of a noiselike signal does not in general have the harmonic structure of voiced sounds.

For all speech sounds, the sound is *filtered* by the vocal tract. That is, parts of the frequency content (spectrum) are enhanced, and parts are attenuated. The vocal tract can be likened to an organ pipe with one end open (Figure 1.5).

The pipe will resonate at those frequencies for which the pressure will be maximum at the closed end and zero at the open end. This will be true of sounds for which the length of the pipe is 1/4, 3/4, 5/4, . . . of the wavelength of the sound. For the average male speaker, this will correspond to resonances at 500, 1500, 2500, . . . Hz (hertz, or cycles per second). For real voice tracts, the location of these resonances varies. That variation is dependent on the position of the *articulators*, namely the tongue, lips, jaw, hard palate, and soft palate (velum). The position of the vocal tract resonances, or *formants*, is fundamental in the identification of different speech sounds. The vocal tract can then be modeled as a filter which changes its resonant character for different segments of speech.

The last main block in the Simplified Speech Model represents the

14   *Talking Chips*

translation from air velocity at the mouth to the transmitted pressure wave.[8] This is called the *radiation* characteristic. Its chief effect is of attenuating those parts of the sound waveform which vary slowly (low frequencies). This characteristic stays roughly the same over time and thus may be modeled by a fixed *high-pass* filter.

[8] Of course, the sound wave has velocity vibrations too, but it's the pressure waveform that's important for hearing. The fluid displacements in the inner ear are responsive to pressure, not velocity. If you stand in a sound pressure null in an acoustically uneven room, it is quieter than other spots even though the velocity waveform would be at its maximum there.

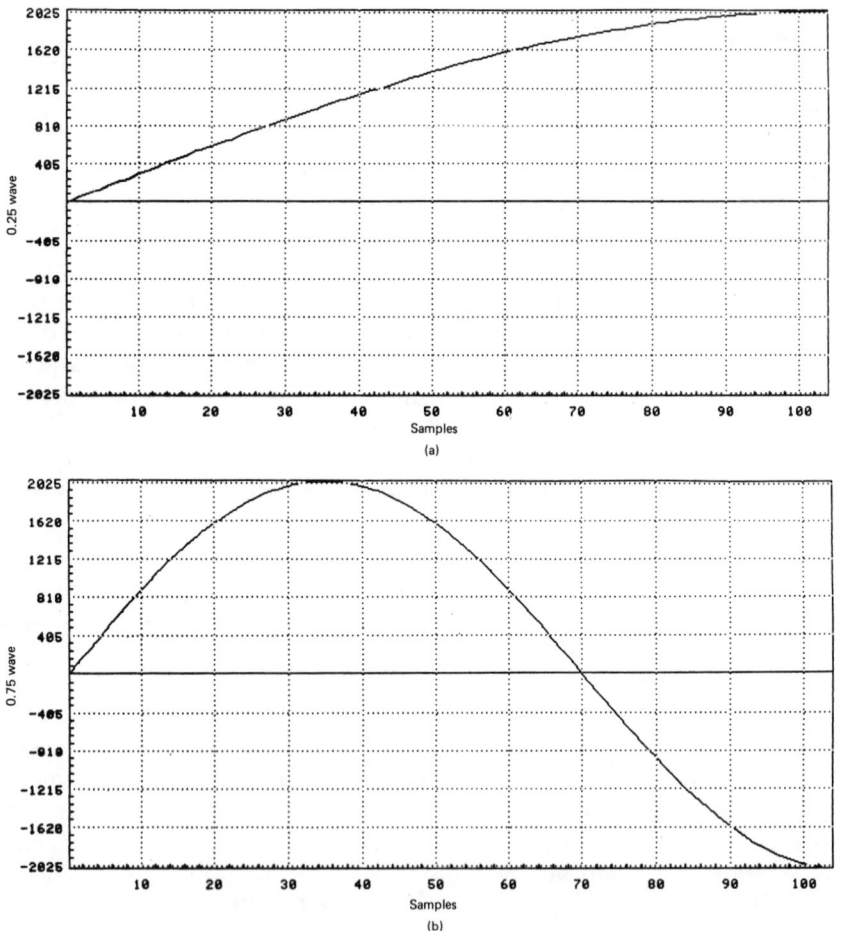

FIG. 1.5. (*a*) 1/4 wavelength for resonant pipe. (*b*) 3/4 wavelength. (*c*) 5/4 wavelength. (*d*) 7/4 wavelength. (*e*) Frequency response of resonant pipe, 0–5 kHz. (*f*) Frequency response of resonant pipe, with velocity-to-pressure radiation characteristic. (*g*) Frequency content of pipe output for typical "voiced" input.

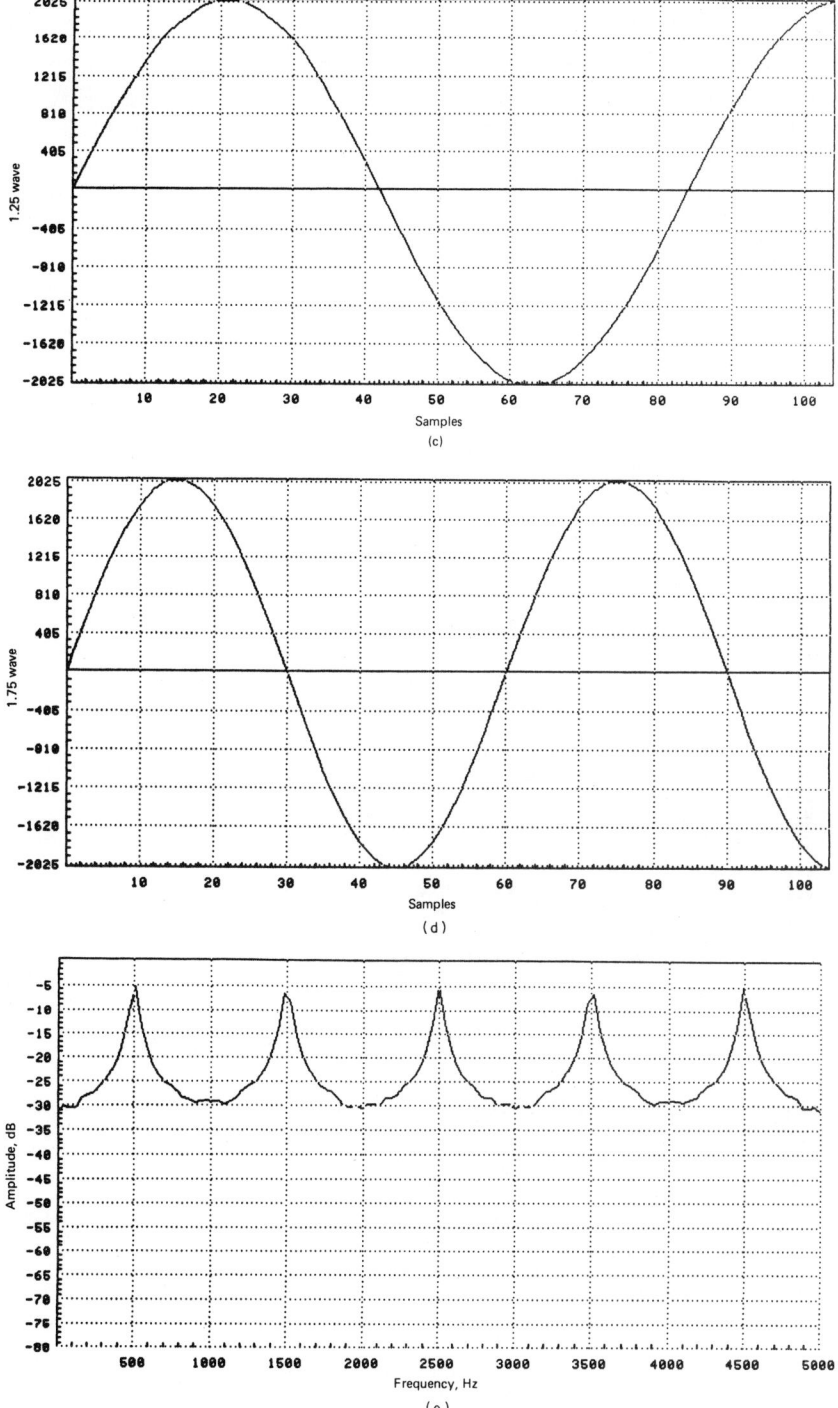

FIG. 1.5. (Cont'd)

16 Talking Chips

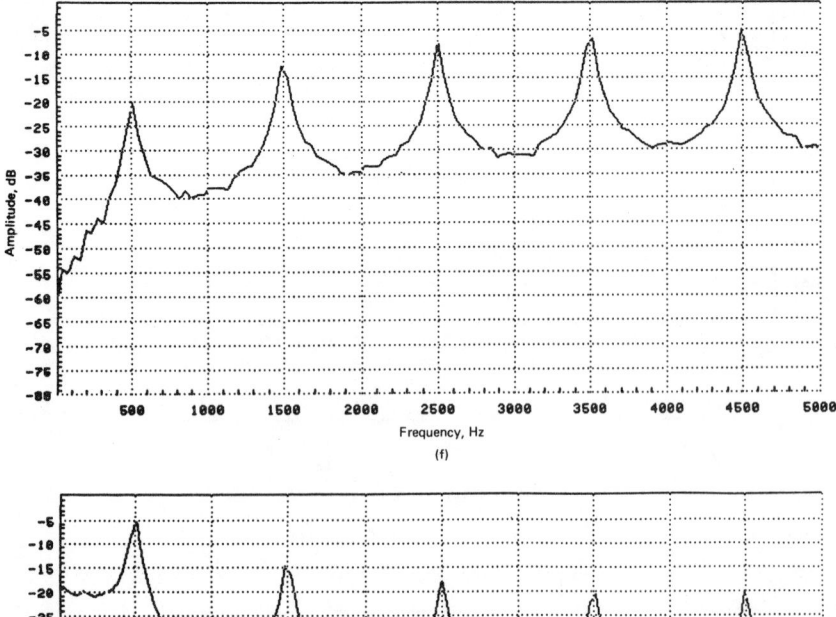

FIG. 1.5. (Cont'd)

If the parameters of this Simplified Speech Model are identified for each segment of speech, we can create synthetic waveforms using the same values. In particular, we must identify:

1. The filter characteristic (at least the main resonances) for the time-varying spectral shaping
2. The voiced and unvoiced switch positions and timings[9]

[9] The periodic or aperiodic character of a sound is important to our hearing even though it may not affect the frequency content very much. A whispered vowel (aperiodic source) and a vocalized vowel (periodic source) have very similar frequency content but sound quite different.

For all major low bit-rate synthesis systems, the aim is to duplicate these features of speech production well enough to satisfy the corresponding requirements of speech perception. *Time-domain* synthesizers (of the low bit-rate type) play back stored waveforms which match these features for the original speech. *Frequency-domain* synthesizers filter waveforms using filter parameters from human speech. Both types approximate the frequency content and the pulse or noiselike quality of each speech segment.

1.3. TIME-DOMAIN SYNTHESIS

1.3.1. Introduction

Some circuits "talk" by playing back waveforms. High bit-rate systems play a stored "image" of the original speech waveform. Low bit-rate systems play waveforms which have perceptually significant features in common with the original speech. In each case, however, the device converts a stored waveform code into a continuous function of time that can be connected to an audio system and heard as speech.

In the following sections, I will start off with the high bit-rate methods at the far right end of the bit-rate chart. I will then proceed to the left, concluding with the main commercial low bit-rate time-domain method, the Mozer technique.

1.3.2. Does a telephone have Buddha nature?

When you speak over a long-distance phone line, chances are you are transmitting and receiving digital signals. Somewhere along the way your voice signal has been converted to a sequence of numbers for transmission. There are physical limits to the number of bits per second which can be transmitted reliably over a given line. You'd expect, then, that the phone company would be eager to use low bit-rate methods to represent the speech.[10] Unfortunately, low bit-rate feature identification techniques fall apart under many real-world conditions. Many sounds, such as two people talking simultaneously, are not modeled particularly well by the switched-source Simplified Speech Model. Background noise can also mess up the analysis. However, the telephone, by its very nature, must be able to handle these conditions.[11]

Because of these problems, most telecommunications systems make

---

[10] Lower bit rates would mean they could fit more calls on a wire. More calls on a wire would mean more money for Ma Bell, because more of you could "reach out and touch someone."

[11] Imagine how much fun it would be to have a phone that could work *only* in a quiet room!

18   Talking Chips

no use of low bit-rate analysis and synthesis. No attempt is made to choose features which will accurately reproduce perceptually significant aspects of the original speech. There is, however, a family of speech storage techniques which produces an approximation of the original waveform. These methods are grouped under the appropriate heading of *waveform coding*. Every technique in this family produces a sequence of numbers which can be stored in a digital memory for later playback as a speechlike waveform.

Let's assume that the speech waveform has already been converted to an analogous electrical function, such as the voltage at the output of a microphone preamplifier. The simplest way to represent this waveform digitally is by storing its amplitude at given moments. These moments are "clocked," that is, separated by uniform time intervals. At these moments, the waveform amplitude is saved in an analog "memory" element, such as a capacitor. This value is then converted to a binary number by a device called an *analog-to-digital converter* (ADC or A/D converter). Those binary numbers can be stored or transmitted and then played back, once every sampling interval, through a *digital-to-analog converter* (DAC). This device produces an analog output quantity (such as voltage or current) corresponding to each input binary code.

How perfectly can a continuous signal be represented by a sequence of numbers? Imagine an arbitrary curve traced through a set of discontinuous dots. If the dots are close enough, they will be a good representation of the curve. Yet how close is close enough? I'd say the dots are close enough if there are no "surprises" on the curve between them. If one could guarantee that a smooth curve drawn between the dots would coincide with the original curve, I would say we had enough dots.[12]

Broadly speaking, then, one must sample frequently enough to capture the quickest variations in the signal. A more exact analysis[13] shows that if the original analog signal is filtered to have *no* frequency content past a frequency half that of the sampling frequency, it can be *perfectly* reconstructed by a filter which removes all portions of DAC output above that same frequency. This latter filter is required because replicas of the signal spectrum are transposed to higher frequencies by the sampling process. If allowed to remain, that high-frequency garbage will sound a little like harmonic distortion. In practice, reconstruction is imperfect. Imperfect filters are used, which permit small amounts of unwanted high frequencies to remain.

There is another important imperfection with this technique. The analog-to-digital converter outputs a number which is supposed to

---

[12] You might not. It's a matter of personal taste.
[13] See Appendix B.

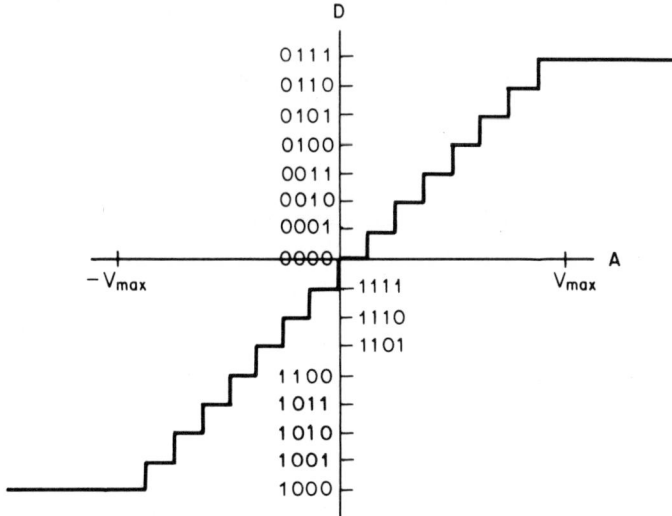

FIG. 1.6. Linear PCM quantization.

represent how big the input is. It can, however, only do this to some finite degree of accuracy. Suppose we use a 10-bit ADC. Even if it is perfect, it can only convert the input to one of 1024[14] digital numbers. Analog input voltages are assigned to one of 1024 ranges, with each corresponding to a number. A 10-bit DAC will convert this number to a single analog value, which we may imagine to be in the center of the original range. Any value of the original signal is approximated, or *quantized* to the values at the center of the ranges, with a maximum error of one-half of the largest range.

In order to minimize the worst-case error for an arbitrary waveform, these DAC output levels must be uniformly spaced. The resulting approximation is usually referred to as *linear quantization*.[15] It is called linear because numbers twice as large represent signals roughly twice as large, within the allowed signal amplitudes (Figure 1.6).

For aural perception, signal-to-error *ratios* are of equal importance at all signal levels. That is, an error of ϵ at signal level x is audibly equivalent to an error of 2ϵ at signal level $2x$.[16] This suggests that with just enough

---

[14] 2 to the 10th power. The maximum number of values that can be represented with 10 bits.

[15] The overall process is anything but linear. Is the transfer curve in Figure 1.6 a straight line?

[16] This is not strictly true. Since the inner ear hears widely different frequencies separately, an error at one frequency will not be covered up or "masked" by a signal at a very different frequency. However, this "epsilon" approximation is good enough for Ma Bell.

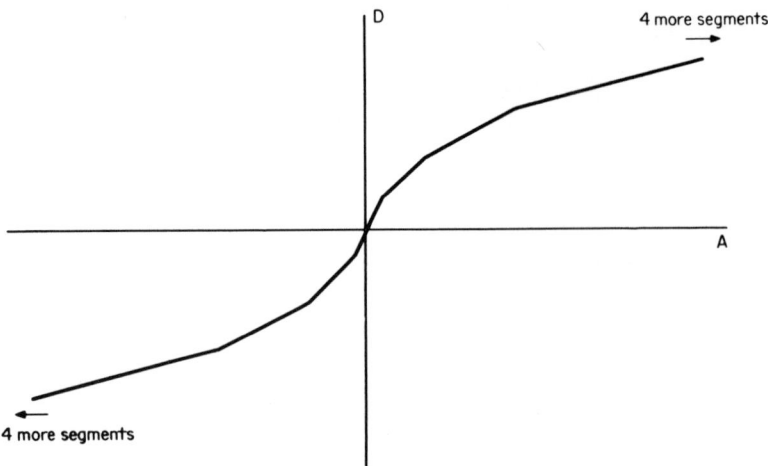

FIG. 1.7. Piecewise linear approximation to mu-law quantization (16 linear steps per segment, not shown).

equal quantization intervals to give inaudible errors for large signals, the errors for small signals will be audible. Linear quantization would only be optimum if a given amount of error was of equal importance at all signal levels.

This leads to a type of *nonlinear* quantization used for telecommunications. An ADC is used which permits large erorrs for large signals, while ensuring small errors for small signals. In this approach, the quantization transfer characteristic is an approximation to a log curve. For such a function, the possible error is proportional to the signal. Thus, signal-to-error ratios are roughly constant for all signal levels. Unfortunately, a *pure* log curve would have an infinite number of quantization ranges between full scale and zero.[17] In addition, extremely low-energy signals are frequently not speech at all, just environmental (or human) noise of some kind.

Figure 1.7 shows the quantization characteristic, often referred to as *mu law*, which is used in the United States. This transfer characteristic consists of 15 linear segments, with slopes decreasing by factors of 2 for each segment further from the origin. Each segment consists of 16 linear steps (not shown). The possible quantization error is dependent on signal amplitude, which is what we wanted.

The complete system for digital waveform storage is shown in Figure 1.8. The overall storage technique is called *pulse-code modulation* (PCM)

---

[17] It would be hard to build a converter that does this, even if you are clever.

and is either *linear* or *nonlinear* depending on the quantization used. Nonlinear PCM, as used by Ma Bell, requires 64,000 bits of storage,[18] which is pretty high up in our bit-rate chart. It doesn't provide low-cost storage, but it *is* universally used for telecommunications because it works well for most kinds of signals under a variety of background noise conditions.

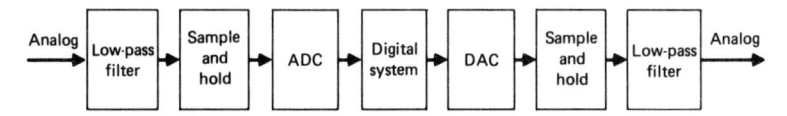

FIG. 1.8. PCM block diagram.

The input portion of the figure is also used by speech analysis systems as the first step in determination of low bit-rate representations of speech.[19] That is, almost every speech analysis method used begins with the waveform sampling and quantization described in this section. Also, all digital synthesizers produce numbers which go to a DAC and a low-pass filter for translation to a continuous speech waveform.

The hardware mechanisms for these converters will be introduced in the next chapter.

1.3.3. Predictive waveform synthesis

Continuing our leftward stroll down the bit-rate chart, we come to the domain of waveform *prediction*. These coding techniques use knowledge about portions of the waveform to describe the waveform with fewer bits. As with PCM, the stored parameters represent the waveforms themselves, rather than perceptually significant attributes of speech.

Consider, as an absurd (but instructive) example, a pure 440-Hz tone (middle A) (Figure 1.9). You know exactly what tone I have described. If I further explain that this signal swings from −1 to +1 V (volt) in amplitude, is 3 s (seconds) in duration, and starts an upward swing at 3 P.M. exactly, then you know all there is to know about it. You may *predict* the values of the waveform exactly. The signal has been completely described by five numbers. Compare this with storing a number roughly every millisecond, as prescribed by PCM sampling requirements, for a total of 3000 numbers!

---

[18] Eight bits a sample for 8000 samples per second. The frequencies over 3400 Hz are thrown away, which is part of the reason for the telephone sound quality we all know and love so well. At least it beats tin cans and string.

[19] That was my real reason for telling you about this stuff. Telecommunications "synthesis" isn't nearly as interesting as talking toasters, unless you have shares of AT&T.

22   *Talking Chips*

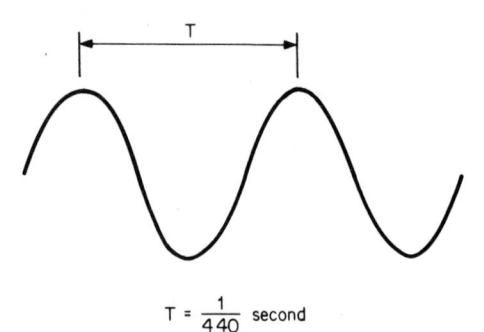

FIG. 1.9. The pitch A, a pure tone of 440 Hz.

$T = \frac{1}{440}$ second

Ordinarily, we do not know enough about a signal to characterize it confidently with five numbers. If, however, we can roughly approximate the signal with guesses based upon reasonable assumptions about its character, we can code the *difference* between our guess and the true signal. If our guess is based on good assumptions, this error will be small and can be described with a small number of bits without causing an unacceptably large overall quantization error. In particular, neighboring samples can be assumed to be somewhat *correlated*. That is, we should (usually) be able to compose a good estimate of the current sample from previous samples. The difference between this estimate and the actual waveform can then be coded. This is what is done in a common form of

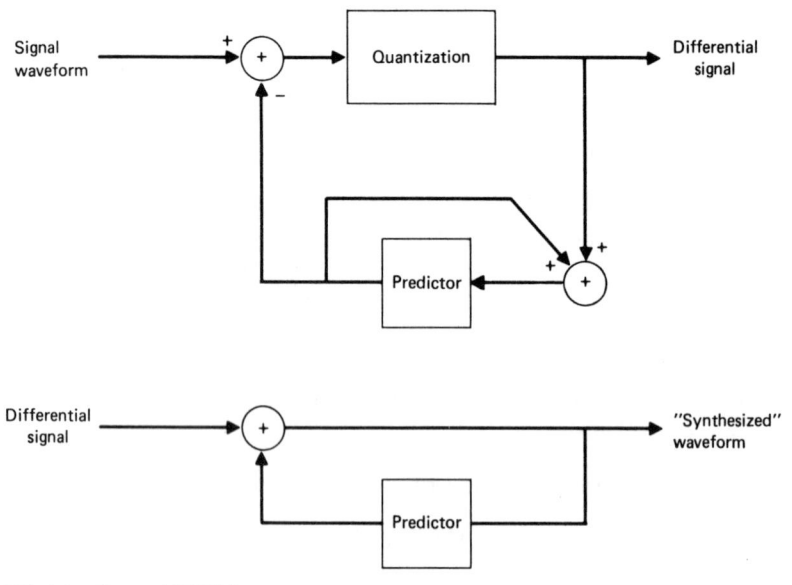

FIG. 1.10. General DPCM system.

FIG. 1.11. Simple prediction system.

predictive synthesis called *differential PCM*, or DPCM (Figure 1.10).

The simplest form of DPCM is a 1-bit-per-sample technique called *delta modulation*. In this approach, the error between our prediction of the next sample and the sample itself is coded with a single bit. The simplest prediction is just the current signal value (as Figure 1.11 suggests).[20] The change between samples may be coded as an increment (delta) up or down.

For such a scheme to work, the waveform must have a restricted change per sample, or slope. Because of this problem, high-quality delta modulation systems use a much higher sampling rate than PCM. Such values as 700 kHz are not uncommon in digital audio applications.

The trade-off between fewer bits per sample and a high sampling rate results in delta modulation having a similar number of storage bits to PCM. However, these systems can be built with much simpler hardware than is used for PCM. One-bit encoding of the *difference signal* does not require a true ADC or DAC, but rather just a comparator (for encoding) and an integrator (which computes a running sum) for playback. Also, the output sampling rate is so high that a *minimal* low-pass filter is required to remove the high-frequency garbage from the DAC output.

With some added system complexity, the bit rate can be further reduced without reduction of quality. In *adaptive delta modulation*

---

[20] This prediction works rather badly at the beginning of each new pitch period, when large waveform values pop up suddenly because of the new vocal pulse.

(ADM), the 1-bit step size is varied, depending on the history. Thus, a string of UP symbols would imply a large slope. A larger step size would then be appropriate. An alternating set of symbols (up, down, up, down, ...) would imply a small slope and would lead to the choice of a small step size.

In all of these schemes, prediction is based on the last sample only. More sophisticated schemes can predict on the basis of other samples as well. Unfortunately, such methods typically require greater hardware complexity.

Typical speech waveform systems of the types described in this section work at rates from 16–40 kbits/s. The exception is the digital audio delta modulation case, which can be as much as 700 kbits/s. These offer mild storage improvements over mu-law PCM, operating at 64 kbits/s. However, violation of correlation assumptions can make even the best of these systems work poorly for *some* sounds. Hence, the preference for mu-law PCM in telecommunications. Yet the concept of *prediction* is a valuable one that we will see again in the frequency-domain synthesizers.[21]

1.3.4. Low bit-rate waveform synthesis: Dr. Mozer rolls his own

In 1970 a Berkeley astrophysicist named Forrest Mozer conceived a sudden curiosity about synthetic speech. He wanted to develop a talking calculator for a blind student. Intending it to be cheap and portable, he had to examine ways of representing the calculator sounds with a small number of bits. He knew that wildly different waveforms would still sound *roughly* the same as long as their magnitude spectrum was the same. From this basic idea, he proceeded through years of work to develop his unusual encoding techniques.

It is interesting to note the extent to which Mozer's line of thought came to deviate from the standard speech wisdom. Waveform-synthesis techniques, such as those described earlier in this chapter, produce speech at bit rates from 16–64 kbits/s. Low bit-rate synthesis techniques have always used time-varying filters to implement a speech production model. No one really thought a waveform synthesizer would be useful at low bit rates.

Mozer's innovation was to merge frequency-domain analysis with time-domain synthesis. The fundamental idea was to find coarsely quantized waveforms (that is, waveforms specified by a small number of bits per sample) with spectra that were close to that of the original speech. As in frequency-domain synthesis, no attempt was made to

---

[21] Again, I had an ulterior motive for introducing a topic. Sneaky devil, no?

match the natural and synthetic waveforms themselves. Mozer's technique was *not*, as it was frequently mislabeled, waveform compression.[22] True, waveform compression does take place, but only on a synthetic waveform that may look nothing like the original speech. The synthetic waveform is chosen to have roughly the same spectral magnitudes as the original speech.

As a fresh approach, Mozer's technique offered certain advantages over frequency-domain synthesis. Like the other waveform-synthesis methods, his does not assume a particular speech production model and so is not limited by the errors of that assumption. On the negative side, Mozer's approach has thus far consisted of a collection of techniques rather than a closed-form solution. As such, it has been rather slow in transferring to new word production sites. This situation is, however, rapidly changing.

The details of the Mozer analysis process, that is, the process of choosing the synthetic waveform to represent a sound, can be found in Chapter 4.

1.4. FREQUENCY-DOMAIN SYNTHESIS

A frequency-domain synthesizer is a direct implementation of a speech production model. It "talks" by playing back pulselike or noiselike waveforms through a filter that is adjusted to give the correct frequency content for each speech segment. The VODER was the first complete example of this, since it successfully modeled connected speech. Modern synthesizers are not too different, except for size and cost. They also have available more sophisticated techniques for computation of the synthesizer control parameters.

Low bit-rate frequency-domain synthesizers do not reproduce all the details of the speech spectrum. Consider the following example: Suppose we wish to synthesize a voiced segment of speech which has a 100-Hz pitch. The waveform is periodic and thus has significant energy at the pitch frequency and its harmonics.[23] If the magnitude of each harmonic in a 5-kHz bandwidth were stored using 4 bits per value, 200 bits would be required. Assuming a new spectrum for each 20 milliseconds, we

---

[22] Such as the example of the 440-Hz tone (middle A).

[23] Any periodic signal can be represented as a sum of pure tones at the repetition frequency and its harmonics. This is the main idea of the summed tones in a Hammond organ. The idea was first worked out by a French mathematician named Fourier, and so the series of harmonics is called the *Fourier series*. The principle was there before he was, though.

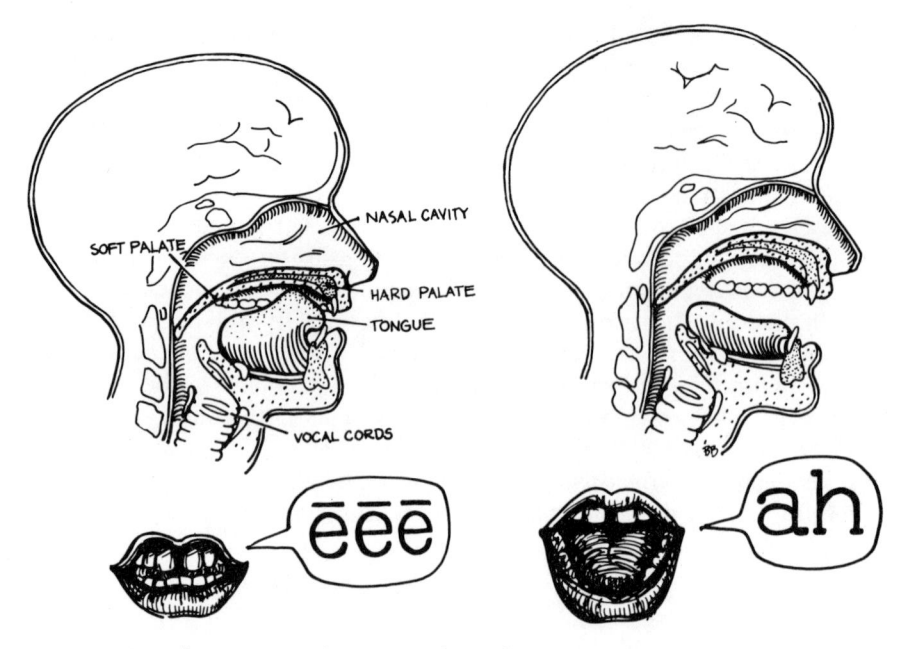

FIG. 1.12. Articulator positions for two vowel sounds.

would have to store 10,000 bits per second of speech. This puts us in the middle of the bit-rate chart.

Commercially successful synthesis techniques use 1000–2000 bits/s. Far fewer than 10,000. In order to reduce the storage this far, we have to determine what features of the spectrum must be preserved to keep the speech useful for communication. When we listen to synthetic speech, we should certainly be able to understand all the words. This is only possible if we can correctly identify each unique speech sound.

Over the range of possible sounds, there are a limited number of linguistic entities. These are called *phonemes*. Examples are the *ah* in father (a vowel phoneme) and the *s* in sit (a fricative consonant phoneme). Each of these phonemes may be pronounced in a variety of ways and still be identifiable as that phoneme.[24] Identification of these elements determines the received speech communication. Thus, intelligibility of the phonemes is the primary measure of goodness for speech-synthesis systems. Low bit-rate speech must preserve those aspects of the frequency response necessary for phoneme identification.

Consider Figure 1.12. The only significant difference between *ah* and

---

[24] See Chapter 5 for discussion of these phoneme variants, called *allophones*.

ee uttered at the same pitch is the position of the articulators (and consequently the position in frequency of the major resonances).

Synthesizers have been built which directly model the motion of these articulators. However, people can usually recognize phonemes when produced by a synthesizer that mimics only a few main resonances. This is why we only need to reproduce major peaks in the speech spectrum. The majority of synthesizers to date have been time-varying filters which are adjusted by the stored parameters to provide a good match to the peaks of the original spectrum.

1.4.1. Simple formant synthesizers

Good reproduction of the vocal tract resonances (formants) is critical if one is to understand what phonemes the synthesizer is saying. *Band center and bandwidth* are convenient representations for each formant. These features vary slowly and smoothly, since they change via motion of articulators (such as the tongue). They can be specified infrequently, thus making formant synthesizers low bit-rate systems. In fact, in the simplest approach, filter bandwidths are determined from the filter number and the band center and are not stored separately. This works because we don't seem to misunderstand synthetic phonemes even when the bandwidth is way off. The band centers are stored for each separate speech segment, where the segment length may vary from 5 to 30 milliseconds (Figure 1.13).

The simplest frequency-domain synthesizers consist of the Simplified Speech Model realized as a pulse generator, a noise generator, three filters in series, and a fixed filter at the output. Formant synthesizers are known for their low bit rates. As an example, the Naval Research Laboratory has done very intelligible formant synthesis at 600 bits/s.

One can also include more resonators to improve the quality. For greater fidelity, the bandwidths may also be stored directly. Synthesizers such as the General Instruments IC use this approach.

It is not always easy to figure out what the formants are for a speech

	F_1	F_2	F_3
ee	270	2290	3010
uh	520	1190	2390
ah	730	1090	2440

FIG. 1.13. Some vowel formant band centers.

segment. For this reason, most commercial frequency-domain synthesizers use a single filter that matches the peaks of the whole spectrum. That way, the individual formants don't have to be identified. The unifying buzzword for this approach is *linear predictive coding* (LPC).

1.4.2. LPC synthesizers

We tend to think of filters as systems that selectively pass different portions of a signal's frequency content. Alternatively, we may think of them as computational units that predict the output at each moment from previous outputs. In the case of a resonator, for example, the output dies down in a very simple and predictable manner (until you put in a new input). Suppose the output is predicted as a weighted sum of past outputs. We can choose the weights to minimize the error[25] between the synthetic waveform and the original speech. The resultant weights can be stored as a representation of the speech, since synthetic speech may be created by driving a prediction filter with the usual source waveforms (as in the formant synthesizer). This scheme is called *linear predictive coding*, or LPC, and the weights are called *linear predictors*. The filter which computes each new synthesis sample as a weighted sum of past samples is called a *direct form* LPC synthesis filter (Figure 1.14).

The concept is similar to the prediction of DPCM.[26] However, in LPC we are trying to identify only key features for the single-source Simplified Speech Model. The speech is represented by the filter coefficients and the grossest features of the source signal, such as its periodicity. Typical bit rates for this method are 800 to 4800 bits per second. That bit rate depends on the accuracy of the coefficients used. It also depends on the length of the segments for which a continuously varying spectrum (as in real speech) is approximated with an unchanging spectrum.

This type of LPC synthesizer is sensitive to coefficient precision. Real hardware can only perform filtering to some limited accuracy. The slight changes caused by coefficient inaccuracy can change the filter characteristic greatly and in a manner that is hard to predict. This change can also make the filter unstable (that is, oscillatory) which is hard to check for without finding the roots of a high-order polynomial (no picnic) or running the filter. This can be a avoided by using many bits to represent each coefficient, but then we have a high bit rate. No good.

---

[25] It's not trivial to define what we mean by error here. In general, we are interested in perceptually significant error. At the very least, this usually means that errors in the position of the spectral peaks should be minimized, since it is these positions that determine our identification of the phonemes.

[26] I told you prediction would be important.

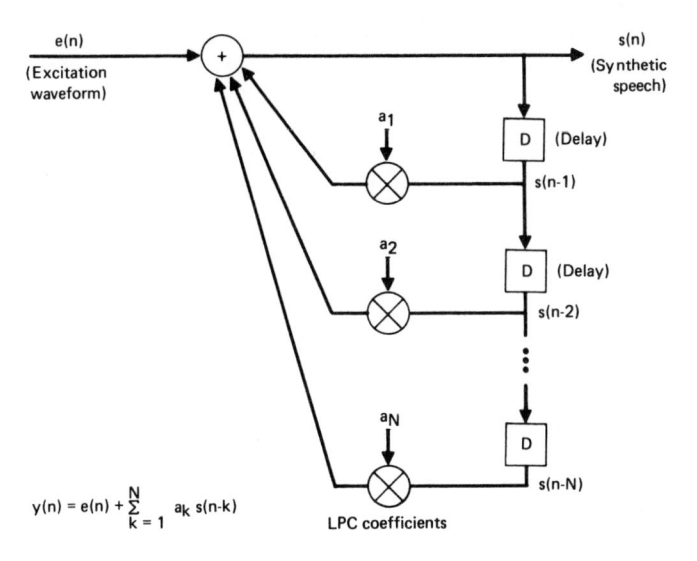

FIG. 1.14. "Direct form" LPC synthesis filter.

An alternative filter structure is called a *lattice*. This structure (as shown in Figure 1.15) has nice sensitivity properties. For one thing, coefficients between 1 and −1 are guaranteed to provide a stable filter. Also, small errors due to coefficient inaccuracies cause only small errors in the output signal spectrum. The lattice can be interpreted as a model of a nonuniform acoustic tube (a cylindrical tube with different thicknesses along its length). To a first approximation, this is a good model of the vocal tract when the velum is closed (that is, when your nasal passage isn't vibrating with the sound). In this interpretation, the lattice coefficients indicate the fraction of the sound (actually the acoustic volume velocity) that is reflected at the discontinuities in the tube. For this reason, these filter weights are called *reflection coefficients*.

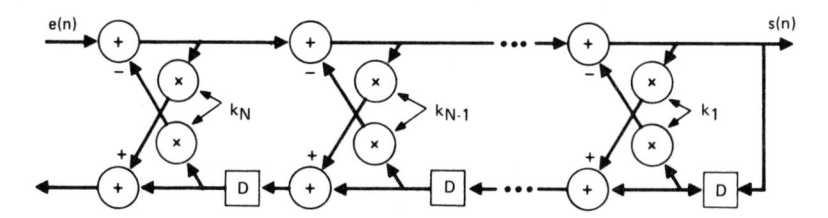

FIG. 1.15. Lattice synthesis filter.

30   Talking Chips

LPC synthesis has a number of significant pros and cons. Briefly stated, they are:

Pros:

1. The lattice is a good model of the vocal tract as a nonuniform acoustic tube. Thus, it is fairly accurate for those vowels and steady-state fricative sounds (such as *sh*) for which the nasal tract is not very significant.
2. Restricting the reflection coefficients to the range between $+1$ and -1 guarantees the stability of the resulting filter. This filter will never oscillate no matter how inaccurate we are, as long as the coefficients are smaller than 1.
3. For lower bit rates, we can store a small number of parameters and interpolate between them for slow speech changes. The resulting filters must be stable, since the interpolated coefficients must also be between -1 and $+1$.
4. The parameters are derived from a closed form[27] analysis technique and can thus be used in a real-time communications application.

Cons:

1. The single-tube model is not accurate for nasals, since the nasal passage is used for these sounds. The prominent antiresonances in nasalized speech are not modeled well by LPC.
2. The single-source excitation model is not accurate for voiced fricatives (like *zh*) or aspirated vowels (like a breathy *ah*). For both of these, both pulselike and noiselike sounds resonate in the vocal tract.[28]
3. While the interpolated values are guaranteed stable, they are non-physical. This results in intermediate values that do not correspond to the natural case.
4. The parameters of the analysis (e.g., decision thresholds) tend to be sensitive to noise, change of speaker, sex of speaker, etc.
5. Nonlinear mechanisms, such as amplitude modulation of the voiced fricative noise source by the pulse source, cannot be accommodated.

---

[27] This means that there is a formula which directly computes the answers, as opposed to some method which iteratively approximates them.

[28] Aspirated vowels can be synthesized by LPC synthesizers if they can mix the sources at the input to the filter, although current commercial integrated circuits do not do this. Voiced fricatives are a result of the filtering of two different sources by two different characteristics, which simply is not possible with a single LPC filter.

So what's the bottom line? LPC synthesizers have proven themselves for low bit-rate production of intelligible speech. However, there are some quality limitations that appear to be fundamental both to the filter structure and to the switched-source speech model upon which it depends. Let's take a look at some more sophisticated models which don't have these problems.

1.4.3. Enhanced frequency-domain synthesis

All of the frequency-domain synthesizers described thus far have been based on the Simplified Speech Model. In these devices, some simplifying assumptions are made about production of speech:

1. Frequency characteristics for all speech segments can be well approximated by an all-pole filter. That is, only the peaks of the frequency response need to be reproduced, not the valleys.
2. The filter-driving function for voiced sounds is a train of pulses at the pitch rate.
3. The filter-driving function for unvoiced sounds is random noise.
4. The above characteristics can be altered at some frame rate of 10 to 30 milliseconds, in accordance with the sluggishness of vocal tract changes.
5. Speech can be band-limited to 4 or 5 kHz without significant loss. This reduction enables the spectrum to be specified with fewer parameters, typically 10 to 14.[29]

These assumptions are only marginally accurate for real speech. They permit simplified hardware and low bit-rate storage. We can spruce up the model with all the clever details we want, but we may not ever be able to analyze the speech well enough to figure out all the parameters, at least using automatic techniques. Nevertheless, a more sophisticated model is practical for several reasons:

1. Text-to-speech systems perform what is called *synthesis by rule* (Chapter 5). In this procedure, parameters for each phoneme are looked up in a library. This library can be generated manually, via trial and error, if necessary. This procedure can take advantage of human observations, manual adjustment, and experimental determination of the enlarged parameter set.
2. Vocabulary production is a lengthy process regardless of the speed of the analysis. Narrators must be directed. Speech must be edited,

---

[29] Limitations 4 and 5 aren't really inherent in the model, but I'm listing them anyway because this is the way synthesizers are usually done because of the need for low bit rates.

transferred, evaluated, etc. A small amount of manual parameter editing will not unduly lengthen the preparation time. Some trial-and-error approaches may also be used to take advantage of the extended model.
3. Future improvements in phonemic recognition should improve the automatic parameter extraction capability. A good model should be ambitious enough to accommodate at least some of these anticipated advances.

Many enhanced speech production models can be postulated. These models should seek to encompass sounds not well described by the simplified model, such as:

1. Sounds where the spectrum (frequency content) is not well represented by all-pole (resonance-only) filters. The most obvious examples are the nasals such as *m* or *n*, which are characterized by prominent antiresonances. A common model enhancement for this purpose is a *side chain* or parallel filter path, which represents the nasal sound path. This provides major nulls in the frequency response of the overall filter.
2. Sounds which are caused by vocal tract excitations other than pure vocal cord oscillation or turbulent noise sources. Most notable are the voiced fricatives, such as *z* or *zh*. For such sounds, turbulence is generated during high-velocity portions of the vocal pulse wave. To accommodate such sounds, a good model should permit mixture of pulselike and noiselike excitations.
3. Transient sounds, changing radically in a few milliseconds. Although the articulators (tongue, jaw, lips, palate) cannot move very fast, the release of built-up pressure that forms a *stop*, such as a *b* or *p* can occur quite quickly. The excitation and filters must change quickly for such sounds to be properly represented. Better speech models have a variable frame rate, longer for steady-state sounds and shorter for transient sounds.
4. The main distinguishing features of sounds like *f* and *th* are at frequencies above 5 kHz. A good speech synthesizer should have some capability at high frequencies (say 6–8 kHz) to produce these sounds. Of course the telephone is band-limited to 3.4 kHz and can certainly communicate quite well without this enhancement.[30] How-

---

[30] Still, try saying "I fought . . ." over the telephone and see who can tell whether you have said *thought* or *fought*. This can really be fun when the background noise is louder than the frequency content below 3.4 kHz in your utterances.

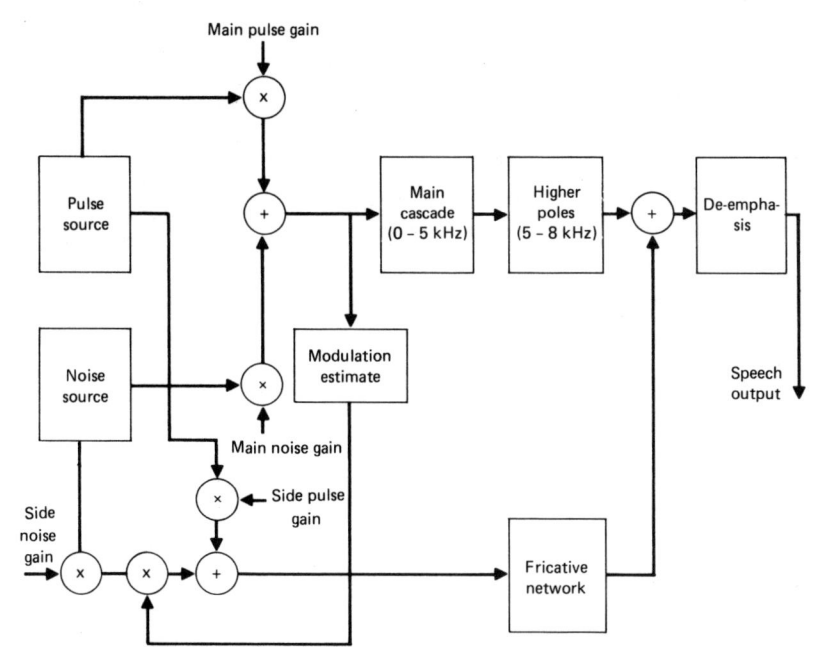

FIG. 1.16. Enhanced speech production model (16-kHz sampling rate).

ever, both intelligibility and quality can be dramatically enhanced in any system with a wider bandwidth.

An enhanced model was formulated by Klatt and implemented in the MITTALK speech-synthesis software, a rule-based system. Current work at National Semiconductor is expected to lead to IC synthesizers which will implement yet another enhanced model, as shown in Figure 1.16.

CHAPTER 2

SPEECH HARDWARE CONSIDERATIONS

2.1. INTRODUCTION

The major revelations in speech science of the past few years have been technological rather than algorithmic. Despite having been built on years of extensive exploration by theoreticians, the importance of these revelations must not be minimized. Those aspects of "mere implementation" have made the difference between usefulness and uselessness for a set of ideas about what is, after all, a practical science.

This chapter will briefly discuss the development of electronic hardware for speech synthesis. The history of this development can be traced through two lineages: that of frequency-selective analog filters and that of the digital computer. Both paths lead to the modern integrated circuit, an innovation which is more than incrementally different from all previous technological advances.

2.2 ANALOG VS. DIGITAL HARDWARE

Early attempts at machine synthesis of speech were based on mimicking the human voice mechanism. When electrical signal representations became possible in this century, researchers designed filters which were analogous to the resonant tube characteristics of the vocal tract. Much as Bell's telephone currents imitated the pressure variations of the human voice, Dudley's VODER circuits imitated the frequency-selective behavior of the human vocal tract.

ANALOG SPEECH SYNTHESIZER

Analog filter theory had developed to the point that virtually arbitrary frequency characteristics could be implemented, using combinations of resistors, capacitors, inductors, and amplifiers. Circuit elements could be varied or replaced by external control, permitting the time-varying spectral shaping required for speech synthesis. With the VODER, this control was exercised by a human operator. In modern devices, digital switching circuits automatically control the frequency characteristic of the speech.

As this century progressed, the field of digital computers advanced rapidly. Initially quite slow and bulky,[1] they were not conceived of as signal processors or synthesizers. Rather, they were used for difficult mathematical problems that had no simple analog or mechanical solution. Since low-complexity speech synthesis was possible using an electrical analog of the vocal tract, the computer was only used for more detailed studies.

[1] ENIAC, the first electronic computer, took over 2 milliseconds to perform a MULTIPLY and weighed 30 tons. Try wearing that on your wrist.

DIGITAL SPEECH SYNTHESIZER

Similarly, storage and transmission of speech waveforms were performed exclusively by analog means until quite recently. Electrical, mechanical (the phonograph), optical, and magnetic analogs of the speech waveform have all been used to represent it. As the sophistication of electronic switching circuits grew, so did the interest in the mathematical behavior of *sampled* signals. If numerical representations of speech could be employed, they would be both more robust[2] and more amenable to further compression than continuous physical analogs. In order to be practical, they would have to be *discrete* numerical representations, that is, a finite list of numbers representing a segment of speech. This is equivalent to saying that we will represent a continuous signal by a series of *sample* values (Figure 2.1).

As mentioned in the last chapter, sufficiently close spacings can be found to represent the signal with arbitrarily small error. In particular, if the bandwidth of the signal spectrum is limited, the signal can be *perfectly* represented by a sequence of speech amplitudes sampled at a rate at least as high as twice the highest frequency in the signal. This

---
[2] A full-bodied, hearty word. It usually refers to an approach that will work well despite unpredictable circumstances, such as noise or hardware variations.

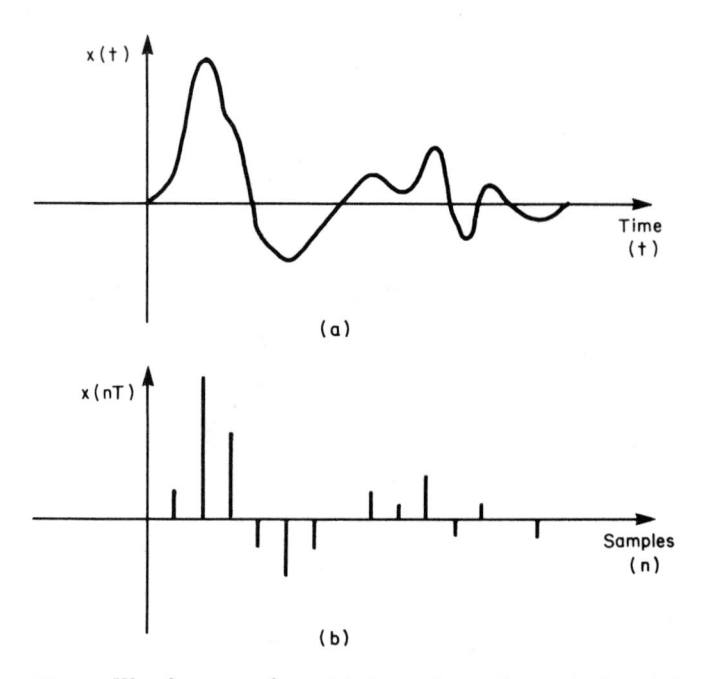

FIG. 2.1. Waveform sampling. (*a*) Original waveform. (*b*) Sampled waveform.

required sampling frequency is sometimes referred to as the Nyquist rate, after researcher Harry Nyquist of the Bell Telephone Laboratories.

A new field was born—discrete time signal processing. In discrete time signal processing, filtering operations are performed on *sequences* rather than on continuous functions. The algebraic manipulations are typically sums and differences rather than the integrals and derivatives of continuous signal mathematics. Filtering is done in the same manner as general numerical work, and thus can now be handily performed by a "number-crunching" computer. Generally, any linear filtering which can be done with an analog system can be equated (for band-limited signals), to any desired degree of accuracy, with a series of MULTIPLYs, ADDs, and DELAYs.

If the signals can take on only one of a finite number of values, they are referred to as *digital*. Digital signal representations are simply sequences of numbers. This means:

1. The processing of signals becomes a *numerical* function, much like payroll computation.
2. Computer simulations (where a general-purpose computer imple-

ments an algorithm which will later be handled by some special-purpose hardware) are the *real thing*. This numerical processing may be used for the artificial production of speech.

Clearly, numerical methods for selectively affecting the frequency components of a sampled signal *can be directly implemented on a digital computer*.

2.3. HARDWARE FOR DISCRETE TIME PROCESSING OF SIGNALS

The early digital computers were huge, expensive, and slow, taking milliseconds for multiplies. While this may not seem like a long time, consider having to perform 100,000 such operations to produce a single second of synthesized speech! In addition to being two orders of magnitude too slow, the cost and bulkiness of these early machines precluded their serious consideration for tasks such as synthesis.

Fortunately, time passed and technology advanced. The relay begat the tube, which begat the transistor, which begat SSI (*small-scale integration*), which begat MSI (*medium-scale integration*), which begat LSI (*large-scale integration*), which begat VLSI (*very large-scale integration*). Until now, when:

1. Hundreds of thousands of switching transistors have been realized on a single IC.
2. Millions of MULTIPLYs per second are easily performed on inexpensive chunks of monolithic silicon.

Today, all the functions required for speech synthesis can be performed on a single IC. What is in dispute is no longer whether it can be done, but how it should be done.

There are three major approaches to this problem: general-purpose digital signal processors, special-purpose digital signal processors, and discrete time analog signal processors.

2.3.1. General-purpose digital signal processors

In recent years, a succession of *digital signal-processing systems on a chip* have appeared in the marketplace. These are essentially tiny number-crunching computers. Like ordinary micros, they are programmable digital systems. However, they usually have a fast hardware multiplier, the lack of which is a prominent weakness in general-purpose microprocessors. The principal *architectural* difference is that these machines are usually of the *Harvard* type, while the general-purpose

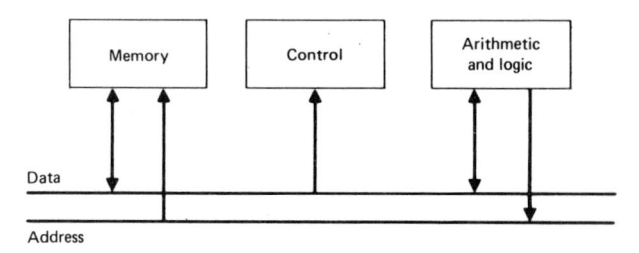

FIG. 2.2. Von Neumann architecture.

micros[3] are almost always of the *Von Neumann* type. What is the distinction between these two?

2.3.1.1. The Von Neumann machine

A general-purpose processor is one which can be reprogrammed to perform a wide variety of operations. The earliest electronic computers actually had to be rewired (via a plugboard) to perform different instructions. In the 1940s, John Von Neumann came up with the idea of using the same memory for both instructions and data. This led to a simpler structure (shown in Figure 2.2), which came to be called the Von Neumann architecture.

The Von Neumann architecture typically refers to a computer with:

1. A single arithmetic unit
2. One memory for both instructions and data
3. One data bus for both instructions and data
4. One address bus for both instructions and data

Because of the common use of solitary computer elements, this kind of computer is usually a *sequential* machine, in which the operations are performed one at a time in sequence. An alternative is a parallel machine, in which at least some operations would be performed simultaneously.

Most machines that we commonly refer to as computers are of the Von Neumann type. They range from micros like the 8080 or 6502 to mainframes like the IBM 370 or CDC 7600.[4] For all of these computers, their architectural simplicity makes many types of operations possible. Virtually any algorithm can be expressed as a sequence of primitive operations. Symbols may be manipulated as conveniently as numbers,

---

[3] Computers come in three flavors: micros (small), minis (medium), and mainframes (large). Although we are already seeing the emergence of the micromainframe.

[4] These mainframes actually employ some parallelism to achieve their speed. However, they are still stored-program computers with common storage and communication paths for instructions and data.

and highly structured and readable languages may be easily employed. However, repetitive numerical operations are slowed by the bottleneck of a single *bus*[5] for instructions and data. Most current microprocessors of the Von Neumann type are too slow for any but the most trivial signal-processing operations.

For signal-processing applications, hardware must perform a large number of arithmetic operations quickly, and most types of symbol manipulation are not important. An architecture is required which can be streamlined for computational speed, without losing programmability for different types of mathematical instructions. One such structure is referred to as the Harvard architecture.

2.3.1.2. The Harvard machine

The unique characteristic of Harvard-architecture computers is that separate *address spaces* are used for instructions and data (Figure 2.3).

The Harvard architecture was used back in the early 1940s in the very first electromechanical computers, called *computation engines*. Professor Howard Aiken of Harvard[6] directed the building of a high-precision calculator of mathematical reference data called the Harvard Mark I. This mammoth computer was used for over 10 years to produce volumes of navigation and ballistics tables. Programs were stored on paper tape, and read/write data were stored in telephone 10-step relays. These rudimentary memory techniques were the primary reasons for splitting program and data into separate memories. Yet, even then, certain features of the Harvard architecture had become apparent.

While the Von Neumann machine is more flexible for general problem solving, the Harvard machine works better for selected applications. When processor usage is narrow and specific, the Harvard architecture's separate address spaces for instructions and data have several advantages:

1. Instructions and data can be fetched simultaneously by using separate buses for each.
2. Address calculations for the fetching of new instructions and for the fetching of new data can occur in parallel. (However, fewer addressing modes are usually provided.)
3. The programming of the machine is still straightforward, since the processing of data and instructions occurs *side by side* instead of in a *pipeline*.[7]

---

[5] A *bus* is a hardware communication path, not transportation for school children.
[6] Just where did you think the Harvard machine was devised?
[7] A *pipeline* is a hardware assembly line. For a repetitive algorithm it increases efficiency, but it can make programming awkward.

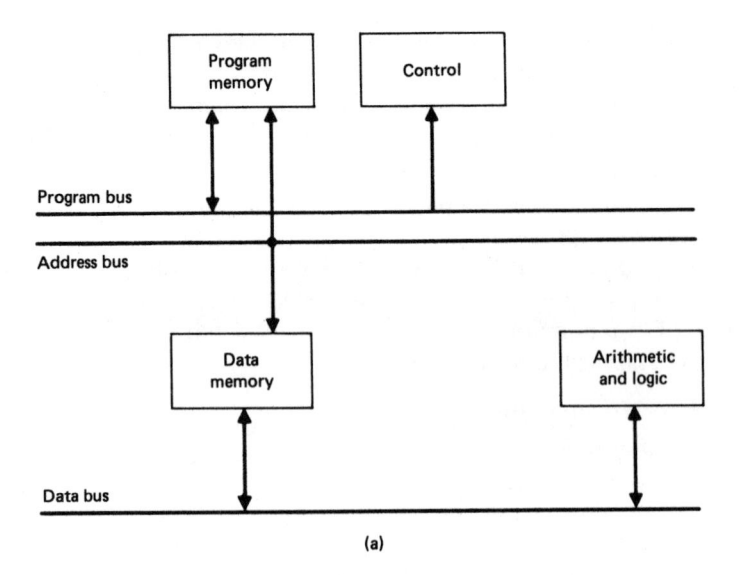

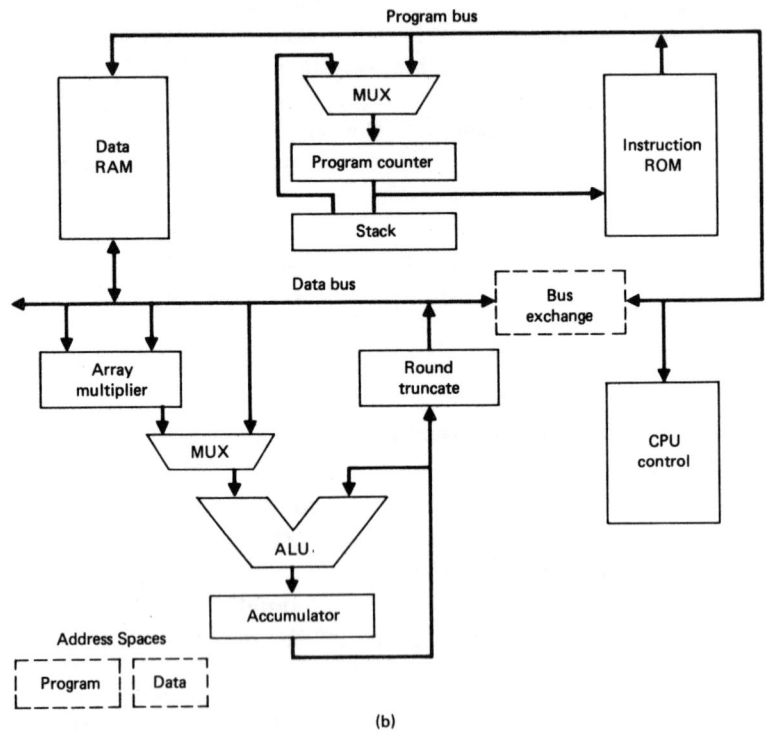

FIG. 2.3. (*a*) Harvard architecture. (*b*) Quasi-Harvard DSP architecture. (Instructions never travel over the data bus.)

4. Instructions can never be misused as data or data as instructions, thus providing better integrity.
5. It's quite simple to share instruction code between many segments of data.
6. Data and instruction widths need not be compatible but may be separately optimized.[8]

The Harvard architecture is preferable in many signal processing applications because of its inherently greater speed in sraight-line numerical programs.

Not all digital signal processors use a strict Harvard architecture. Many have augmented the architecture to provide data paths between the program and data bases. The TI 320 DSP chip is a good example of this approach.

General-purpose *digital signal processing* (DSP) chip designers may someday opt for the slightly lower computational rates but inherently greater flexibility offered by the more common Von Neumann machine. Nevertheless, the Harvard machines currently dominate most signal-processing and control applications.

2.3.1.3. DSPs in the '80s

Digital signal-processing systems have been built for a number of years. Ben Gold, of MIT's Lincoln Laboratory, has pointed out that when the application is not precisely known, simple sequential structures using fast hardware technologies are frequently better than a highly parallel architecture. This is true because

1. Development of sequential programs is generally easier.
2. A fast parallel structure which works well for some algorithms will work terribly for others.

For reasons such as these, the general-purpose signal processor is one of the more attractive applications for IC technology. Such a processor *sequentially* implements a number of signal-processing operations on a numerical signal representation. Since the machine is sequential, programming for a large class of operations is relatively easy. The inclusion of fast arithmetic capability makes many real-time (or near real-time) functions possible. Since the IC is photographically produced on a single piece of silicon and is essentially just a somewhat specialized micro, the

---

[8] While data and instruction widths can be different in a Von Neumann machine, they must still be simply related, such as 15 bits for instructions and 60 bits for data. In Harvard machines, no simple relation between the two is required.

final product has the potential of becoming competitively inexpensive.[9] Several companies are currently banking on this and have produced IC's of this type. Three of these are described in Chapter 3.

2.3.2. Special-purpose digital processors

Research scientists have gotten very excited over the idea of programmable signal processors. If they were in general use for signal processing, applications could be updated by altering software in existing products. Such generality, however, means an increase in the size (and consequently in the cost) of the IC. Also, given a large size, a greater architectural generality must be traded off against speed in performing particular tasks. The hardware design can certainly be more efficient if the algorithm to be performed is strictly limited. Until now the rule has been: If a widget is intended to do some particular function, we expect to have to design that widget, rather than reprogram an old widget.

While the prospect of new, low-cost, programmable signal-handling hardware is certainly exciting, the reality is still that of yesterday. Most high-volume commercial signal-processing applications are still being handled by special-purpose chips. In particular, all of the high-volume talking chips are special-purpose processors of some kind.

The simplest special-purpose signal processors perform a single arithmetic function. An example is the multiplier-accumulator IC, which can easily perform a *scalar product* of two vectors. A scalar product is the sum of the products of each of the components of two vectors. That is, for $\mathbf{x}(n)$ and $\mathbf{y}(n)$, two vectors of length N, the scalar product is

$$SP = \sum_n \mathbf{x}(n) \cdot \mathbf{y}(n)$$

This operation is used for autocorrelation, for example, a common operation in signal processing, particularly in LPC analysis (see Chapter 4). By having a single component capable of performing this operation at a high speed [200 ns (nanoseconds) per product], high-performance systems may be constructed.

The main problem with such systems is that they are optimal only for a very restricted class of algorithms. Although the autocorrelation operation may dominate the execution time of some procedures, other functions may be of sufficient complexity to reduce the importance of the fast single-function chip. For instance, if a MULTIPLY AND ACCUMU-

---

[9] There will be a big market for them if they're cheap. They will be cheap if there is a big market for them.

Speech Hardware Considerations 45

LATE take 200 ns but the address calculation and memory fetch to provide the multiplicand take 10 μs (microseconds), the speed will be wasted. This is an obvious mismatch. In practice, the usual system consideration is much less obvious. If the signal-processing function can be sufficiently well defined to *hard-wire* the entire system with fast parts, there will be fewer performance trade-offs than in a fully programmable system.

If the sales volume for the application is sufficiently high and the performance requirements sufficiently low, the entire system can be integrated on a single chip. This has been the case with speech-synthesis systems. Single-chip *codecs* and *modem* filters[10] have been in use for several years. In each case, the signal-processing algorithm had to be frozen, and in return, the manufacturers were able to provide an inexpensive product.

The design costs and complexities of these systems are skyrocketing. It may become infeasible to follow the changing needs of the equipment manufacturers using the current long-cycle IC design process. Their needs are changing quickly, and chip complexity is growing explosively. With tens or hundreds of thousands of transistors on a VLSI circuit, the problem of interconnection alone is mind-boggling. It can, in practice, take years to make a new VLSI design into a reality.

Some suggest that the answer to this inflexibility lies in the general-purpose chip, since it can be reprogrammed for different functions. However, as has already been pointed out, such chips necessarily use more silicon "real estate"[11] than a special-purpose chip providing the same function. This means a higher base cost for manufacturing. It would appear that special-purpose chips can be expected to dominate the market for some time to come. This is particularly true if the design and manufacture of IC's can be streamlined from the present state of affairs.

Special-purpose digital signal processors tend to be inflexible by microprocessor standards. For instance, memory-addressing capabilities are usually very limited, and there are frequently no conditional branches in the control flow. However, these sacrifices[12] simplify the design, which makes the chip smaller, easier to test, and quicker to get to market.

Most commercial speech synthesizers are currently implemented with special-purpose digital chips. A number of these are described in the next chapter.

---

[10] *Codecs* are described later in this chapter. A *modem*, or modulator-demodulator, is the device with which computers communicate over telephone lines.

[11] A quaint term that circuit designers use to describe the area of a silicon chip. It does not refer to beach property.

[12] They aren't *really* sacrifices, since the function is specified well enough that we don't need much flexibility. I was just being dramatic.

2.3.3. Analog signal processors

For the analysis and synthesis of speech, there is always at least some analog signal processing. At the very least, the original speech signal must be filtered and digitized, both of which require analog processing. A digital synthesizer must also feed its output through a DAC, another analog system, to reconstruct an analog signal.[13]

It is obviously more economical to implement a task with analog hardware if that hardware is less complex than the conversion hardware (ADC and DAC) required for digital processing of analog signals. In many other instances, it is still more expensive to implement an algorithm with digital than with analog hardware.

Over the last decade, a series of techniques have been developed which perform sampled data processing using charge, as opposed to binary numbers, for the signal representation. These are the only analog sampled data techniques which have been implemented on integrated circuits. Circuits which perform these operations are called *charge-transfer devices* (CTDs). A common CTD is a type of analog delay line, called a "bucket brigade." This delays an electric charge representing the signal and uses an integrated circuit structure of capacitors connected by switches. Such a mechanism can be used for applications such as audio reverberation.

In recent years, a new class of charge-transfer devices has been developed, called *switched-capacitor filters*. A common interpretation of these filters is as a resistor approximation. That is, one could design an analog-active filter with resistors, capacitors, and op amps (*operational amplifiers*), and then replace the resistors with capacitors switched back and forth to transmit charge. The switched capacitor, then, acts like a sampled data resistor. More precisely, a switched-capacitor filter is the analog counterpart to a digital discrete time filter. All of the sampled data mathematics is the same as for digital filters.[14] However, the signal is represented by electric charge instead of by symbolically stored numbers.

For instance, take the digital flow graph in Figure 2.4.

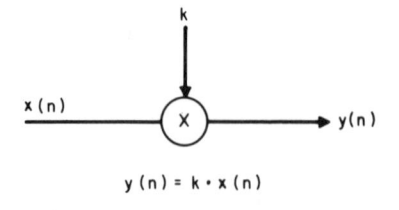

FIG. 2.4. Digital flow graph of a MULTIPLY.

$y(n) = k \cdot x(n)$

---

[13] Unfortunately, we don't as yet have a good way to directly "hear" digital data.

[14] Digital filters compute their output as a weighted sum of past outputs and inputs. See Appendix B for an introduction to this math.

It shows that $y(n) = a \times x(n)$. This can be implemented as an analog circuit as shown in Figure 2.5.

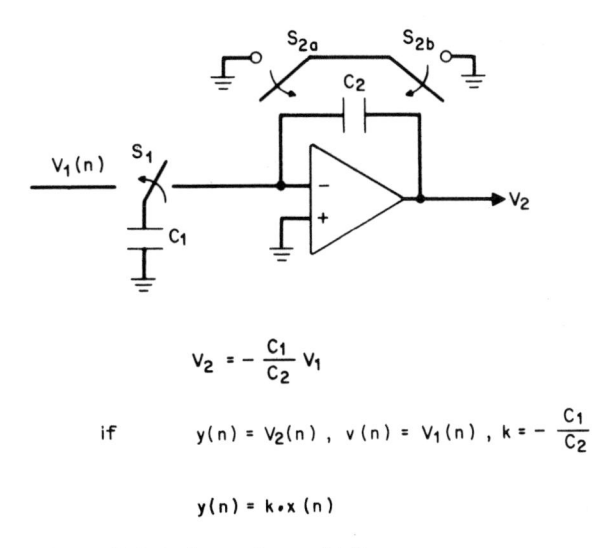

$$V_2 = -\frac{C_1}{C_2} V_1$$

if $\quad y(n) = V_2(n)$, $v(n) = V_1(n)$, $k = -\frac{C_1}{C_2}$

$$y(n) = k \cdot x(n)$$

FIG. 2.5. Switched-capacitor multiplier.

If the amplifier is an ideal op amp, the total charge dumped on the input capacitor when S_1 is closed must be balanced by the charge pulled from the output capacitor. Since charge is capacitance times voltage, we get

$$C_1 \times V_1 = -C_2 \times V_2$$

therefore $V_2/V_1 = -C_1/C_2$

The capacitor *ratio* determines the signal multiplier. This ratio tends to be stable over the usual variations in the fabrication process, although the absolute size of the capacitances may vary quite a bit.

Addition can be performed by dumping charges from other capacitors. Integration is performed if the output capacitor is not "cleared" after each arithmetic cycle (the capacitor acts as an analog accumulator). Lossy integration (as in a low-pass filter) can be performed by throwing away some of the integrated charge each cycle.

Figure 2.5 can be considered a low-pass filter (actually an integrator) if we do not zero the output capacitor. The frequency response will go infinite at zero frequency, since any dc voltage will increase the output without limit. It is an analog implementation of the digital flow graph (Figure 2.6).

Because of this equivalence, virtually any digital signal flow diagram

48   Talking Chips

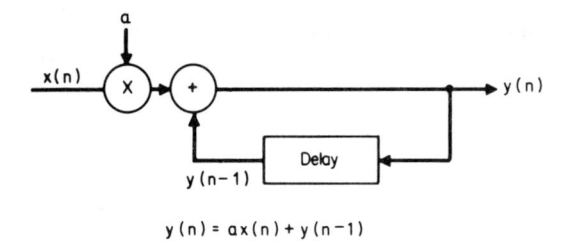

$$y(n) = ax(n) + y(n-1)$$

FIG. 2.6. Integrator flow graph.

can be implemented by a switched-capacitor filter. In particular, if any filter can be described as a combination of integrators, it can be efficiently implemented and can be designed to be resistant to effects from process-dependent parasitics (which ordinarily limit the accuracy of capacitive circuits) (Figure 2.7).

The advantages of the switched-capacitor techniques include high speed, small filters, and easy interface to the analog world. In comparison to other analog techniques, they can implement filter characteristics that depend very predictably on a clock and an easily controlled physical parameter, the ratio between two capacitor sizes. The disadvantages include built-in inflexibility and the restriction to a small class of algorithms. For simple tasks, such filters carry much less overhead than digital versions.

Switched-capacitor techniques have also gained popularity in the implementation of some functions which are fundamentally analog, such as data conversion (digital-to-analog and analog-to-digital).

The simplest talking chips are digital-to-analog converters which play back digitized and stored speech. It is instructive to consider the

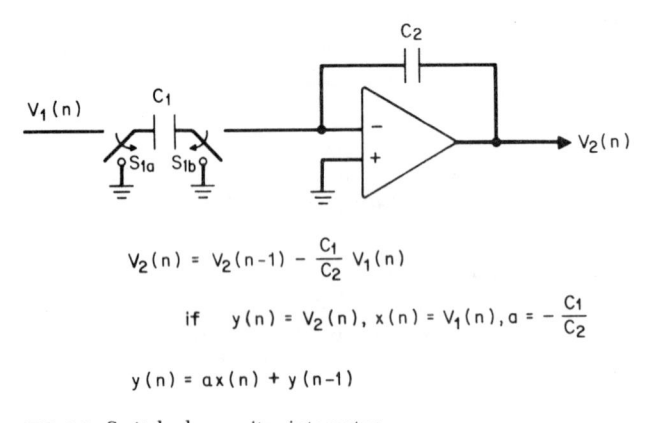

$$V_2(n) = V_2(n-1) - \frac{C_1}{C_2} V_1(n)$$

$$\text{if} \quad y(n) = V_2(n),\ x(n) = V_1(n),\ a = -\frac{C_1}{C_2}$$

$$y(n) = ax(n) + y(n-1)$$

FIG. 2.7. Switched-capacitor integrator.

functional hardware for these devices, the precursors to the low bit-rate synthesizers.

2.3.3.1. Codecs

Integrated codecs were one of the first applications of LSI circuit technology to a speech communications problem. Codec stands for *coder-decoder* and is the nonlinear (*mu law* or *A law*)[15] ADC-DAC mediating between speech and the *pulse-code modulation* (PCM) data stream.

Until the mid-1970s, these functions were performed by expensive high-speed converters which were shared by many analog channels. Thanks to rapid improvements in IC technology, such as the switched-capacitor filters, it became possible to put both the ADCs and DACs onto a single chip. In 1975 an experimental NMOS[16] IC encoder was produced at Berkeley using switched-capacitor techniques. After this, numerous manufacturers began producing similar ICs. Some used switched capacitors, some used resistor strings, and others used combinations of the two approaches.

The current generation of codecs now includes an antialiasing filter on the chip. Typically, this is also implemented with switched capacitors.

As a codec contains both an ADC and a DAC, I shall discuss each in turn. First I shall provide a brief description of the process of D/A conversion, along with some generic approaches. Then I will show A/D conversion to be an operation employing the same structure and, in fact, containing a DAC.

DACs change a numeric representation of a signal value into some physical circuit quantity. The digital input determines how switches are set in an analog circuit. This in turn produces an output voltage, current, or charge which is used as the analog signal.

One of the simplest DACs is a *resistor string* (Figure 2.8). For an N-bit converter, this is a series connection of 2^N resistors.

The digital word simply decodes to the proper tap of the resistor string for the correct output. While having many desirable characteristics, this method does require many resistors for high values of N. It can also be difficult to ensure that all those resistors are accurate enough.

In other approaches, *binary-weighted currents* are added (Figure 2.9). This can be implemented by a resistive structure called an R-$2R$ ladder. Each section (one R and one $2R$ resistor) can contribute a current corresponding to one of the bits of the digital word (Figure 2.10).

Notice that the current divides in half at each internal node, yielding

---

[15] *A law* is a European nonlinear quantization rule. It's very similar to *mu law*.
[16] *N-channel metal-oxide semiconductor*. This describes the kind of field-effect transistors that are available for the fabrication process.

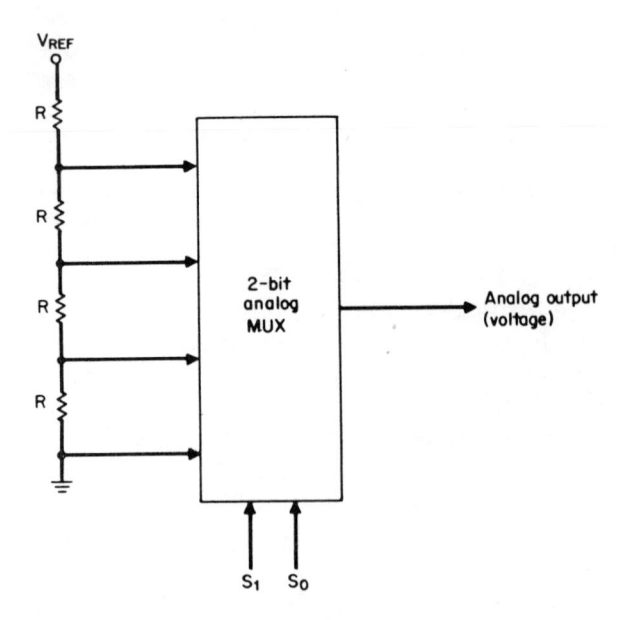

FIG. 2.8. Two-bit resistor-string DAC.

the binary-weighted currents. That is,

$$i_{out} = I_{REF}(S_{N-1}/2 + \ldots + S_0/2^N)$$

where the S coefficients are the bits of the digital word, and I_{REF} is $V_{REF}/3R$.

This approach has a parallel in the switched-capacitor domain. Instead of switching in currents, we now switch in *charge*. For the 2-bit case again, consider the switched-capacitor DAC in Figure 2.11.

For capacitors:

$$Q = C \times V$$

where Q = electrostatic charge stored, coulombs
C = capacitance, farads
V = voltage, volts

When the C capacitor is switched from V_{REF} to GND, there is a new

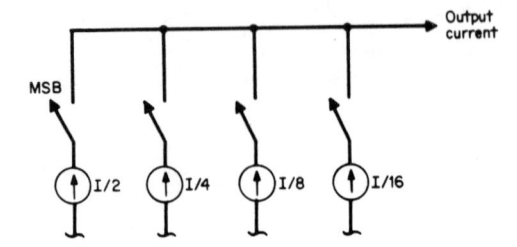

FIG. 2.9. Four-bit binary-weighted current DAC.

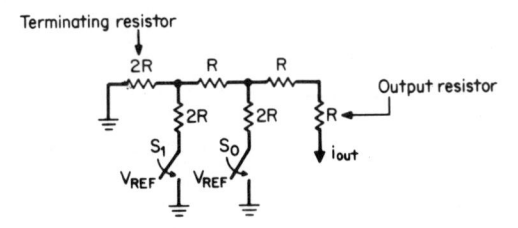

FIG. 2.10. Two-bit resistor-ladder DAC.

charge stored on the 2C capacitor:

$$Q_{2C} = (2C) \times (-V_{REF})$$

Since essentially no charge flows to or from the op amp, all of this charge comes from the output capacitor. Thus,

$$Q_{out} = -Q_{2C} = 2C \times V_{REF}$$

which is the internal signal representation. Clearly, the half-sized capacitor will contribute half as much charge to the output. Thus, the charge on the output capacitor will be an analog representation of the digital word which switched in the capacitors.

This output is generally sensed as the op amp *voltage*. For the 2C contribution case above:

$$V_{out} = Q_{out}/C_{out} = V_{REF}/2$$

The capacitor chain may of course be extended in powers of 2. Each such additional binary-weighted capacitor yields proportional voltage contributions to the output.

All of the DACs shown thus far have been linear. That is, they have implemented a transfer curve[17] that is linear. Telecommunications' DACs implement the piecewise linear approximation to mu law, as

[17] A curve showing the relation between input and output amplitudes for a systems.

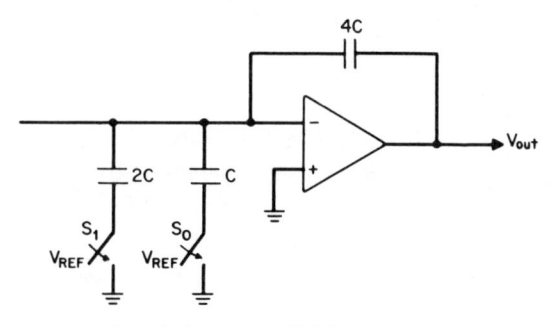

FIG. 2.11. Switched-capacitor DAC.

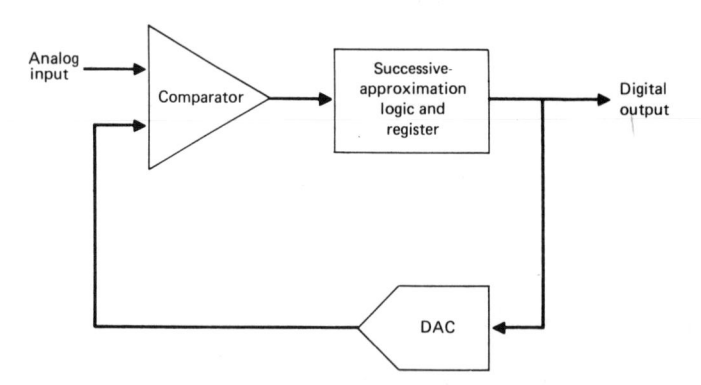

FIG. 2.12. Successive approximation A/D converter.

described in Chapter 1. The *least significant bits* (LSB)[18] are converted by a 4-bit linear DAC. The segment (or range) is chosen by changing the control parameters for the DAC via another DAC-like circuit.

The most commonly used A/D technique for medium-speed applications such as speech[19] is called *successive approximation*. Digital words are generated and are corrected bit by bit. Correction is performed after comparison between the DAC output for the trial binary word and the analog voltage to be converted. The three major parts of an ADC are:

1. The successive approximation register that holds the digital "guess"
2. The DAC that converts this guess to an analog parameter (such as voltage for comparison to the input)
3. The comparator that generates a 1 when DAC output is less than analog input, and a 0 otherwise (within the accuracy of the converter) (Figure 2.12)

The guesses are generated in a typical *binary search*. First, 1 0 0 0 0 ... is tried. If this is too high, the first bit is cleared. Otherwise, it remains set, and so on for each bit. After N such guesses, the register will hold an N-bit word that is the best available approximation to the ideal conversion value for the analog voltage at the input.

2.3.3.2. Switched-capacitor synthesizers

The filters of a frequency-domain synthesizer may be implemented in switched-capacitor technology. A number of companies have chosen this route, and two such chips are described in the next chapter. There are currently some advantages to this approach, such as low power and area

---

[18] To paraphrase Orwell, "Some bits are more significant than others." The least significant, or lower bits, are those that represent the lower powers of 2. Much as in the number 15, 5 is the least significant digit.

[19] As opposed to instrumentation (low speed) and video (high speed).

for simple filtering algorithms. However, the superior flexibility of digital approaches will probably be victorious in the end.

We can expect to be seeing far more complicated systems implemented in silicon. As the systems get more complicated, it becomes more awkward to squeeze the algorithms into the limited set of operations which can be conveniently performed via analog techniques.

2.4. AUTOMATED DESIGN TOOLS

General-purpose signal processors are desirable when the algorithm is variable. Special-purpose processors are more efficient when the algorithm is known. The latter's advantage is restricted by the current difficulty in implementing new designs for complex signal-processing systems. Their future is dependent upon advances in what is called *computer-aided design* (CAD).

Engineers have been trying for many years to streamline design of VLSI circuits by the use of sophisticated software tools. More recently, researchers have attempted to open up IC design potential to the system designer.[20] Many academic and industrial groups have devoted serious effort to the creation of software aids for high-level designers. The most optimistic have visualized a design tool, called the *silicon compiler*. Ideally, this program would compile our high-level system description into the *machine language* of the patterns for IC fabrication.

[20] Who may not know an N^+ diffusion from his grandmother's mustache.

Some programs like this have been designed, such as FIRST and MACPITTS. Detractors point out that these compilers produce very large chips (much as an inefficient compiler could turn out a large machine-code program) and that they have for the most part produced ICs that don't work. Supporters feel that these defects are temporary and point to the AGC chip of Joel Feldman, designed in three weeks with MACPITTS, as an example of things to come. All would agree, however, that the trend in computer-aided design is to provide a flexible mechanism for reprogramming new algorithms *at the level of chip design*. Standard cells are continually being developed for elementary functions (RAM, ROM, multiplier bit slices, etc.). By using automatic routing programs for interconnection, the design of new special-purpose processors can become much faster. If this approach is successful, it may give researchers the design flexibility they need without burdening the product itself with unnecessary features.

Toward this end, CAD-based design projects have been sponsored at a number of leading universities, among them MIT, Stanford, UC Berkeley, Cal Tech, and Carnegie Mellon. Students design ICs down to a computer-aided layout, then send off these designs to sponsored silicon "foundries" for fabrication.

The level of sophistication of CAD software has increased by leaps and bounds over the last few years. The basic blocks of a functional CAD system are:

1. *Register transfer level simulation.* Data flow check at an architectural level
2. *Logic simulation.* Logic design check of boolean outputs given boolean inputs
3. *Schematic capture.* Extraction of node interconnections from schematic
4. *Circuit simulation.* Circuit design checks of given node interconnections
5. *Layout graphics editor.* Graphics tool for quick layout using repeated cells
6. *Circuit extraction.* Extraction of circuit values from layout for a repeat of circuit simulation.

Procedures based on such software can take the IC from the architectural stage to a tape ready for the mask-making process. While designers must still actively participate in the intermediate stages of design, it is still undoubtedly true that the overall process is greatly speeded by these tools.

In the nitty-gritty world of industry, these techniques have just begun to be implemented. Researchers in academia have already had some notable successes with these techniques. A speech IC designed at UC Berkeley is a good example of what can be done.

2.5. THE BERKELEY VOCODER

Bjorn Solberg, Steve Pope, and Bob Brodersen at UC Berkeley have designed an LPC (*linear predictive coding*) vocoder[21] IC. This chip performs real-time LPC analysis and synthesis using an adaptive lattice technique. In this approach, the reflection coefficients are estimated at every sample point. The chip was built using the conservative design rules[22] of Mead and Conway, on a silicon-gate NMOS process. The resulting die is 225 × 265 mils (about 60,000 square mils). While not a small die, it is the first such complete implementation on a single IC. The designers did not attempt to reduce the size by aggressively minimizing the implementation of each section. One can reasonably assume that a commercial version could be made quite a bit smaller.

The chip does LPC analysis (consisting of pitch tracking and an adaptive estimation of the coefficients for the synthesis filter) as well as synthesis from received parameters. The analysis is performed digitally on the input sequence.

The bulk of the processing is done by three computational units. These blocks are identical in basic design but differ in details of configuration, such as word length and size of data memory. Each block processes full data widths in parallel but communicates to other blocks via serial buses to simplify interconnect. All three are controlled by a single processor block. Special-purpose circuits perform those functions not easily done by the three main blocks. These occupy a relatively small percentage of the die and so were designed using a small library of *standard cells*, which were bit serial and thus easily expandable to various word lengths. This differs from the full custom fashion of design, yet was achieved without a large area penalty.

The die photo in Figure 2.13 is labeled to show the major blocks on the chip. The three main processors are the *filter*, *correlator*, and *pitch tracker*. The filter is used in filtering for the analysis, synthesis, and pitch tracking. The correlator estimates the analysis filter parameters. The pitch tracker implements the Gold pitch-tracking algorithm,[23] which determines the excitation type and the pitch period for voiced speech.

---

[21] This term stands for VOice CODER and was coined by Homer Dudley in 1936 to describe a speech analyzer-synthesizer.

[22] Design rules are restrictions on the minimum size and separations of the geometrical patterns used in the layout of a chip.

[23] Briefly described in Chapter 4.

56   *Talking Chips*

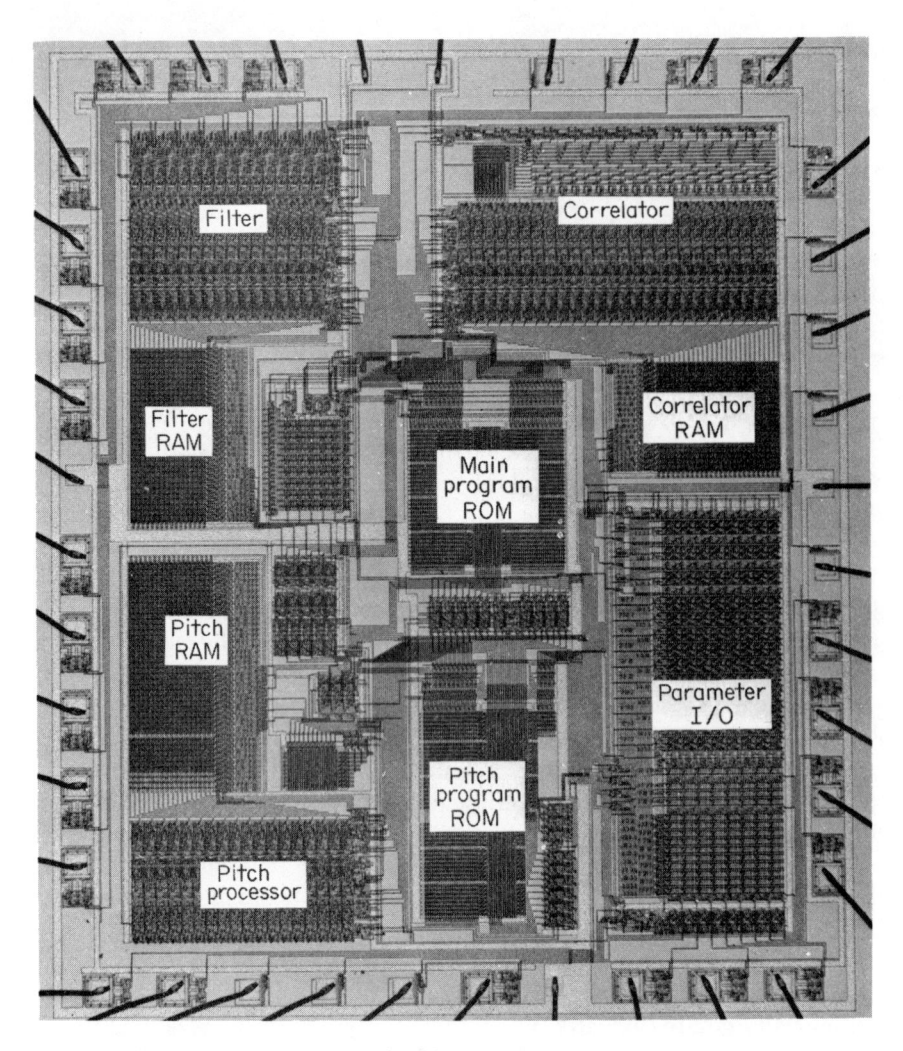

FIG. 2.13. Die photo of Berkeley vocoder IC.

The Berkeley vocoder illustrates that the computer-aided design approach is eminently workable. As a further benefit, projects such as this are developing libraries of standard signal-processing functions which may be applied to future IC's

While the successes of this project and that of others, such as the RISC (*reduced instruction-set computer*) IC, suggest that automatic IC generation is on its way, a true silicon compiler still lies well in the future. Even if the architecture-to-layout phases were streamlined, the algorithm-to-architecture transferal is far from trivial. An IC cannot be guaranteed to work when the layout is done, even for "conservative" design rules. IC fabrication is a lengthy, complex, and sensitive process, and changing parameters can make designs fail. In industry, design engineers have worked closely with process engineers to ensure that their chips would work. The ideal of a silicon compiler feeding a silicon foundry is dependent on a tight coupling, at least at the software level, between the two ends.

Most university VLSI projects to date have not actually worked, possibly because of this problem. However, recent successes suggest that these difficulties are temporary. New speech-system designs are being strongly affected by this increased capability to design special-purpose ICs quickly, using the silicon-compiler types of design tools.

SILICON REAL ESTATE OFFICE
SELLER MOTIVATED!
33,000 MIL^2!
DON'T MISS THIS ONE!
ONLY 20,000 MIL^2
200 NSEC MULTIPLIER
11-9-72
12-72
100,000 MIL^2
GENERAL PURPOSE SIGNAL PROCESSOR
WITH A POLYSILICON VIEW!
12-3-72
QUALITY
SPEECH SYNTHESIS
ONLY 30,000 MIL^2!!
PERFECT FOR CHILDREN
B.B.

CHAPTER 3

SOME REAL CHIPS

3.1. INTRODUCTION

In the last chapter, we described the major types of speech-processsing hardware. When these concepts are translated to silicon, new constraints arise. In particular, there is a major trade-off between die area and design time. A quickly designed working part can get the jump on the competitor. On the other hand, more time might be devoted to optimizing the size of the part. Size is a crucial consideration for these devices, because larger chips require a larger defect-free hunk of silicon and larger defect-free masks for critical photographic steps of the fabrication process. Consequently, the *yield*, or number of good die per wafer, decreases exponentially with size. While prices can be substantially affected by market conditions, the wafer cost can dominate when the pricing gets tough. Historically, once a product matures, the pricing *does* get tough. Ergo: the dominance of the concern about "silicon real estate." Small is beautiful.

This chapter will skip through some of the major products that have been built for speech synthesis. While certainly not exhaustive,[1] it should be sufficient to give the reader the general idea of the design trade-offs for this area.

[1] My apologies to those who have been skipped. At least I didn't say anything bad about you.

3.2. GENERAL-PURPOSE DSPs

3.2.1. Introduction

While general-purpose *digital signal processors* (DSPs) are currently not competitive with special-purpose synthesizers, many proponents of this approach insist that it is the wave of the future. Could be. Three of the major examples of this genre are described here.

3.2.2. The Intel 2920

The Intel 2920, first introduced in 1979, was an analog and digital signal-processing chip specifically designed to replace analog subsystems. The chip had a 9-bit analog data-acquisition system with four analog inputs and eight analog outputs. Using a switched-capacitor comparator, the chip could compare analog inputs against those of a folded resistor string DAC. Limit comparisons, comparisons at the *transistor-transistor logic* (TTL) level, and successive approximation were available input techniques under program control (Figure 3.1).

The 2920 was the first chip to incorporate both analog and digital signal-processing techniques. Usual digital signal-processing chips used off-chip converters to transform analog signals into their digital equivalents. To really replace analog subsystems, the Intel designers had to provide an on-chip analog interface.

The digital signal-processing section of the chip is simple in nature and is used to implement algorithms such as filters, oscillators, or modulators.

The instruction *read-only memory* (ROM) is 24 bits wide. Each word provides two 6-bit addresses for operands, a 4-bit shift constant, 3 bits for the *arithmetic logic unit* (ALU) function, and 5 bits for control. There are 192 words of instruction ROM available. Addresses for instructions are generated in a very direct way. The program counter starts at zero, executes the first instruction, and is incremented to the next instruction. When a reset instruction is executed, the program counter is reset back to zero. No other jumps, conditional or unconditional, are possible. The theory behind this is that signal-processing routines are so regular that they require no conditional branches.[2]

The data *random-access memory* (RAM) is 40 words of 25 bits each, giving a wide numeric range. This is sufficient storage for the implementation of 20 second-order sections, a 40-tap transversal filter,[3] or a 20-stage lattice filter. The RAM has dual ports, so both operands for the ALU

---
[2] Try writing a program like that sometime!
[3] A filter for which the output is the weighted sum of past inputs.

Some Real Chips 61

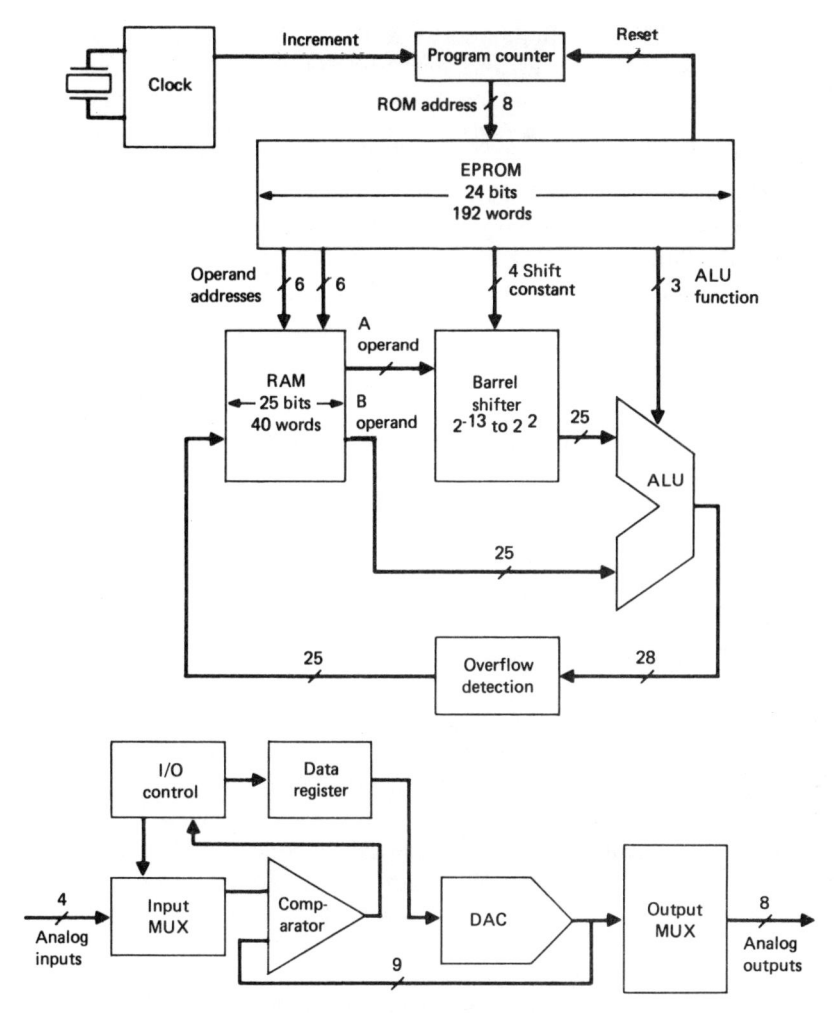

FIG. 3.1. Block diagram of the 2920 by Intel.

are fetched simultaneously. The A operand is passed through a barrel shifter (where multiple bits can be shifted in a single cycle) to be scaled by a binary number from 2^{-13} to 2^2. The B operand goes directly to the ALU where arithmetic, logical, and magnitude functions (absolute magnitude or limit functions) are performed.

The ALU result is checked for overflow before returning to the data RAM. It is stored in the address location previously occupied by the B operand. Other than binary scaling via shifts, no multiplication operation is provided. The Intel designers reasoned that the multiplication of a

RAM value by a filter coefficient constant could be done with reasonable accuracy by several scaling and accumulation operations. Since the processor was to replace analog components with limited accuracy anyway, why build a large-array multiplier with tremendous coefficient precision?[4]

The chip was fabricated in NMOS silicon-gate EPROM technology in a die area of about 46,600 square mils. It was an interesting experiment and certainly educational for everyone in the industry. As a high-volume analog subsystem, however, it clearly lost out to switched-capacitor filters.

3.2.3. The Bell DSP

The Bell digital signal processor chip was introduced in 1980 as the first chip of a family developed by Bell Laboratories for internal telecommunication applications. This processor was built in silicon-gate NMOS with a die size of approximately 110,000 square mils. Running with a 5-mHz clock, the Bell DSP can churn out 1.25 million operations per second. This is fast enough for 40 second-order sections at an 8-kHz sampling rate (Figure 3.2).

A 16 × 20 array multiplier and 40-bit accumulator give the Bell signal processor great numeric precision. The data RAM is 20 bits wide, giving a numeric range of more than a million for each word stored. The 128 words of on-chip RAM provide sufficient memory for most filter applications.

The storage ROM for instructions is 16 bits wide and can be used to hold constants and filter coefficients. The 312 words of ROM data are the maximum that can be fetched for an 8-kHz sample rate. In some applications, however, other sections of ROM code may be executed as data is processed. The Bell designers were thereby able to justify 1024 words of instruction ROM, allowing three entirely separate programs to reside on the same chip. The arithmetic unit is also pipelined in three stages. Data transfers, multiplications, and additions all occur simultaneously after the pipe is full. Programming the chip to take advantage of these features requires some thought.

The chip has been successfully programmed to implement a speech synthesizer and low-speed data modems. It has also been programmed to act as a dual-tone multifrequency receiver. It is still expensive,[5] but Bell

---

[4] Because it is cheaper to perform simple low-accuracy analog tasks with analog components. The applications that are interesting for digital signal processing generally require a lot of accuracy.

[5] The production cost is high. As of this writing, Bell is not yet permitted to offer the chip for sale to the general public.

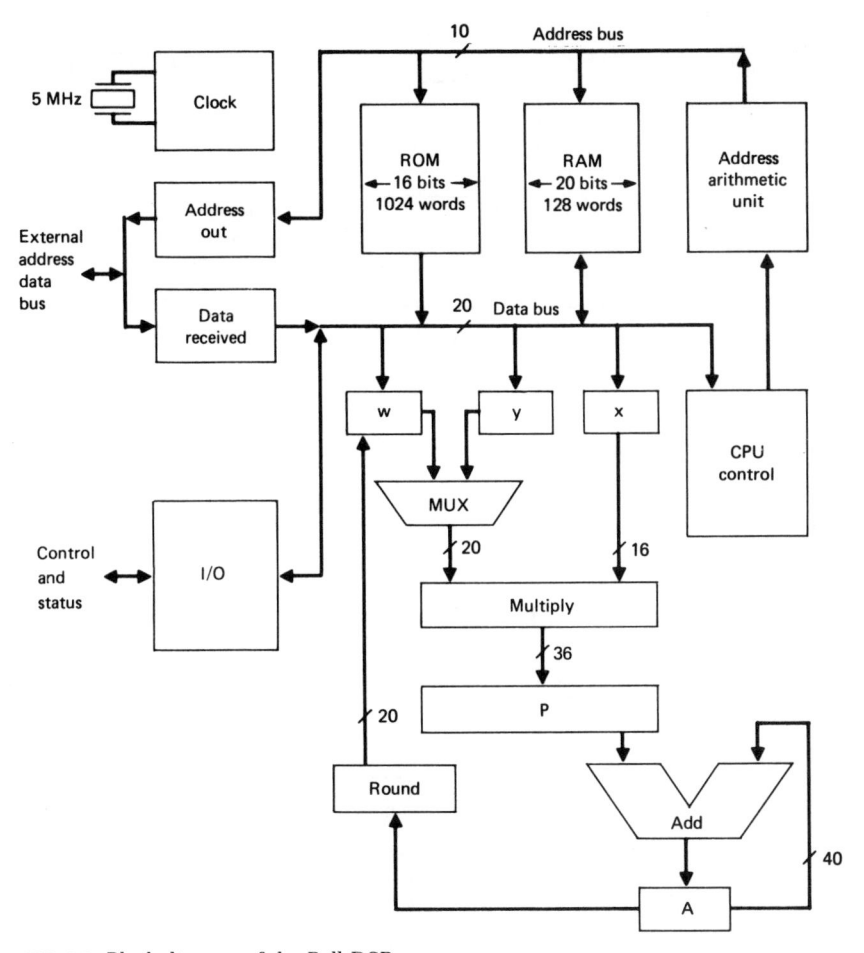

FIG. 3.2. Block diagram of the Bell DSP.

engineers anticipate large price reductions in the coming years. This would make it feasible to put such chips in each subscriber phone.

3.2.4. The TI 320 DSP

In late 1982, Texas Instruments, Incorporated (TI), announced a general-purpose digital signal processor that immediately received rave reviews. The TI DSP chip was a powerful number cruncher, with a simple, easy-to-program architecture. This combination, the TI engineers reasoned, would initiate enough volume to bring the price down to $10, which would really blow open the DSP market (Figure 3.3).

The TI DSP chip, operating with a 10-mHz clock, executes 5 million

64 *Talking Chips*

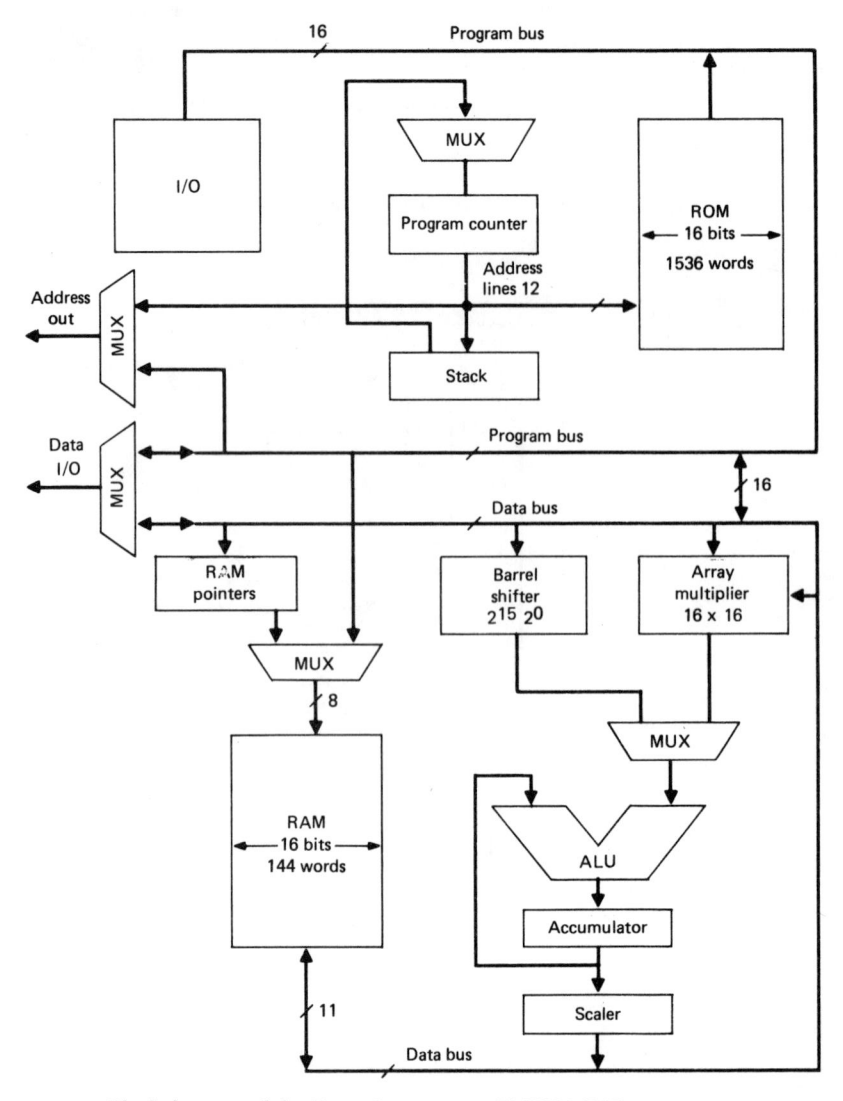

FIG. 3.3. Block diagram of the Texas Instruments TMS320 DSP.

instructions per second. An instruction can typically be executed in a single 200-ns cycle, and several operations may execute in parallel. Speed is its middle name.

The TI designers chose a Harvard architecture to permit simultaneous fetch and execution of instructions. TI did allow transfers between program and data buses. Constant data stored in program ROM may be given to the data RAM, and the contents of the accumulator may be given to the program counter for computed address branches. These simple modifications eliminated many of the problems of the strict Harvard architecture. However, the addressing modes were quite limited.

The TI chip offered over 1500 words of on-chip ROM, with expansion off chip to 4000. The instruction and data widths were 16 bits. This compatibility made programming and off-board expansion easier.

The data RAM was 16 bits wide and 144 words deep, allowing for 128 filter coefficients with RAM left over for program linkage. The numeric computation unit sported both a 16 × 16 array multiplier and a 16-bit barrel shifter. The ALU was a full 32 bits wide and offered logical as well as arithmetic functions. Either the low or the high 16 bits of the accumulator could be stored in data RAM.

High-speed I/O enabled the chip to transfer 2.5 million words per second to or from external memory or from program ROM to data RAM.

The TI chip was fabricated in silicon-gate NMOS with a die size of about 70,000 square mils. TI expects to shrink the chip down to approximately 57,000 square mils, which will increase its speed to over 7 million operations per second.

3.3. DEDICATED DIGITAL SYNTHESIZERS

3.3.1. Introduction

Thus far, almost all speech-synthesis ICs are of this type. Some are time-domain synthesizers (National, Sharp), some are frequency-domain (TI, General Instruments), but all are special-purpose microcomputers which talk. Their story follows.

3.3.2. Digitalker® the chip

In the summer of 1978, Dr. Forrest Mozer signed a contract with National Semiconductor Corporation of Santa Clara, California. National would buy the exclusive right to use his patented method of time-domain synthesis for three years. Dr. Mozer would use his basement laboratory to encode a customer's vocabulary into a ROM pattern, and National would build both the speech ROM and the synthesizer.

Mozer detailed the workings of his time-domain synthesizer to the MOS LSI custom-design group in November of that year. The original Digitalker® chip (Figure 3.4) was fabricated in metal-gate NMOS technology, the same process as the General Instruments (GI) chip, described later. Like GI, National had expertise in NMOS ROMs and simple controllers. Building the synthesizer in NMOS would allow easy expansion to a single-chip synthesizer with ROM on board.

The National engineers did not have to design the digital filter required

66   *Talking Chips*

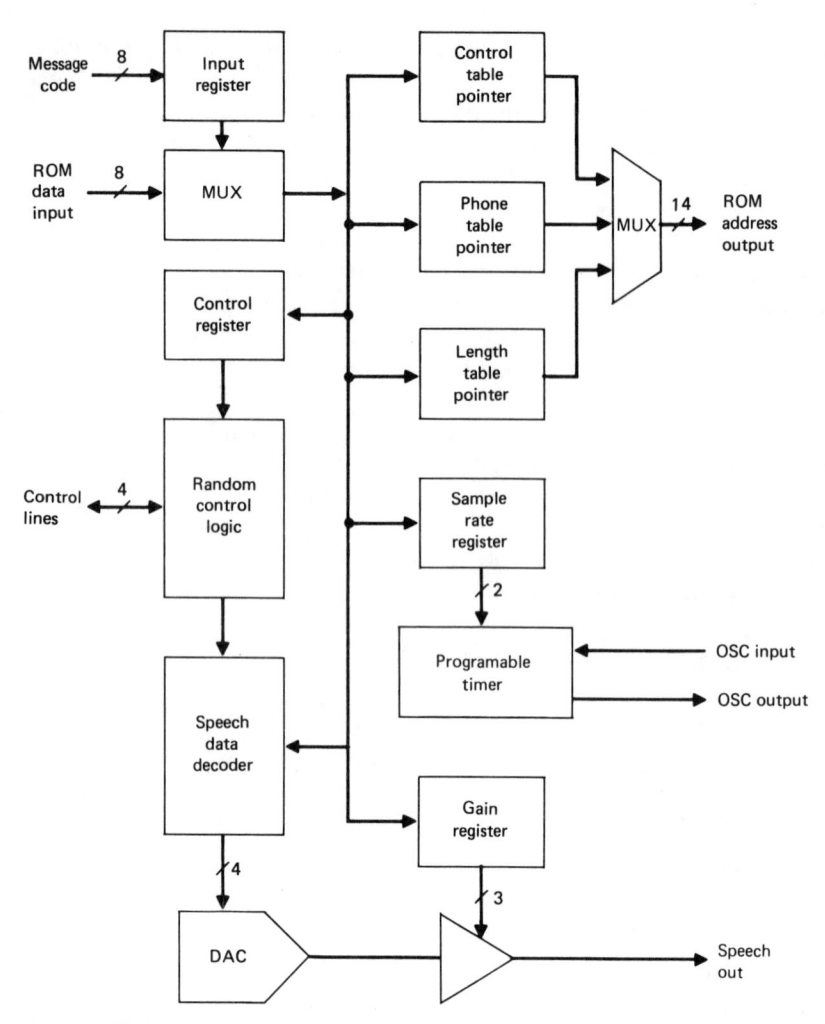

FIG. 3.4. Block diagram of the Digitalker® speech synthesizer by National Semiconductor.

by their competitors using *linear predictive coding.* The time-domain synthesizer would read in a message code and then extract amplitude sequencing and waveform data from an external ROM, building up a speech waveform by concatenation. Rather than use special-purpose ROMs, like the very slow TI ROM or the serial-mode GI ROM, National decided to use a standard ROM interface. By using general-purpose off-the-shelf ROMs, National hoped to keep the prices down by increasing the volume of an existing product line. Using standard ROMs also made customer development much easier. A customer could easily develop his speech product with *erasable programmable read-only memories* (EPROMs) or standard vocabulary ROMs and then interface them with Digitalker®. Both TI and GI had special-purpose ROMs that interfaced to their speech chips, so their customers could not use standard EPROMs without extra hardware.

The price National paid for this standard ROM interface was a larger package. The 14 address lines, 8 data lines, 8 message lines, and the normal control lines were all required. This meant that a 28-pin package was insufficient, and National had to use the more expensive 40-pin package. The extra packaging cost and board space were considered less significant than the increased flexibility for EPROM interface. Now a customer could change his vocabulary at the last minute or build several hundred prototypes of a product without committing to a custom ROM from GI or TI. This strategy paid off. Many companies that couldn't afford mask-tooling changes, and many larger companies that were still evaluating speech products, now jumped onto the bandwagon. Giving the customer a simple interface to standard ROMs allowed many new entries into the speech market. Talking toasters had a chance to compete with Speak and Spell.[6]

The Digitalker® synthesizer was really just a large controller. An 8-bit message code on the input pins specified one of 256 different words or phrases. The message code was an index into an entry table where a control pointer and length table pointer were stored. These stored pointers were extracted from ROM and loaded into the control table pointer and length pointer in the synthesizer. The control pointer addressed a packet of information that described the utterance. The first field of information in the control packet was the address of the waveform data. This address was extracted and loaded into the phone table pointer.[7] The synthesizer then loaded control information, such as duration and sequencing rules, into the control register. The duration was specified as a number of stored periods to play and a number of repeats for each period. Different phone types also had different sequencing rules to adjust the ordering of the output sequence.

The next information field loaded by the synthesizer from the control package was the sample rate. Unlike LPC synthesizers, the Digitalker® was able to dynamically change sample rates at phone boundaries. This allowed fricatives (both voiced and unvoiced) to be played at a 13-kHz sample rate and normal voiced sounds to be played at a 10-kHz rate. Since there was no multiplier requirement to limit speed, the Digitalker® was able to increase the bandwidth for those speech signals which

---

[6] Can you spell "burned"?

[7] Phones are speech sounds. This table is a library of such sounds used for a particular vocabulary.

contained high-frequency components. The sample-rate register could also reduce the bandwidth down to 8 kHz for limited bandwidth channels, such as the telephone. This bandwidth reduction had a corresponding data-rate reduction, allowing the synthesizer great flexibility in data rate and sound quality trade-offs.

The length table pointer addressed a table in ROM that contained pitch data. The pitch of the speech signal was determined by the amount of silence between fixed-length segment playbacks. This was adjustable on Digitalker® II. Digitalker® I had no pitch adjustments, which meant that the same word with two intonations had to be stored twice. Also, by adding the pitch adjustment, words could more easily be concatenated into phrases having a more natural cadence.

In very low data-rate applications, words of approximately the same duration could use the same pitch table information. This gave each word the same intonation but eliminated storing pitch data for each word.

The final pointer into ROM was the phone table pointer. This pointer accessed a library of compressed waveform data. A 3-bit gain coefficient at the beginning of each period gave a nonlinear scaling of the speech data stored. The speech waveforms were stored either as 2-bit or 4-bit quantizations. These would be expanded either by nonlinear ROM lookups or by delta encoding. Delta encoding was dropped for Digitalker® II, as some complexity and some types of distortion were partly due to this technique. The selection of these coarsely quantized waveforms is discussed in Chapter 4.

After expanding the speech data out to its final value, the synthesizer loaded the data into a 4-bit resistor-ladder DAC followed by a 3-bit switched-capacitor gain control. Off-chip filtering would be needed for antialiasing and signal deemphasis.

The speech chip occupied about 30,000 square mils of area, larger than expected since there was no digital filter hogging silicon real estate. The problem with this first chip was that the interconnection of the random control logic took up more area than the logic itself. Still, the product held up in the marketplace. The key question was, Could time domain survive in an ocean of frequency-domain research and product lines?

The next affirmative answer to that question came from our friends across the sea.

3.3.3. Japanese time-domain synthesis

In the summer of 1980, Sharp announced a new single-chip synthesizer. Like many other Japanese companies, Sharp chose CMOS (*complementary metal-oxide semiconductor*) technology for chip implementation. Metal-gate CMOS was a reliable, production-worthy process with millions of digital watches testifying to its low wafer cost and high yields (Figure 3.5).

While slightly less dense and higher in cost than its cousin, metal-gate NMOS, CMOS had a couple of very attractive features. First and foremost was low power consumption. While most NMOS synthesizers used 200 milliwatts or more, the Sharp synthesizer ate up a mere 4 milliwatts when operating and only 3 *microwatts* in standby mode. Fifty times less power in operation and 10,000 times less power when standing by is nothing to sneeze at, especially if you're building portable products.

A second feature of CMOS was its wide supply range. While TI's first synthesizer used -12 V (National's used $+7$, and GI's $+5$), Sharp's needed only 2.7 V. Now two AAA batteries could power a speech synthesizer with on-board ROM. CMOS has other advantages as well. It has a wider temperature range and better noise immunity than NMOS. Low power remains the principal advantage, however. With this feature, Sharp was able to add speech to a wide range of products including watches that "told the time."

The Sharp designers saw time-domain synthesis as being very attractive. Medium-quality speech for male and female adults and children was achieved using about 2000 bits/s. Tones, chimes, and sustained musical sounds were easily done without the power- and area-consuming digital filter required by frequency-domain techniques like LPC. Influenced by the work of Forrest Mozer, Sharp decided to synthesize by playing back

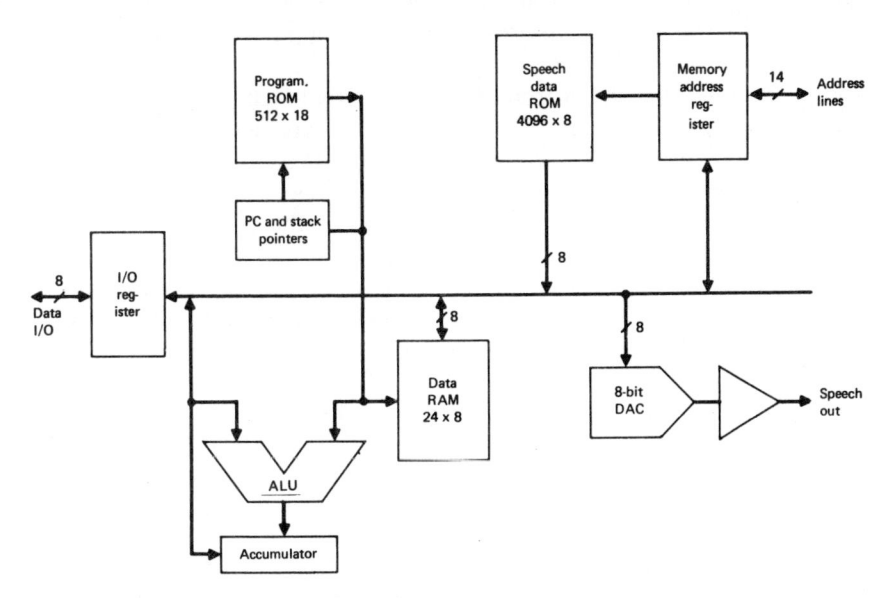

FIG. 3.5. The Sharp CMOS speech synthesizer.

low bit-rate waveforms. Unvoiced sounds were encoded by storing zero-crossing information with 2 bits of amplitude. Voiced waveforms were represented by 4 bits of *adaptive differential pulse-code modulation* (ADPCM) information. Amplitude information was stored separately, and the stored waveforms were frequently repeated. Unlike the Mozer technique, waveforms were not symmetrized by phase adjustment during the analysis process. Ignoring the phase, Sharp was not able to cluster waveform samples near quantization levels. This deficiency meant an increase in quantization noise. As compensation, each pitch period used a unit step size which maximized the signal-to-noise ratio.

By skipping phase adjustment, Sharp hoped to sidestep those parts of Mozer's patented process that yielded very distinct-looking waveforms. By not paying a royalty to Dr. Mozer and not having the digital filter required by LPC, Sharp's designers hoped to produce the lowest-cost product.

National Semiconductor had faced an interconnect problem due to the extensive use of random logic in their first time-domain synthesizer. Sharp instead designed a special-purpose microcomputer whose architecture, instruction set, arithmetic, and address capability were optimized for their chosen synthesis technique. The microcode ROM which held the instructions for synthesis was 18 bits wide, so little decoding had to be done for control. The 35 instructions and small number of addressing modes gave a simple yet elegant solution to the problem of pasting together time waveforms. The processor stepped through the data ROM, expanding waveforms and repeating pitch periods as directed by the microcode. The RAM, ROM, and ALU were connected by a single 8-bit data bus. This structured-architecture approach paid off. Very little of the chip was wasted on interconnect. Large dense blocks were linked to a common bus. Only the addition of an 8-bit DAC made the Sharp chip a synthesizer and not just another microcontroller.

On a less dense CMOS process and with double the on-board ROM, Sharp's chip was several thousand square mils smaller than that of its closest competitor, GI. While National's chip had been somewhat smaller, the Japanese IC included an on-board speech ROM. Some would say that the Sharp speech quality suffered from the lack of the phase-oriented analysis. Nonetheless, the concept of building a special-purpose computer for speech synthesis was definitely the product of some "sharp" minds.

Naturally, National struck back.

3.3.4. Microtalker synthesizer

As of this writing, the design has been completed for National Semiconductor's new speech-synthesizer family called Microtalker. With increasing competition from Japanese and domestic chip suppliers, National decided to cut die size and increase synthesizer performance. The Microtalker synthesizers were built on a 4-micron XMOS technology, a proven silicon-gate NMOS process with higher yields than the older metal-gate process. The technology choice, along with some of the design decisions described here, made possible a very small synthesizer with 4000 bytes of on-board speech ROM. Like the Sharp synthesizer, the Microtalker (Figure 3.6) was actually a microcomputer designed for concatenation of waveforms.

The biggest problem facing the designers was how to reduce the interconnect area. Connecting the various functional blocks on the Digitalker® had actually taken up more area than the blocks themselves. A new way of reducing the number of data and control lines had to be developed if a really small synthesizer was to be realized. Historically, microcomputers used a central *programmable logic array* (PLA) to decode the microprocessor instructions. This block would usually fetch instructions from program ROM and activate control lines to perform data transfers and data processing operations. However, as instructions become more complex, both PLA size and the number of control lines grow quickly. Snaking control lines around the chip was an odious task.

In Von Neumann machines, instructions and data travel over the same bus. Since the data bus already interconnects the data ports of major blocks, why not multiplex the bus to carry control information as well? If the major blocks of the chip (RAM, ROM, ALU, and output DAC) could control themselves instead of being controlled by a single PLA, the number of control lines could be greatly reduced.

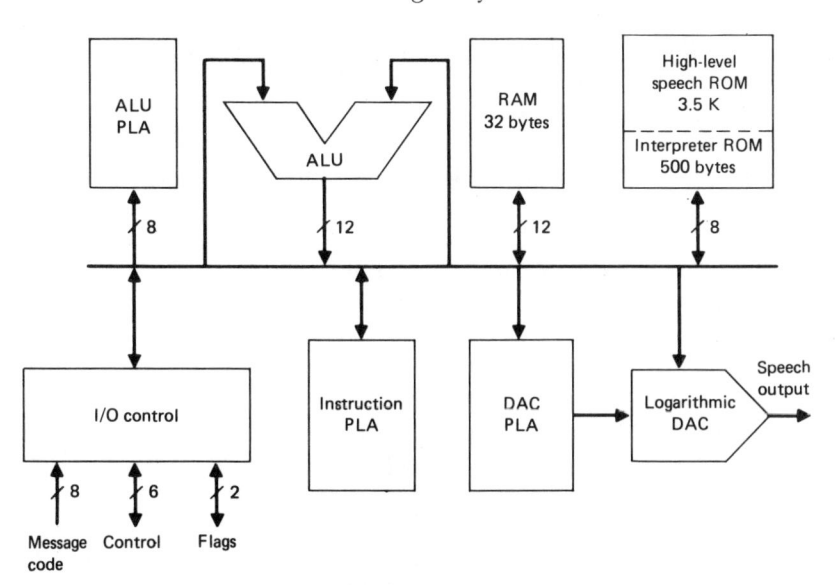

FIG. 3.6. National Semiconductor's Microtalker speech synthesizer.

The designers decided that large dense blocks of independent logic would occupy less area than small blocks strung together by control lines. The data bus would now transfer four types of information: data, addresses, instructions, and control words. For example, the ALU would receive over the bus one or two operands and a control byte. The ALU PLA would decode the control byte and perform the operation without any help from the instruction PLA.

Many advantages of the idea soon became apparent. Independence of major blocks meant that layout for each one could be separate. This speeded up the overall design. As had been hoped, interconnect and random logic were now a small amount (about 10 percent) of the total die area. In addition, the distributed processing concept allowed each block to run at a slower rate so that minimum-sized devices were used almost everywhere.

The designers decided to steal several hundred bytes from the speech ROM to implement an interpreter. This permitted efficient speech storage as parameter lists. The interpreter would link these lists together to implement nesting, repetition, indirection, and other high-level programming concepts to lower the data rate. It also provided a flexible user interface. Words could be called as subroutines, or linked together into phrases, without a host controller.

The strategy paid off. At only 23,000 square mils (including over 30 seconds worth of speech parameters), the Microtalker was half the size of the Sharp time-domain synthesizer.

Besides execution of the waveform concatenation algorithm, the microcomputer monitored and manipulated flag I/O lines. These were controlled by the user program contained in the on-board speech ROM. This code could make the synthesizer repeat a message when a flag input went high, or set a flag output for a warning light during an emergency message. Since both speech code and program code resided in the same ROM, both could be customized by the same mask, which further reduced system cost.

The Microtalker chip can accept any of 256 message codes from an 8-bit message port in either a parallel or serial mode. The message code is an entry vector into the interpreter, which translates high-level speech commands into machine code for the synthesizer. Pitch data was now completely separate from waveform data, so a word could be stored once and played back with different pitch contours, and the same contours could be used for different words. Pitch control consisted of loading the starting address of a desired pitch contour. When speech was generated by the play instruction, inflections in pitch would be computed at run time.

The microcomputer core of the synthesizer would use eight pointers to gather speech data from the on-board ROM. Eight general-purpose registers were used for processing and manipulation of control and speech data. Eight memory locations provided temporary storage for raw and processed data.

Since a large part of Mozer synthesis is simply the repeating of waveforms, a special smart DAC was designed for this purpose. The DAC could expand coded waveforms into "normal" waveforms and repeat conversions both forward and backward in time. This DAC capability freed the main processor for other work. The DAC used a 4-bit linear resistor ladder with 4 bits of logarithmic gain to achieve almost 10 bits of dynamic range. Since the synthesizer had a wide range of applications, four sampling rates between 8 and 13.3 kHz could be used. A special PLAY instruction also allowed arbitrary waveforms to be stored in a ROM and played without expansion. The IC also puts out a clock signal for an MF-4 switched-capacitor antialiasing filter, so that the latter can track the sampling rate of the synthesizer.

With Microtalker, a very flexible synthesizer on a small die, National could get down in the trenches and fight out the price wars with the Japanese.

3.3.5. Can you spell L–P–C? The story of Speak and Spell

3.3.5.1. *Case history: The first major consumer speech product*

In the fall of 1978, TI announced a 3-chip system to synthesize human speech. The chip set consisted of a speech synthesizer, read-only memory, and a controller. It was to be used in a teaching aid for spelling called Speak and Spell.

There were several startling aspects to this system. First, the overall data rate was only 1200 bits/s. Second, concatenation of words was very simple. And third, the entire chip set was fabricated using low-cost PMOS[8] technology.

For the first time, the consumer market of toys, calculators, and appliances could afford an interface based on digitally produced speech. Speak and Spell consisted of an alphanumeric display, keyboard, speaker, and chip set assembled into a red plastic case for $59.95. Until this time, speech synthesis had been difficult enough to choke a powerful general-purpose computer. Several companies—such as Votrax, Computalker Consultants, and Telesensory Systems—all produced board-level systems that talked. But the TI chip set was extremely low in cost compared to these systems.

Two of the three chips used innovative design techniques to push the limited performance of PMOS. The TMC0270 controller was a slightly modified calculator chip. The controller was specifically designed to interface with the speech synthesizer by using five special lines to transfer data and commands such as SPEAK, TEST/TALK, and BEGIN SILENCE. The number of pins on the controller was reduced from 40 to 28 by multiplexing the I/O. The controller was also slightly modified to enhance its binary-coded-decimal (BCD) arithmetic capabilities. The TMC0350 ROM chip was a completely new design which packed 128,000 bits on a 47,000-square-mil die. This was four times the memory of existing technology and was achieved by letting the access time slip to 80 μs, several hundred times slower than a standard off-the-shelf ROM (Figure 3.7).

The ROM also had several unique I/O features. The address input to the ROM was a 4-bit nibble port which accepted 14 address bits and 4 chip-select bits. The latter allowed any one of 16 different ROMs to supply the speech data. The ROM had a built-in sequencer which would automatically increment to the next byte in ROM when accessed. This meant that only the starting address of a sequence had to be loaded. Finally, either a serial output mode or nibble (4-bit) output mode could be selected by mask programming. Even though it was housed in a 28-pin package, one entire side was left unused to limit on-chip interconnection.

Since the ROM could be clocked by the synthesizer, the entire array was made dynamic, which would lower power-supply current and help reduce the cell size to 0.225 square mil per bit. By customizing the ROM for this application, the TI designers squeezed just about everything out of it that they could.

---

[8] The TI chip used a metal-gate PMOS process, a slow but cheaply fabricated chip technique (sort of like a dinosaur kicking around the back room).

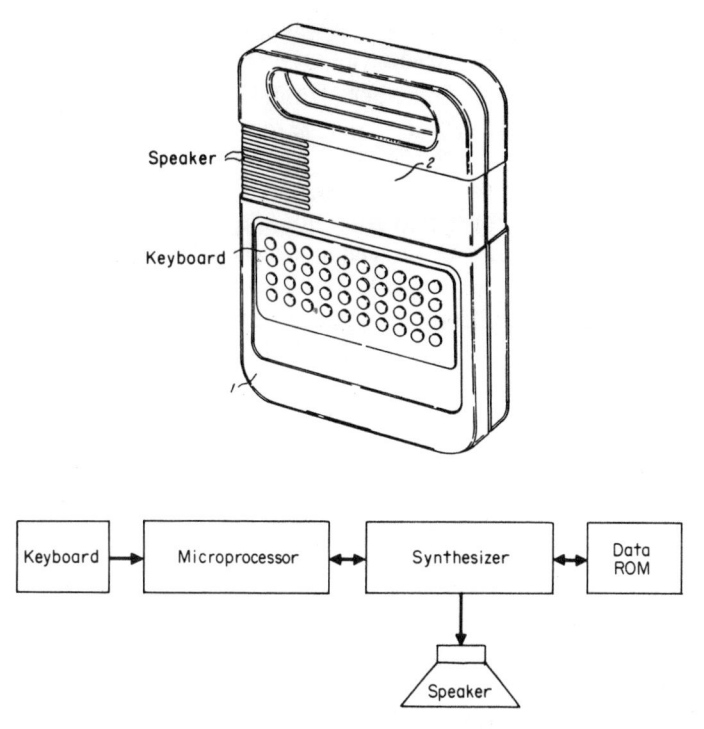

FIG. 3.7. The Speak and Spell system.

The key chip of the set was, of course, the TMC0280 speech synthesizer. The synthesizer not only spoke but also controlled the speech ROM, allowing the controller time off to play the game. The controller could start a phrase, go away and calculate the starting address of the next phrase, and then test the see when the current phrase was completed.

The synthesizer was not merely the core of the system; it was the spark of the product. Without speech, Speak and Spell would be just another dumb teaching machine.[9]

3.3.5.2. The Speak and Spell Chip

Since cost was a major constraint of the Speak and Spell product, low-cost PMOS technology was chosen as the process. Although very production-worthy for large chips, PMOS is slow and uses a nonstandard supply of -9 V. The nonstandard supply was not an issue because the entire chip set, controller, synthesizer, and ROM were all built with the PMOS process. The slow speed, on the other hand, would be the biggest problem the TI designers had to overcome.

[9] Imagine trying to market a device called "and Spell."

The design team had to build a 10-stage digital lattice filter running at a 10-kHz sample rate. This meant the hardware had to perform 200,000 MULTIPLYs per second, a similar number of ADDs, and (to top things off) parameter interpolation of 96 points every 20 ms. Even in Texas that was a tall order.

The first job was to partition the circuit into manageable pieces. Since the digital filter would occupy over half the chip and use a complicated pipeline scheme, a separate linear interpolator was added to smooth parameters within frames.

Speech frames would come in from an external companion ROM every 20 ms. These frames would normally contain 48 bits specifying the 12 speech parameters: amplitude, gain, and 10 reflection coefficients.

The data rate of 2400 bits/s could be reduced in three special cases. First, by using a repeat bit which allowed repetition of the old reflection coefficients. Only pitch and gain coefficients, 10 bits total, would be sent. Second, by sending only 4 reflection coefficients for unvoiced sounds. An unvoiced frame was specified by pitch equal to zero. This frame would have only 28 bits instead of the usual 48. Third, by using an energy value of zero to denote silence. This meant that only a 4-bit frame would be used. By cleverly using all three of these techniques, the data rate could be cut in half to only 1200 bits/s. Certainly quite a feat for a low-cost synthesizer in the spring of 1979.

The block diagram of the synthesizer (Figure 3.8) shows both simplicity and power. As data comes in from the outside world, it is held in an input register while the chip decides if it is control or data information. Control bits denoted such things as "repeat equal one," "energy equal zero," or "pitch equal zero." Encoded speech data was stored as is in a parameter buffer. By storing encoded data, less RAM was used than would be in storing expanded data. Since the speech parameters had varying bit lengths, each RAM address had a word length to match its parameter. For example, pitch was stored as 5 bits, while energy used only 4. Each of the 12 parameters that was held in RAM would be used as a pointer into a partitioned lookup ROM. This means, in effect, that each parameter had a custom lookup, just as if 12 ROMs were used, with each parameter used as an index into the ROM. The ROM lookup value had a constant 10-bit length, which was accurate enough for the digital filter and pitch controller.

The most complicated section of the entire chip was a massive lattice filter which performed the hundreds of thousands of MULTIPLYs and ADDs needed every second. Digital signal processing is difficult enough with a fast technology such as NMOS. Building a circuit in PMOS, inherently three times slower than NMOS, would require a special circuit

Some Real Chips 77

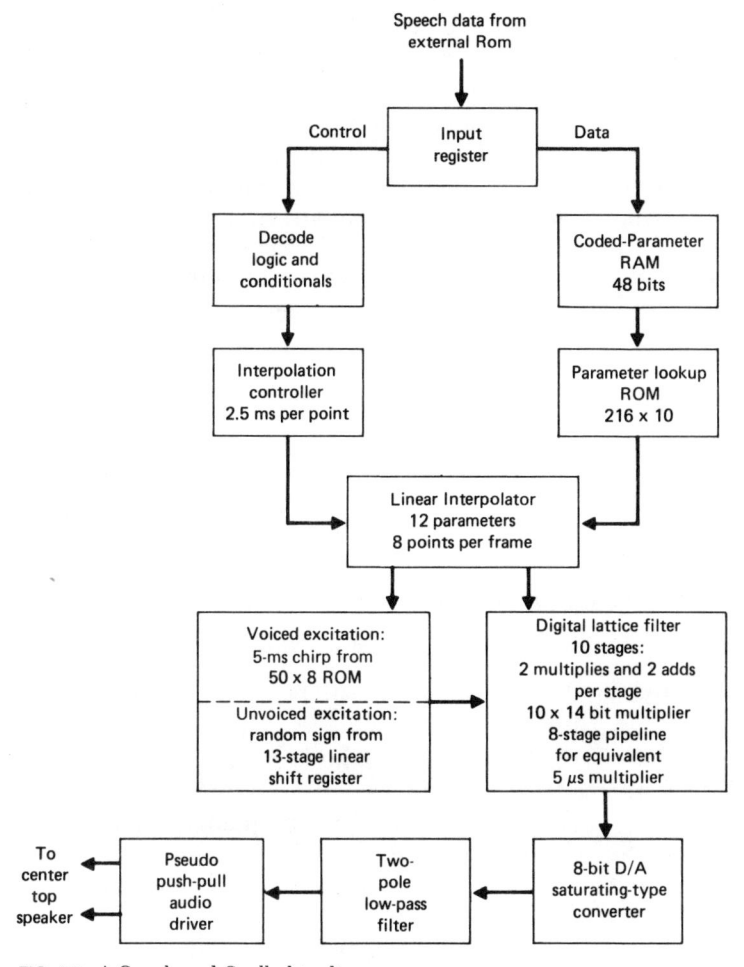

```
                    Speech data from
                     external Rom
                           │
                           ▼
        Control      ┌──────────┐      Data
       ┌─────────────│  Input   │─────────────┐
       │             │ register │             │
       ▼             └──────────┘             ▼
  ┌──────────┐                         ┌──────────────┐
  │  Decode  │                         │Coded-Parameter│
  │logic and │                         │     RAM      │
  │conditionals│                       │    48 bits   │
  └──────────┘                         └──────────────┘
       │                                      │
       ▼                                      ▼
  ┌──────────────┐                    ┌──────────────┐
  │Interpolation │                    │Parameter lookup│
  │ controller   │                    │     ROM      │
  │2.5 ms per point│                  │   216 × 10   │
  └──────────────┘                    └──────────────┘
       │                                      │
       │        ┌──────────────────┐          │
       └───────▶│Linear Interpolator│◀─────────┘
                │  12 parameters   │
                │ 8 points per frame│
                └──────────────────┘
                   │            │
                   ▼            ▼
         ┌────────────────┐  ┌──────────────────┐
         │Voiced excitation:│ │Digital lattice filter│
         │ 5-ms chirp from │  │     10 stages:    │
         │   50 × 8 ROM    │  │2 multiplies and 2 adds│
         ├────────────────┤  │     per stage     │
         │Unvoiced excitation:│ │10 × 14 bit multiplier│
         │ random sign from │─▶│  8-stage pipeline │
         │  13-stage linear │  │   for equivalent  │
         │  shift register  │  │   5 μs multiplier │
         └────────────────┘  └──────────────────┘
                                      │
  To    ┌────────┐  ┌──────┐  ┌──────────┐
center ◀│ Pseudo │◀─│ Two- │◀─│ 8-bit D/A│
 top   ◀│push-pull│  │ pole │  │saturating-type│
speaker◀│  audio │  │low-pass│ │ converter │
        │ driver │  │filter│  │           │
        └────────┘  └──────┘  └──────────┘
```

FIG. 3.8. A Speak and Spell chip diagram.

technique called *pipelining* to compensate. The pipeline multiplier was composed of four 15-bit adders which could add 2, 1, or 0 times the multiplicand. This hardware was used to implement Radix 4 Booth Recoding, a common multiplication algorithm. Using eight stages of pipelining, a 40-μs multiply was effectively reduced to 5 μs. The only remaining problem was chip real estate. Although four-phase dynamic logic was used to minimize the area, the digital filter was still over 20,000 square mils. But large cheap chips is what PMOS was good at (as years of calculator production had proved), so the project went on.

The frame update rate was kept low to keep the data rate down, so a linear interpolation was done on each parameter, 8 times during a frame. This gave an interframe update every 2.5 ms, even though a frame was 20 ms long.

The voiced excitation ROM supplied a 50-element digitized "chirp" to excite the filter. This waveform was more spread out in time than a pulselike signal, so it made better use of the filter dynamic range. It also had a spectrum which compensated for other synthesizer requirements, including some of the nonidealities of the low-cost speaker.

Unvoiced excitation consisted of a constant-magnitude pulse whose sign was controlled by a 13-stage shift register containing a 3-EXCLUSIVE-OR feedback circuit. This simple white-noise generator provided an even spectrum of energy with a sufficiently long period.

The lattice filter structure was used. This digital filter topology was guaranteed stable with only moderate coefficient accuracy requirements. The coefficients of this filter structure could also be interpolated without too much error in the frequency response. This lattice was composed of 10 identical sections with two MULTIPLYs, two ADDs, and one DELAY per stage. Excitation data was the input, and speech data was the output. Ten reflection coefficients provided 10 poles of filtering to model the vocal cavity. This is equivalent to five resonances, or four with some overall shaping.

The output of the lattice was truncated to 10 bits and given to an 8-bit converter that would saturate on large numbers. The converter had ½ least significant bit of accuracy and used the logic supply as a voltage reference. The resultant analog signal was buffered and sent to a 2nd-order low-pass filter to reduce unwanted high-frequency components. The natural loudspeaker response was also used to attenuate these signals. A pseudo push-pull audio buffer delivered 100 milliwatts into a 100-ohm, center-tap speaker.

A one-chip synthesizer that could be manufactured in high volume for low cost had been achieved.

Since its introduction in 1979, the TI synthesizer has been challenged many times by NMOS synthesizers with 10 times the speed and 3 times the density. Yet because of its simple manufacturing on inexpensive equipment, the TI synthesizers continued to hold a strong share of the synthesizer market against these smaller, more agile contenders.

The real challenge came several years later when NMOS synthesizers incorporated all three chips—the controller, ROM, and synthesizer—on the same die. Stuck at the limits of die size already, the TI designers will probably offer new chips in NMOS to meet the competition. However, the original chip has done its job well. More than a new chip had been introduced; a new age had been ushered in.

3.3.6. The General Instruments synthesizer

3.3.6.1. Summary

In the spring of 1981, TI met its first frequency-domain competitor, General Instruments from Hicksville, New York. Having just completed a semicustom speech chip for Milton-Bradley, the GI designers had the missing piece for a new type of synthesizer. By combining their normal products of 4-bit controllers and custom ROM design with the digital signal-processing experience just gained, the GI designers would develop the first "combo" chip. Incorporating a 4-bit controller, 2 kbytes of custom speech ROM, and a 12th-order digital filter on a single die, GI could battle larger competitors offering multichip solutions (Figure 3.9).

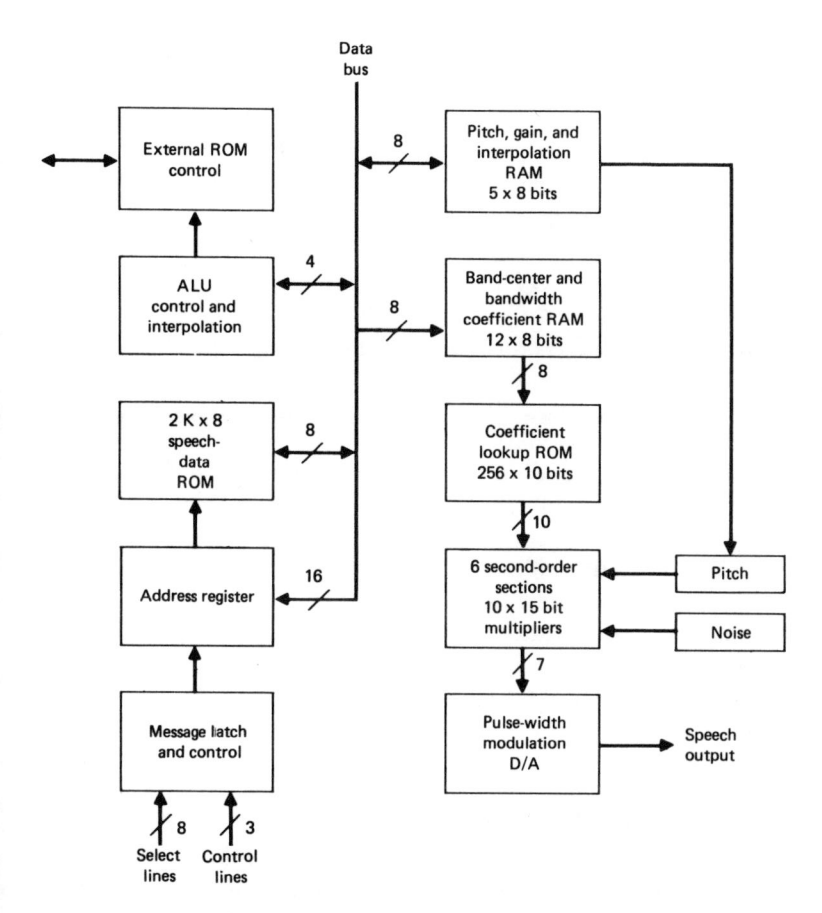

FIG. 3.9. Chip diagram of a speech synthesizer by General Instruments Corporation.

Choosing metal-gate N-channel technology rather than the P-channel circuitry used by Texas Instruments, the GI designers reaped several benefits.

First, N-channel metal gate was still a simple, high-volume process that could produce inexpensive devices. Although not as inexpensive as PMOS, NMOS yields had improved steadily. Most important, the NMOS metal-gate process was very good for both controllers and ROMs. Selecting a process that produced small and inexpensive ROMs was now a major factor, since half of the chip would be speech ROM. The controller consumed the lion's share of the remaining real estate, leaving the synthesizer a weak third in priority.

Second, NMOS has many times the speed and almost double the density of PMOS. The large pipeline multiplier used by TI could be replaced by two much simpler and smaller serial-parallel multipliers, drastically reducing the synthesizer size. Third, NMOS uses a standard 5-V supply. This makes chip interface much simpler. Finally, PMOS technology had reached the end of its growth. The TI designers could not hope to build a chip with both the synthesizer and the ROM together. The GI designers could not only mate a synthesizer with a 2 kbyte ROM, they could expand into a 4 kbyte ROM at a later date without pushing the technology. Clearly NMOS would replace PMOS as systems became more integrated and complex. The question, of course, was: Would it be cheaper?

GI's chip also used a different form of LPC synthesis from TI's. Instead of by a 12th-order lattice filter, the processing would be done by six 2nd-order sections. Although both filters could produce identical spectra, several important gains could be realized using the latter filter structure. The filter coefficients for a 2nd-order section have a simple relation to the band center and bandwidth of a resonance. Each of the six sections could be thought of as independent filters with variable band-center and bandwidth controls. Lattice filters, on the other hand, have no simple relation between filter coefficients and resonances. By using a filter that had band-center and bandwidth controls, the GI chip could implement three different types of speech synthesis. The first was a simple variation of standard LPC. Factoring the LPC spectrum into separate resonances, the spectrum could be described by resonator parameters instead of lattice coefficients. Unfortunately, these parameters are not as easily interpolated, since they cannot be guaranteed to correspond with the true ordered formant values (which would lend themselves nicely to interpolation). The TI chip interpolates filter coefficients eight times per frame, which gives smooth transitions between frames. Interpolation gives smooth-sounding synthetic speech for relatively large frame sizes. The GI chip relies, then, on interpolation of the pitch periods and amplitude only. The filter coefficients could be supplied in one of two ways. If large changes in the filter were needed, new coefficients from the speech-data ROM would be supplied. However, when only small changes of the coefficients were required, only *delta* information in the form of small 2s complement integers would be supplied. Slowly varying spectra could be easily updated using delta encoding of band-center and bandwidth coefficients. Delta encoding of parameters was just the first of several different methods available using the resonance description of the spectrum. Since the frequency response was now being determined by six independent filters, only those filters needing update were changed on frame boundaries. This also lowered the overall data rate.

The second type of speech synthesis was a throwback to the simple formant synthesizer. Of the 12 filter coefficients, 6 primarily supply bandwidth information, which is perceptually less significant than band-center location for each formant. By storing only band-center coefficients in the speech-data ROM and having the controller algorithmically generate bandwidth coefficients by using a rule such as BW = 50 Hz + (BC − 2000)/10 (as used by Kang of the Naval Research Labs), the data rate could be cut from over 2 kbits/s to less than 1 kbit/s. The speech quality suffered, to be sure, but the degradation was far less severe than cutting out six lattice (reflection) coefficients.

Now there was an option. One could easily trade off quality and data rate, squeezing out every bit of the on-board ROM essential for high-volume applications. The final method of synthesis was again made possible by the new filter configuration. Votrax had long used analog filters in *phoneme synthesis*, in which a library of sounds was categorized by band-center and bandwidth patterns. These sounds could be strung together by simple blending rules to create very low bit-rate speech. Robotic and choppy speech at 100 bits per sound is better than no speech at all.[10] The on-chip ROM could hold a hundred or so allophones as a library. The controller could compute simple blending methods under the supervision of an external host processor. Years later a complete text-to-speech transformation would be possible using a single-chip microcomputer with the GI synthesizer.

The resultant flexibility of having six programmable filters, a controller, and 2 kbytes of ROM on a single 44,000-square-mil chip was made possible by the shift to NMOS processing. The ability to program one chip into three different synthesizers with various operating modes was made possible by using software, not hardware, to control the synthesizer parameter loading. The GI speech chip was directly targeted for games, toys, and appliances. There it would hold its own against the synthesizers

[10] Sometimes.

of larger companies such as National Semiconductor and Texas Instruments.

3.3.6.2. Chip description

A message code specifying one of 256 utterances could be loaded into the message latch by either mechanical switches or the controlling microprocessor. This code would point to speech data on a 4-byte boundary. The ALU could increment the address register, load it for jumps, or save it in a single-level stack for one level of subroutine call. Subroutines are very useful because one sound could be stored once and used by many calling routines. Although only 2 kbytes were stored on the original chip, a full 16-bit address for 64 kbytes of speech data would be used. The controller part of the chip could serially ship out speech-data addresses to a special GI speech ROM. The speech data could then be serially loaded back into the chip. The speech ROM could increment the current address and save one address on an internal stack, so address transfers occurred only on jumps. The ALU interpreted the data from the ROM by unpacking and calculating interpolated parameters. The ALU could load a new address into the address register for jumps and subroutines. The speech-data instructions were organized so all or part of the 15 speech parameters could be updated. Pitch, gain, and repeat information were held in one set of registers. The 12 filter coefficients were in a second set of registers. The filter coefficients were transformed by a 256 × 10 bit lookup ROM before being used by the digital filter. The band-center coefficients would be multiplied by two when used by the digital filter, since their range is double the bandwidth coefficient range.

Scaled impulses would excite the digital filter for voiced sounds, and noise from a pseudo-random sign generator would be used for unvoiced sounds. Improvements on these simple excitation techniques, such as ROM-driven excitations and simultaneous excitation of several sections, would be used by later designs for higher quality in some sounds.

The output of the filter was truncated to 7 bits before being given to a *pulse-width modulation* (PWM) type of *digital-to-analog converter*. The DAC would generate constant period pulses of varying duty cycles. When filtered, high-duty cycles would deliver a high voltage, and low-duty cycles would deliver a low voltage, hopefully in a linear manner. This extra stage of filtering was done off chip, as was the low-pass filtering and amplification. Since the DAC was basically a digital circuit and no on-chip filtering was attempted, the entire GI chip was digital in nature. Having a purely digital chip made testing easier and increased yields. It also provided such inherent digital features as better noise immunity, better temperature performance, etc.

The GI chip was the first complete speech-synthesis system on an IC.

By choosing NMOS, the GI designers were able to integrate the core system of each speech-synthesis product on a single chip. Placing the ROM, controller, and synthesizer together gave GI a technical, marketing, and pricing advantage over their competitors. The TI chip, built in PMOS, was at the process limit when it was introduced. By choosing NMOS, GI was not only able to introduce a more complex chip at the outset but was able to introduce a chip with twice the ROM two years later.

3.3.7. Telesensory Systems

In the spring of 1980, Telesensory Systems Inc. (TSI) of Palo Alto, California, announced a pair of special-purpose NMOS ICs for high-quality synthetic speech. Targeted for a text-to-speech system for the blind, these ICs had many interesting capabilities. The chip set had a host-interface chip called PDSP-B and a number-crunching chip called PDSP-A.

The host-interface chip could control two signal processing chips, which doubled the computational power. A single A chip could synthesize a nine-formant OVE III synthesizer, while two A chips would be needed for a cascade/parallel Klatt synthesizer.

A unique feature of the chip set is that controlling microcode could be downloaded into the chip set, along with the normal coefficients and excitation. By downloading different microcode, many different synthesizers could be realized. All of the major synthesis structures—such as lattice, cascade, and parallel resonator arrangements—could be implemented with no hardware changes or ROM alterations.

This extra flexibility forced the synthesizer to be split into two pieces with extra RAM and D/A, but TSI figured that the board-level product had to have an advantage over the VLSI products of semiconductor companies.

3.3.8. Japanese LPC synthesizers

Unlike their American competitors, Japanese semiconductor companies did not look to low-cost processes like PMOS or metal-gate NMOS for fabricating speech-synthesis chips. By using very advanced CMOS processes, some with 3-micron feature sizes, the Japanese were able to pack more ROM and synthesizer capabilities on a smaller die.

Good examples of this are the CMOS synthesizers of Sanyo and Hitachi. Both chips have 4 kbytes of on-board ROM, use an upgraded LPC-10 digital lattice filter, have 9-bit DACs, and draw only 30 milliwatts in operation from a 3- to 5-V power source. Both allow for ROM expansion, and the Hitachi chip includes a keyboard interface.

By using a 3-micron process, Hitachi was able to cram 4 kbytes of ROM on a synthesizer with more capability and in less area than the American Microsystems analog IC.

All of this performance and technology came with a low price tag. The Japanese companies were able to enter with low-power single-chip synthesizers with cheap ceramic oscillators, eliminating expensive crystals, for only $3 a chip in quantity.

Can you say Nedzumi-bashira?

3.4. ANALOG SPEECH SYNTHESIZERS

3.4.1. Introduction

In an increasingly digital world, it is interesting to note that some tasks still have more efficient analog solutions. Some manufacturers have felt that this was the case for speech synthesizers. Behold the two principal examples.

3.4.2. AMI synthesizer

In the summer of 1981, AMI (American Microsystems, Inc.) of Santa Clara, California, announced their entry into speech synthesis. AMI had built switched-capacitor telecom products with a double-poly 5-micron CMOS technology and now decided to build an LPC synthesizer using analog rather than digital techniques. AMI claimed that the use of switched-capacitor filters resulted in 30 percent less area than a fully digital filter. A second advantage of using analog filters on a CMOS process was the inclusion of a 3.5-kHz low-pass filter for output smoothing and a 30-milliwatt power amplifier which could directly drive a 100-ohm speaker.

The CMOS chip (Figure 3.10) had a 5-bit input code to select one of 32 phrases from a 2.5K × 8 on-board ROM. Pitch, amplitude, repeat data, and reflection coefficients were all interpolated four times across a 20-millisecond frame. The LPC filter used a switched-capacitor SAMPLE AND HOLD technique with a 9-bit multiplying DAC to implement the lattice filter. A single op amp per filter stage balanced the charge on a feedback capacitor when a programmable input capacitor was discharged on the op amp inverting input. Charge was delayed, added, and scaled by filter stages in much the same way numbers were manipulated in a digital filter.

This chip, at 48,000 square mils, was considerably larger than Japanese digital CMOS synthesizers with more ROM. This casts some doubt on the claim of greater die efficiency for an analog filter.

Some Real Chips 85

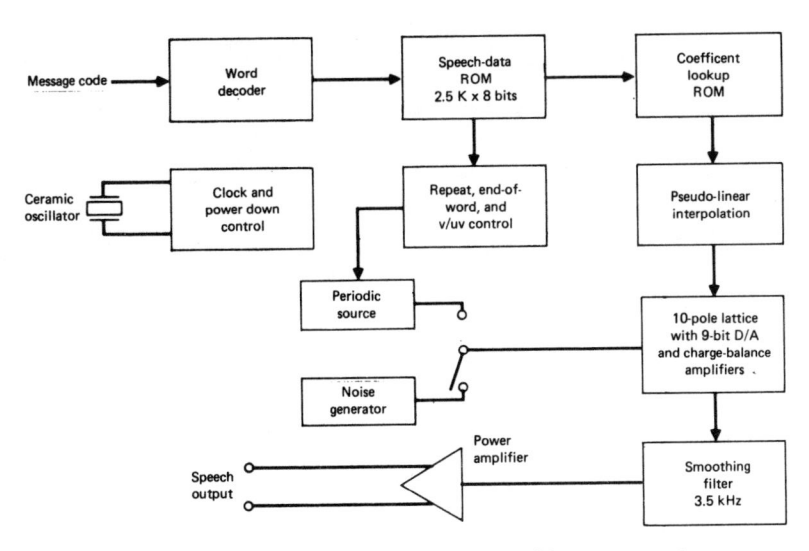

FIG. 3.10. Chip diagram of a synthesizer by American Microsystems, Inc.

3.4.3. Votrax

In the summer of 1980, Votrax, a division of Federal Screw Works,[11] announced a single-chip synthesizer. Unlike competitive chips from TI, GI, National, etc., the Votrax SC-01 (Figure 3.11) was a phonemic synthesizer.

The SC-01 permitted user input of 64 different phoneme codes. The resulting phonemes were concatenated by the chip and transformed into formant parameters which controlled a switched-capacitor filter. Votrax had built board-level products for many years before this, but now a single chip performed unlimited vocabulary synthesis at very low bit rates. Votrax contracted Silicon Systems of Tustin, California, to design and build the CMOS synthesizer. Silicon Systems had previously built telecommunications products in CMOS and had both analog and digital design expertise.

The designers used switched-capacitor filters with programmable center frequencies and bandwidths as the model of the vocal tract. These analog filters were not as flexible as digital filters but were (at the time) considerably smaller. Unlike digital filters, their accuracy was limited by circuit tolerances. However, the control parameters for the filter were derived from a very simple vocal-tract transition model which was even more inaccurate than the filters.

---

[11] Really. I wouldn't kid you.

86 Talking Chips

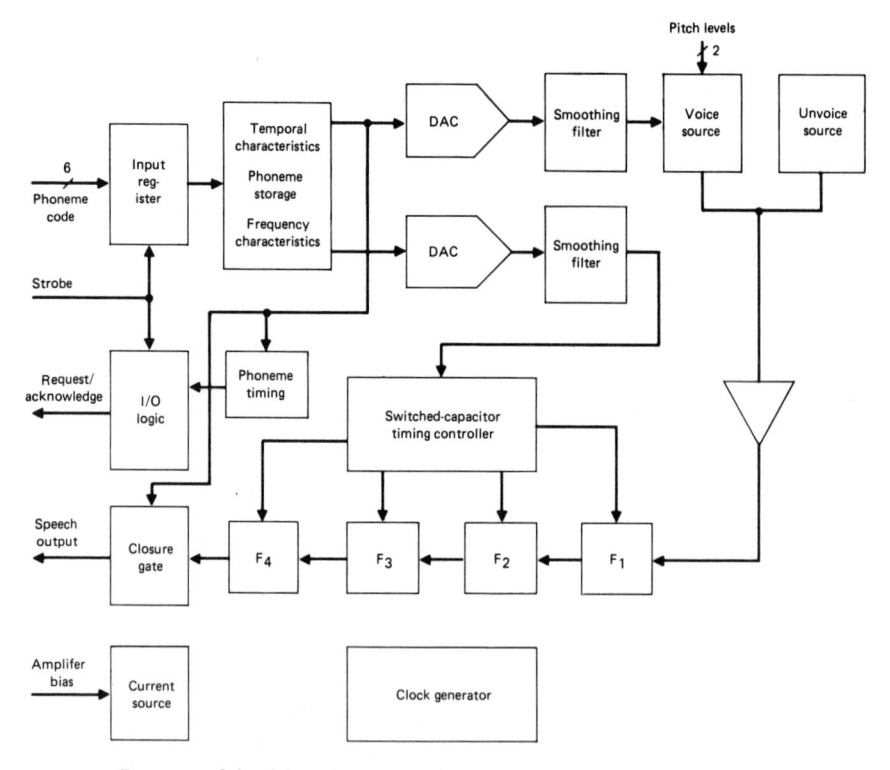

FIG. 3.11. Diagram of the SC-01 Votrax synthesizer.

The Votrax SC-01 chip receives an input byte from an external host through its phoneme code port. Sixty-four phonemes with four pitch levels each can be specified by the host. The host usually receives keyboard input strings of phonetic symbols. The host computer will usually manipulate the input strings using a synthesis-by-rule program. In a very simple system, the host can translate phoneme symbols into phoneme codes for the SC-01.

The SC-01 has on-board ROM where both frequency and time characteristics of phoneme sounds are stored. Frequency characteristics—such as formant locations of vowels, nasal resonances, and fricative spectral shapes—are looked up and passed through a smoothing filter. The long time constant of this filter smooths out the abrupt jumps from one phoneme lookup to the next by smearing the phoneme parameters together. A separate ROM lookup contains the temporal characteristics of phoneme sounds—such as vocal closure times, amplitude, and pitch.

These parameters are converted into voltages by a DAC at the output of each ROM. The DAC outputs are smoothed by transition filters. The frequency characteristics are passed through filters with relatively long time constants corresponding to the sluggish motion of the vocal tract. Temporal parameters are smoothed by filters with shorter time constants, since time events such as stops can occur relatively quickly.

The excitation consists of a periodic source with four pitch levels. These can be set by a 2-bit code provided by the host. A shift register with EXCLUSIVE-ORs provides a maximal length pseudo-random sequence for the noise source in fricative sounds. The vocal-tract model is implemented by four 2nd-order low-pass switched-capacitor filters in series. The output of the filter cascade passes through a closure gate which can abruptly reduce the output amplitude for stop consonants.

The SC-01 is the main component of the Votrax Type 'N Talk system.[12] This product translates English into synthetic speech. While the unit itself produces monotone speech (not much fun over an extended time), external software can provide inflections for better sounding speech, since the SC-01 is certainly capable of varying the pitch.

The SC-01 was built in low-cost metal-gate CMOS and consumed less than 10 mA from a 9-V supply. This permitted inclusion into portable products. The latched phoneme-code inputs could be driven from 5-V CMOS outputs, making a simple interface to the host computer. With a die size of only 24,000 square mils, the SC-01 became the core component of many small systems that needed unlimited vocabularies.[13]

---

[12] Trademark of Votrax.

[13] See Chapter 5 for an introduction to the creation of speech from phonetic rules.

CHAPTER

4

ANALYSIS FOR SYNTHESIS

4.1. INTRODUCTION

We have seen some of the methods by which synthetic speech may be produced. However, nary a sound would be heard without first finding the correct numbers to represent the speech. These parameters may be determined in one of two ways:

1. Analysis of natural speech.
2. Application of phonetic rules to the concatentation of library sound parameters.

Even in the latter case, some analysis of natural speech must have been performed in order to build up the original library. This chapter will introduce some of the major methods for this analysis. We shall first look at determination of the short-term spectrum and then at the methods of classification and pitch tracking.

4.2. SPEECH SPECTRUM ESTIMATION

4.2.1. A brief review

In Chapter 1, we saw that synthesizers generate speech which has certain *perceptually significant characteristics* in common with the original speech. Most important of these is the short-term spectrum

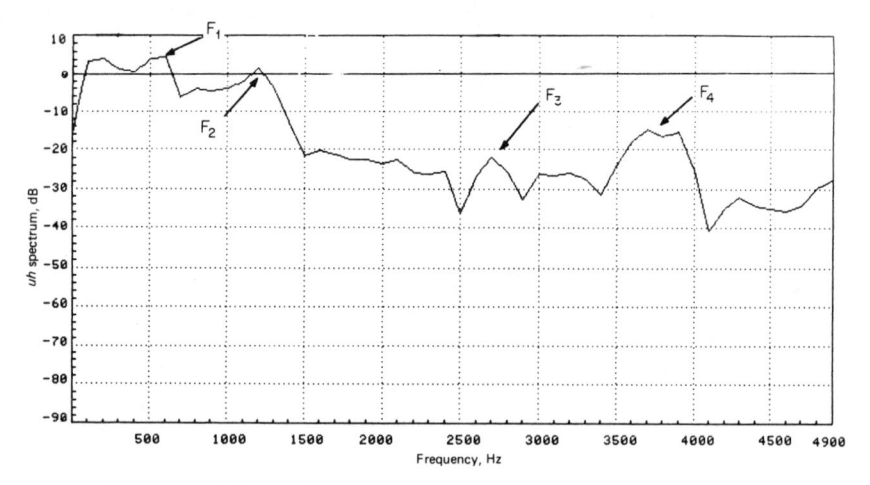

FIG. 4.1. Spectrum of *uh* sound.

(frequency content of a short segment of speech). The difference between natural and synthetic spectra is the main error criterion for all major low bit-rate analysis techniques.

Straightforward techniques exist for computing the frequency content in a finite length sequence of numbers.[1] However, as shown in Chapter 1, merely storing the spectrum for each speech segment results in a medium-to-high bit rate.

Any spectral analysis technique which specifies the major peaks of the spectral envelope will sufficiently define the synthesis parameters. As described in Chapter 1, this analysis is essentially equivalent to finding the vocal-tract resonances, the formants.

4.2.2. Formant estimation

One such approach is called *formant tracking*. In this process, the vocal-tract resonances are estimated for each time window (typically 10–40 ms) of speech (Figure 4.1).

Estimation is made using a per-frame spectral analysis as well as a between-frame continuity assumption. That is, the initial estimates of formant frequencies are usually modified by requirements that the formant frequencies change in a smooth manner over time, since their positions are determined by the articulator positions. The spectral analysis itself should be restricted to those methods which yield a smoothed estimate of the frequency content, since formants shape a spectrum that is complicated by many other less phonetically significant factors.

[1] In particular, the discrete Fourier transform, defined in Appendix A.

Either in the form of the derived resonances, or in some other representation of the smoothed spectrum, parameters can then be stored which represent the phonetic content of the speech to great accuracy and with very few bits.

An obvious approach to derivation of formant values is called *peak picking*. This term refers to any procedure which examines the speech spectrum and picks out significant peaks as the vocal-tract resonances. While seemingly straightforward, any such technique is actually quite complicated because of the multitude of heuristic rules that must be developed to really make it work.[2] Neither will such a procedure be error-free. For instance, when two formants are close enough together, they will form a single peak in the frequency response.

As with other formant estimation techniques, peak picking is not feasible without smoothing the spectrum to reduce the granularity of pitch harmonics and other local features which obscure the overall envelope. The three main techniques for estimation of smooth speech spectra are:

1. Sampling outputs of overlapping bandpass filters (Figure 4.2). The overlap ensures a smooth-looking frequency response.
2. Smoothing the ripple in the log spectrum by *liftering*, which is a cute term for filtering in the log spectral domain referred to as the *cepstrum* (Figure 4.3).

[2] Such as: If F_2 not found in expected region, then expand F_1 region and look for second-highest peak. If no second peak is found, then set F_2 peak to 200 Hz over F_1 peak. (F_1 is the first formant band center, F_2 is the second, etc.)

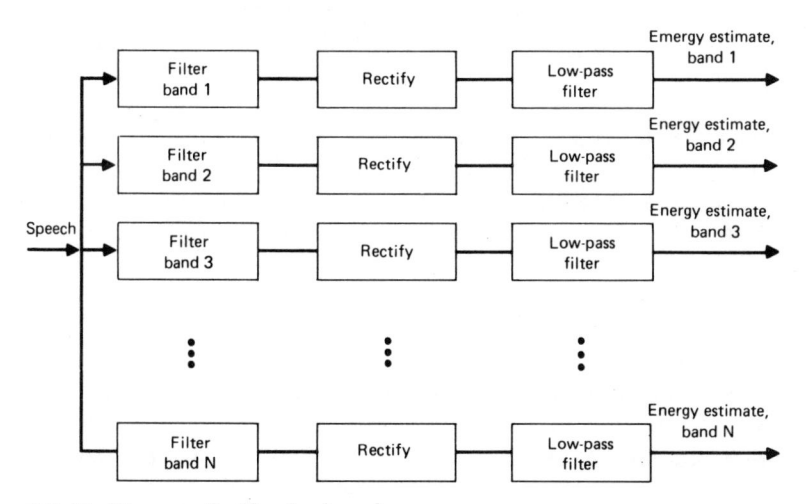

FIG. 4.2. Diagram of a filter-bank analyzer.

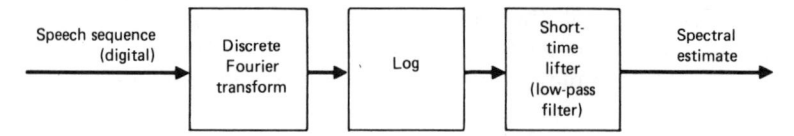

```
Speech sequence                          Short-
   (digital)     Discrete                time        Spectral
   ─────────▶    Fourier   ──▶  Log  ──▶ lifter  ──▶ estimate
                 transform              (low-pass   ─────────▶
                                         filter)
```

FIG. 4.3. Cepstral analyzer.

3. Analyzing the speech to find a set of linear filter parameters which will minimize the square of the error between the original speech and the signal "predicted" by those parameters. This technique is called *linear prediction* and is shown in Figure 4.4.

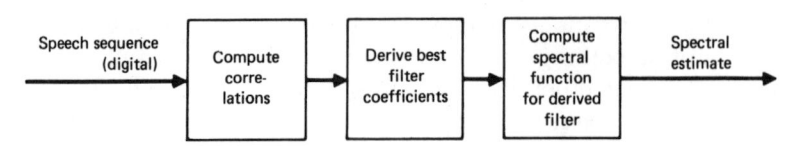

```
                                          Compute
Speech sequence  Compute    Derive best   spectral     Spectral
   (digital)     corre-  ▶  filter     ▶  function  ▶  estimate
   ─────────▶    lations     coefficients for derived ─────────▶
                                          filter
```

FIG. 4.4. Linear predictive spectral analyzer.

Each of these techniques may be used to compute an estimate of the overall frequency response for a speech segment. Peak picking may then be used to find the formant positions. Each approach can also be used for synthesis without the intermediate step of peak picking formants. Filter bank outputs may be used for what is called a *channel vocoder*. In this device, the energy in each synthesizer filter band is determined by the energy of the corresponding analysis filter output. Thus, the short-term spectral envelope is roughly duplicated, given a sufficient spread of filters across the speech bandwidth. Cepstral techniques may also be used to generate spectra for synthesis by filter or mathematical-transform techniques.

The dominant spectral analysis technique is, by far, linear prediction. Like the other estimation techniques, it provides a smoothed version of the frequency response of a speech segment. Unlike the others, it inherently favors an accurate matching of the peaks of the frequency response rather than the valleys. This is appropriate for formant estimation. Peak-picking techniques can be used to find the formants from this spectrum.

The linear prediction analysis itself can also yield filter parameters which can be implemented by a synthesizer to produce speech with the same spectral envelope. This latter approach has been the preferred method over the last few years. Systems have either implemented this using *lattice* filters, as described in Chapter 1, or with serial or parallel configurations of resonators. The latter requires the factoring of the linear predictive spectrum into its component resonances (typically done by finding the roots of a polynomial, usually of order 10 or 12). Fortunately, modern high-speed computers make this factoring a relatively easy matter.

4.2.3. Linear predictive analysis

As a mathematical technique, linear prediction has a long history, dating back to the least-squares methods of Gauss. As an engineering technique, it should probably be associated with Weiner's work in control theory during the 1940s. In the last 15 years, these ideas have been applied to speech processing by researchers such as Itakura and Saito, Atal and Schroeder, Makhoul and Wolf, and Markel and Gray.

For short durations of speech, the filtering action of the vocal tract may be regarded as time-invariant (that is, unchanging over time). This filter is approximately linear, or a filter for which a composite input yields an output that is a sum of the outputs which would have resulted from the pieces of the input, if taken separately. That is:

$$\text{if } x_1 \rightarrow y_1 \text{ and } x_2 \rightarrow y_2$$
$$\text{then } (ax_1 + bx_2) \rightarrow (ay_1 + by_2)$$

For many such systems, the output at any one time is due not only to the current output but also to the previous states (or outputs) of the system. Incorporating this, the current value of the output is then:

$$y(t) = F\,[y(t-s), x(t)] \qquad \text{for } 0 < s \leq t$$

assuming $x(t) = 0$ for $t < 0$

where s is the variable representing how far we are gazing into the past. In the linear sampled data case, we could say

$$y(n) = x(n) + a_1 y(n-1) + a_2 y(n-2) + \ldots + a_N y(n-N)$$

Acoustic analysis of the I/O characteristics of a lossless tube (no energy lost at the boundaries, no side branches) yields a relation of the form shown above. To a first approximation, the vocal tract behaves this way for sounds that are not nasalized. The time-varying filter in the speech-production model of Figure 1.2 can be assumed to be of this form.

The least-squares minimization approach is a mathematical technique designed to choose coefficients for the above system such that the error (here defined to be the energy or sum of squares for the error signal) is minimized. In applied mathematics, we frequently have the problem of minimizing some error function by choosing the best values for some independent variables. The simplest approach is to take partial derivatives (with respect to the variables, which are in this case the LPC coefficients) of the error function and set the resultant expressions to zero. This is justified since these derivatives should be zero at minima, as they are the slope of the function. These operations yield N equations in N unknowns, which can be solved for the optimal coefficients.

These thoughts can be expressed compactly with a little algebra. If $s_n(n)$ is the natural speech sequence and $s_s(n)$ the predicted speech sequence using N optimal predictor coefficients to weight N past values of the speech, and the a's are the predictor filter coefficients, then:

$$e(n) = s_n(n) - s_s(n) \quad \text{(the error signal)}$$

$$E = \sum_{\substack{\text{all } n \\ \text{in} \\ \text{interval}}} e^2(n)$$

$$= \sum_{\substack{\text{all } n \\ \text{in} \\ \text{interval}}} [s_n(n) - s_s(n)]^2 \quad \text{(the error energy)}$$

$$= \sum_{\substack{\text{all } n \\ \text{in} \\ \text{interval}}} \left\{ s_n(n) - \sum_{i=1}^{N} [a_i s_n(n - i)] \right\}^2$$

where the predicted speech signal has been replaced by the weighted sum of past values for the speech. Taking partial derivatives with respect to each a, get N equations of the form

$$\sum_{j=1}^{N} [a_j \phi(i, j)] = \phi(i, 0) \quad \text{for } i = 1, 2, \ldots, N$$

where $\phi(i,j)$ is a correlation sum between versions of the speech segment delayed by i and j points.

The details of the efficient solution to these equations are well covered elsewhere (see More Advanced Reading). For our purposes, it is sufficient to remark that there exist low-complexity techniques for solving these equations yielding solutions that are optimal in the sense of the error criterion of minimum mean-squared error, assuming the correctness of the acoustic tube model. The overall approach is referred to as LPC analysis of speech.

4.2.4. Other methods: Mozer analysis

As mentioned above, linear prediction only does a good job with estimation of the *peaks* of the frequency response. While this is desirable for most speech sounds, for others, the valleys are also significant. Linear

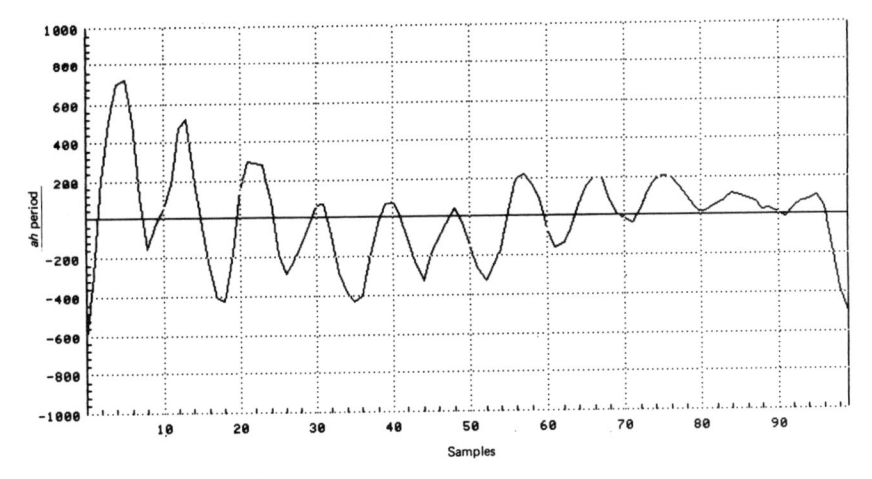

FIG. 4.5. Period of voiced speech.

prediction techniques are not easily adaptable to those speech sounds. The model used with such systems is also the simple one of Figure 1.2, which does not correctly implement sounds which are simultaneously voiced and noiselike.

Over the years, other working systems have been developed which rely less on model assumptions, while still resulting in accurate reproduction of formants. Usually such systems are either more computationally intensive or result in higher bit rates, yet frequently perform well over classes of speech segments which are difficult for techniques such as LPC. An example of such an algorithm is analysis by synthesis, which iteratively converges to synthesizer parameters producing speech to match the short-term frequency response of the original speech.

A relatively new type of analysis by synthesis is the frequency-domain analysis for the time-domain synthesis of Forrest Mozer.

Imagine a period of voiced speech as shown in Figure 4.5.

In the sampled data domain, this could be represented as a sequence of N numbers. For example, Let $N = 64$. If we take a DFT (*discrete Fourier transform*) of this sequence (Figure 4.6), we will get another 64-point sequence where each element is a complex number, that is, a number with a magnitude and a phase.

By the assumption of the ear's phase deafness,[3] we can alter the phase of each of these numbers without appreciably altering the sound of the corresponding time sequence. Therefore, the phase of each number, or the phase of each frequency component in the speech segment, may be regarded as a free parameter to be altered for playback.

---

[3] Easily disproved, but approximately correct.

96   *Talking Chips*

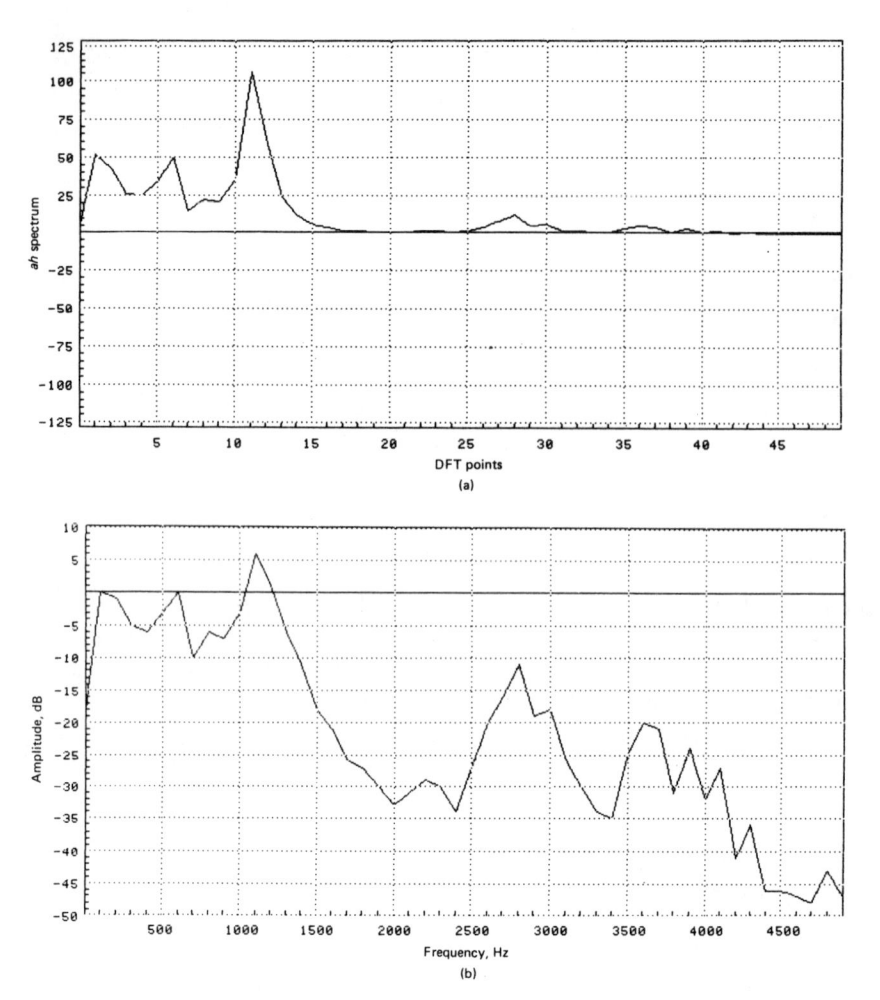

FIG. 4.6. (*a*) discrete Fourier transform (DFT) of speech period, (*b*) log DFT in dB, with respect to a 10-kHz sampling rate.

In the example of a 64-point waveform, imagine that the sequence came from a speech segment sampled at 12.8 kHz. The period is 5 ms long, and the DFT gives the amplitude and phase of harmonics of the 200-Hz fundamental. The *phase deafness theorem* implies that a signal composed of cosines of any phase, given the same amplitude as those for the original signal, will sound roughly the same as that original signal.

Particularly useful choices for phase are 0 or 180 degrees. These selections mean that the harmonics will all be cosines, with the choice of phase determining the polarity, as seen in Figure 4.7.

These choices are particularly fortuitous, as they result in a symmetrical or *even* waveform. The second half of such a waveform is the *mirror image* of the first. Thus, only *half* of the waveform need be stored. Playback is achieved by first playing this (half) waveform forward and then backward (a straightforward hardware option). Another factor-of-2 bit-rate reduction is accomplished, without any error in the magnitude spectrum.

Now that the phases are restricted to 0 or 180 degrees, we see that each of the 32 frequencies may be added with one of two polarities. That is, the synthetic waveform will be a sum of 32 cosine functions, each of which is either added to or subtracted from the total waveform, depending on the polarity. There are 2^{32} waveforms that all have the same magnitude spectrum. The rest of the Mozer technique is concerned with the choice of these available waveforms for low bit-rate playback.

The next step consists of choosing the cosine polarities to reduce the amplitude of the summed waveform at the edges of the segment. If the waveform amplitudes are sufficiently low in the 1st and last quarters, they may be set to zero with little or no perceptible degradation.

Finally, the high resolution (16-bit) levels of the waveform must be reduced to a low resolution representation, such as 4-bit, both to reduce bit rate and to facilitate low-cost playback. Simple quantization would

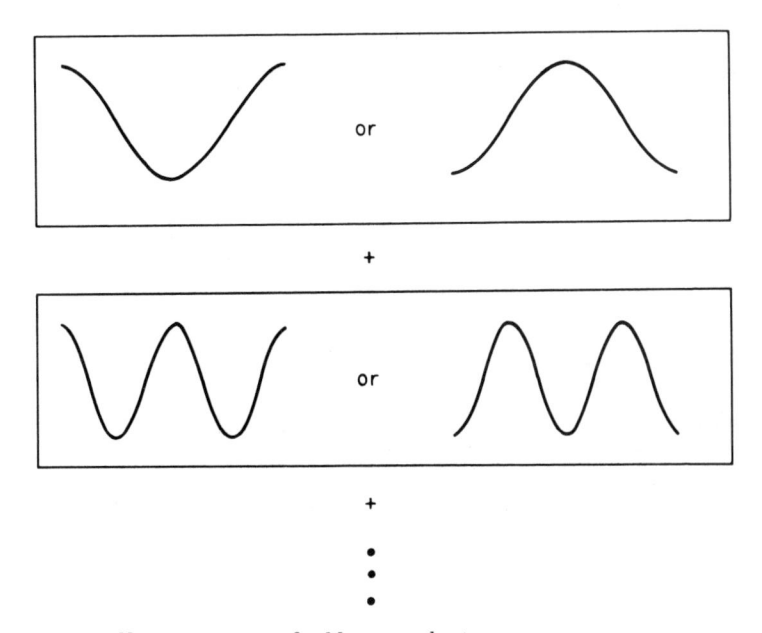

FIG. 4.7. Harmonic cosines for Mozer synthesis.

98   *Talking Chips*

give rise to a large error. However, by choosing cosine polarities which result in sequence values near the coarse quantization steps, the quantization may be done with low error (Figure 4.8).

For a 16-bit unsigned number X, we search for polarity choices resulting in a sequence which has values close to 0, 4096, 8192, etc. Clever search techniques must be employed to avoid the exhaustive

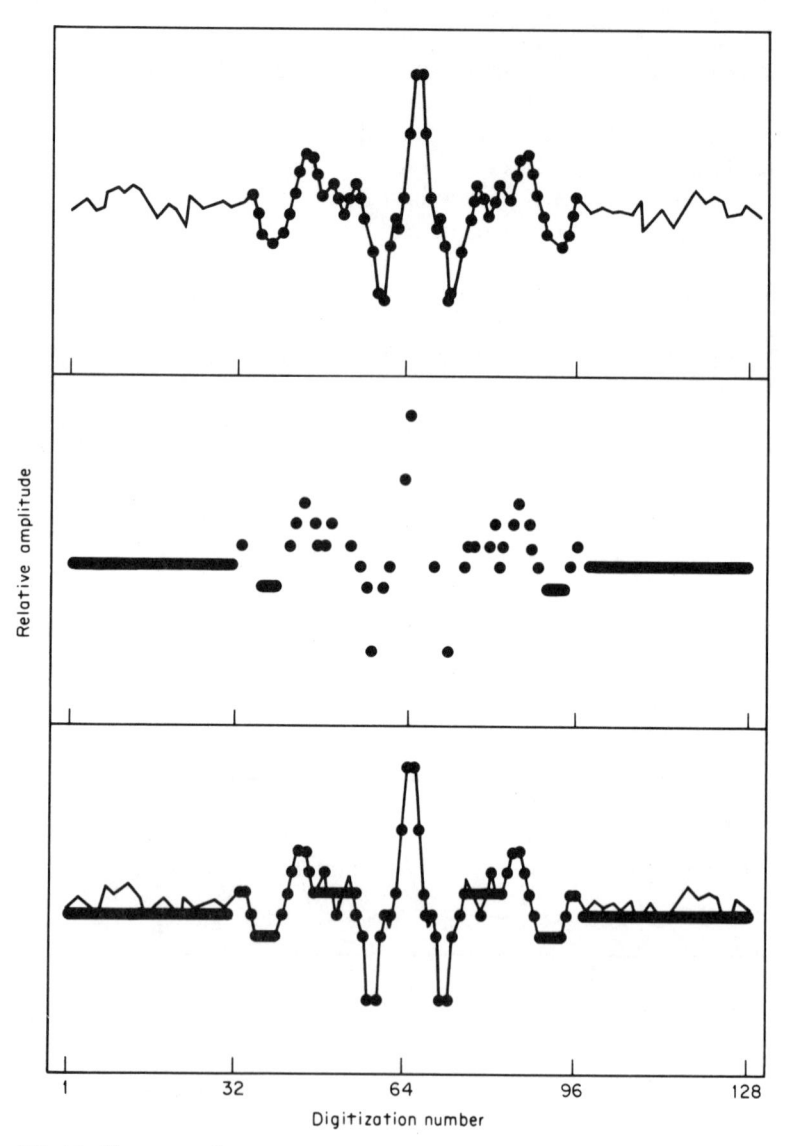

FIG. 4.8. Mozer waveforms.

search through 2^{32} waveforms. If such a sequence can be found, the 64-point waveform will have been represented with sixteen 4-bit numbers (or 1 bit per sample) but little perceptible error. In practice this can nearly always be done. In fact, we can frequently represent these numbers with 2 bits each, resulting in 0.5-bit-per-sample storage.

Assuming the 12.8-kHz sampling rate, this example results in a representation of 6.4–12.8 kbits/s. While a considerable reduction from the PCM rate of 100 kbits/s or mu-law PCM of 64 kbits/s, it still does not give a low bit rate comparable to LPC.

Final reduction is achieved through two mechanisms:

1. Library storage and retrieval
2. Frame repeats

For the first, libraries of sounds are created. These are used whenever possible to build desired words. Factors of 4 are typical reductions, in that, on the average, each sound can be used four times in a vocabulary. The average bit rate can be reduced to 3200 bits/s by this step. The unvoiced sounds are actually shared much more than voiced sounds.

For the second, individual frames (which are pitch periods in the case of voiced speech segments) may be repeated several times (in general) without much perceptual degradation. This is true because the spectrum variation is a function of the *speed* of talking, as opposed to the pitch. For normal rates of speech, the speech spectrum does not change appreciably (for most sounds) over 30 ms, which is usually several pitch periods. In practice, the bit rate may be reduced by a factor of 3 or so by this technique, resulting in a system of 1 kbit/s. This is the average bit rate for the Digitalker II® system, while the older system required roughly twice the storage as a result of using 128-point periods.

Note that the Mozer technique depends on a *perceptual* model (the usual magnitude-of-spectrum assumption) but not explicitly on a speech *production* model. While this dependency precludes formant coding, etc., it also means that the technique is not subject to the limitations of a pole-only, single-source model. Thus nasals (which have significant antiresonances) and voiced fricatives (produced by noise *and* pulse excitations) are coded as easily as vowels.

4.3. CLASSIFICATION AND PITCH TRACKING

4.3.1. A brief review

The preceding sections have been concerned exclusively with characterization of the short-term frequency content of speech. This is roughly equivalent (for a formant or LPC approach at least) to a modeling of the spectrum of the vocal tract. Speech analysis must also characterize the *source* or *excitation*, which drives the vocal tract. In the context of the simplified model already described, we must learn whether the excitation was *pulselike* or *noiselike*. In the former case, we must learn the repetition frequency of the pulses, called the *pitch*. There are two steps to determination of these excitations. The first is a classification step, called the *voiced-unvoiced determination*. The second is a calculation step, called *pitch tracking*.

There are many techniques to do both of these determinations. Sometimes they are joined together in a single algorithm which yields both classification and pitch. The major classes of techniques follow.

4.3.2. Periodicity measures

One approach is to look for periodicity in the speech. Since voiced speech results from the quasi-periodic oscillation of the vocal cords, some measure of that periodicity should show not only the periodic nature of the source but also the length of the period. Autocorrelation is one of the simplest of these methods. This refers to the calculation of lag product, or the scalar product between the speech segment and delayed versions of itself. The maxima of such a sum of products will occur for lags which will match the signal up to similar versions of itself.

For example, when a perfectly periodic waveform is correlated with itself, the peaks of the result will be at delays of zero, one period, two periods, etc. (when correlation is graphed as a function of delay).

Thus, correlation peaks show the period of a waveform. In the case of a

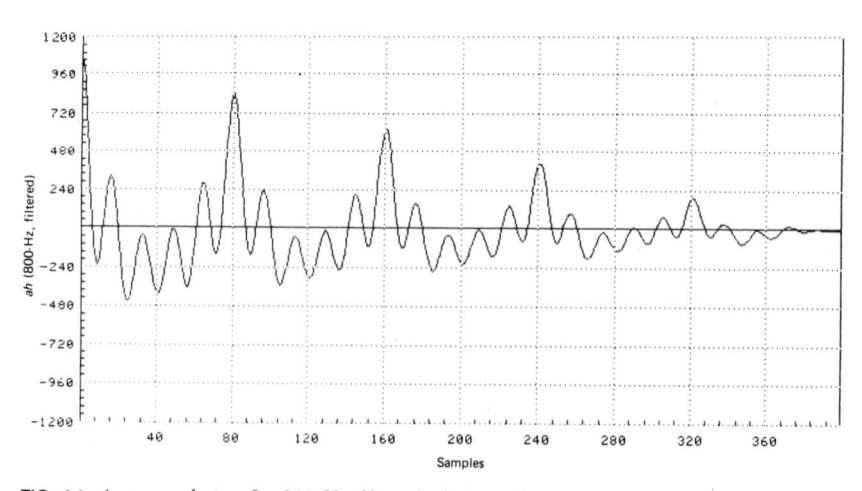

FIG. 4.9. Autocorrelation for 800-Hz filtered *ah* (periodic).

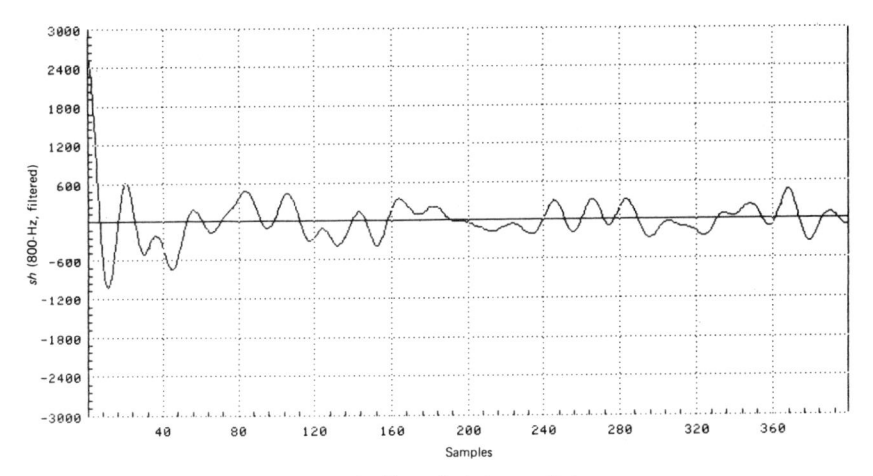

FIG. 4.10. Autocorrelation for 800-Hz filtered *sh* (aperiodic).

quasi-periodic waveform, in which succeeding speech segments bear close resemblance to one another, the *size* of the first major autocorrelation peak (after the zero delay peak) is a measure of the correlation between neighboring periods. (See Figures 4.9 and 4.10.)

This suggests a simple pitch detection technique. The autocorrelation function can be computed for a section of a speech waveform.[4] Then, based on the size of *later* peaks in the expected range of delays (typically 4–20 ms for a male voice), a voiced/unvoiced decision can be made. If the segment is determined to be voiced, then the position of the dominant peak yields the pitch period.

This has been a simplified description of the method. The mathematics is not as difficult as the proper choice of a decision threshold for the size of the autocorrelation peak. In practice, it is difficult to make reliable voiced/unvoiced decisions over a variety of speakers using a periodicity detector such as this.[5] Assuming a correct classification, however, these pitch-period measurements are relatively immune to the noise and distortion of the original speech input.

4.3.3. Pattern recognition

Instead of determining periodicity, voiced/unvoiced decision procedures can evaluate the statistical or spectral features of the two types of sounds, even within a single period.

---

[4] Actually, the speech is usually filtered first to remove frequency content that will not be useful for this determination.

[5] Another method is the *cepstral* approach, which measures periodicity by the periodic ripples in the log spectrum at harmonics of the pitch frequency. It sometimes fouls up real-world classifications quite badly, too.

Talking Chips

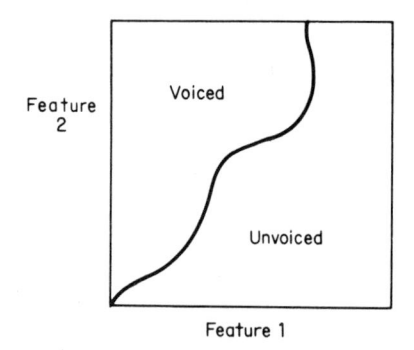

FIG. 4.11. Decision function for two classes and two features.

A training procedure can be instituted to develop a *decision rule* based on parameters extracted from the speech. Typical parameters are energy, zero-crossing rate, the first few terms of the autocorrelation function, or anything else that explicitly or implicitly specifies the spectrum (Figure 4.11).

Such a rule will be the one that best classifies this training data. *Best* will generally mean closest to the decisions made by a human using aids that are visual (waveform and *spectrogram*)[6] and aural (the sounds themselves).

The rule is validated by experiments with new speech. If this test is performed using new speech from the same talkers, the decision rule is only validated for those people's voices. If a broad sample of people is used for source speech, statistical conclusions can be drawn about the overall accuracy of the rule on a talker-independent basis. If new training can be instituted for each talker, however, the decision rule can be optimized for higher performance. Such new training is useless for a real-time communications system but is very helpful for the stored-speech synthesis applications of the current generation of talking chips.

This pattern-matching approach is independent of any periodicity assumptions or ad hoc choices of decision thresholds (although the optimizations should at least begin with reasonable guesses). It has been implemented in different forms with great success. The only real drawback to the idea is its relative complexity.

Some researchers have found that techniques of this kind do not perform as well as the periodicity type of algorithms under extreme conditions of noise or distortion. To counter this weakness, it is perfectly reasonable to require high-quality original recordings. Such a requirement is a small price to pay for the increased accuracy of decisions.

---

[6] This is a display that shows the variation of spectrum over time, usually by using the vertical axis for frequency, the horizontal axis for time, and intensity for amplitude.

Analysis for Synthesis 103

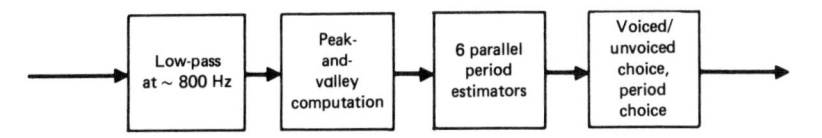

FIG. 4.12. Gold-Rabiner pitch detector.

4.3.4. Waveform measurement

A trained human operator can classify voiced and unvoiced segments and pick out a period with only a waveform to look at. Pitch detectors have been designed which incorporate similar techniques. They extract parameters which are the positions and amplitudes of peaks and valleys of a smoothed (low-pass filtered) version of the waveform. The smoothing is done to remove rapid amplitude variations which could be mistaken for major peaks and valleys.

One such scheme was proposed by Gold and Rabiner (Figure 4.12) and has since been frequently implemented in software and hardware. It makes six different pitch guesses based on the peak and valley measurements, then makes a voice/unvoiced decision depending on the degree of agreement between these guesses. It is markedly faster in software and simpler in hardware than nearly all other methods. It is not as accurate as some of the more complex methods, nor is it as robust under noise or distorted conditions. However, it does work well enough for automatic pitch detection in real-time communications.

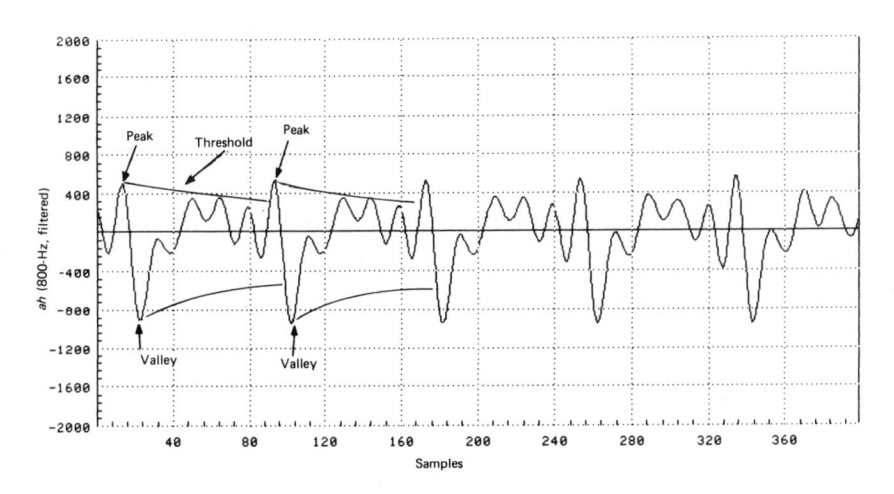

FIG. 4.13. An 800-Hz low-pass-filtered waveform with exponential peak thresholds.

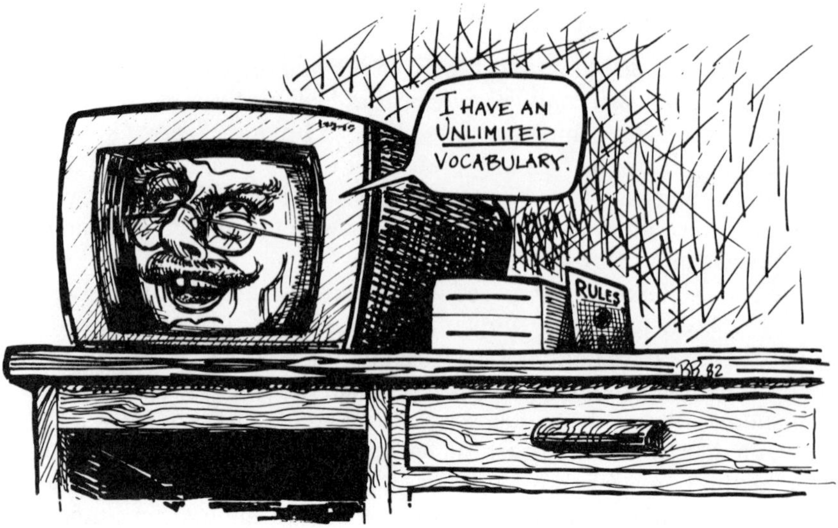
I HAVE AN UNLIMITED VOCABULARY.
RULES

CHAPTER 5

SYNTHESIS BY RULE

5.1. INTRODUCTION

Many different techniques have been described in the preceding sections for coding and representing the information in speech signals. Such coding allows that information to be stored or transmitted for later reconstruction as synthetic speech. Depending on the quality of the coding, transmission, and reconstruction, the resulting speech will normally sound quite close to the voice which was originally analyzed.

We can also create sequences of parameter values directly in the computer, rather than by analyzing a real speech signal. This possibility gives us a new freedom and flexibility that didn't exist before, the ability to create new words and sentences, to create sound not derived from recorded speech. We can generate the parameter patterns directly from the sequence of phonemes to be reproduced. Almost as a side effect, by using a phoneme representation rather than coding the parameters directly, the bit rate is reduced by a factor more than 10 to 1. This can result in speech storage at less than 200 bits per second.

There is, however, a price for all this wondrous creative power. The intelligibility of the speech resulting from our generated sequences of parameter values depends critically on our understanding of the parameter model and the underlying mechanisms of the speech process.

Since the time of Noam Chomsky's work at MIT in the late 1960s and early 1970s, our knowledge of linguistic processes has been represented in the form of collections of rules. These rules express the many detailed relations between sound features, phonemes, word patterns, and sentence patterns. In particular, Chomsky and Halle published an extensive model of the relations between different classes of sounds, word prefix and suffix structures, and stress and intonation patterns for the English language.

One might imagine that a simple set of rules for generating parameters for a formant synthesizer model would be no more than a list of the formant values for each of the phonemes of the language. Before discussing the problems of this approach, we will need to browse for a moment in the arcane world of phonetic features, coarticulation, and allophonic variation.

5.2. MAJOR CONSIDERATIONS FOR FORMANT RULES

5.2.1. Phonetic features

We have seen in previous discussions of speech models that different speech sounds have different properties and to some extent require different reproduction mechanisms. An example is the distinction between the buzzy quality of voiced sounds and the noiselike quality of the fricatives. All the sounds of speech can be categorized into a dozen or so overlapping classes, based on such properties as the positions of the tongue and lips, the nature of the airflow mechanism, and the action of the vocal cords. These properties, which serve to group sounds into distinctive classes, are known as *phonetic features*. The phonetic features include *voiced* (vocal cords vibrating during most of the duration of the sound), *nasal* (an opening at the velum between the mouth and nasal cavities), and *consonantal* (some constriction exists in the airflow pathway).

One of the major classes of consonants is the *stop*. These sounds are characterized by a period of silence, followed by a burst (a small explosion of air pressure) when the point of closure is released. The stop consonants are further subclassified according to the position of the tongue or lips used to produce the closure. In English, the major closure positions are *labial* (lips brought together as in *p* and *b*), *alveolar* (tongue pushed against the alveolar ridge just behind the teeth as in *t* and *d*), and *velar* (tongue bunched up against the velum in the back of the mouth as in *k* and *g*). Since airflow completely stops for some period of time during these sounds, there are no meaningful formant values. Proper output of the synthesizer during this time should be silence. Additionally, the formant values for the nonsilent portion of these sounds are affected by the surrounding sounds. This case is not covered by the simple formant-frequency-list model. A parameter generator mechanism must be capable of modeling this pattern of events correctly in order to produce intelligible speech output.

Fortunately, the parameter patterns we need to generate have many common characteristics across all the sounds of a class. It is, therefore, economical to use these phonetic features in the design of a set of rules. As examples of the patterning inherent in the feature mechanism:

1. The switch described in Chapter 1, which selects either the periodic source or the noise source in the synthesis model, will be operated most of the time by one of the features *fricative* or *aspiration*.
2. The class of nasal sounds—in English, those written as *m*, *n*, and *ng*—uniformly are voiced, have a medium amplitude less than that of a vowel but greater than that of a voiced stop consonant, and always exhibit a low first-formant frequency.

Phonetic features such as these may then be generated for each type of sound, including the stops.

5.2.2. Coarticulation

If we construct a system which generates parameter values phoneme by phoneme, accounting for patterns like the above, we find the result still unsatisfactory. In fact, if the parameter values are *constant* for the duration of each phoneme, the result is worse than unsatisfactory, it is unintelligible. Some kind of smoothing is necessary so that the generated values blend properly to make one sound follow the next. After all, the tongue does not move in jumps.

The term *coarticulation* refers to the effect each phoneme has on its neighbors, that is, the smearing of articulatory events across more than one phoneme. A fairly straightforward case of this is the motion of the formant frequencies during a vowel, just before or following a consonant closure. Each of the closure positions has an associated characteristic pattern of formant frequencies, even though for most of the duration of a stop no formants are detectable. The formant patterns for the stops are evidenced by the motion of the formants toward or away from these positions to their respective positions in the neighboring vowel, although these motions actually occur entirely during the vowel.

As another example of coarticulation, consider the velar opening, between the mouth cavity and the nasal cavity. This opening changes size at the beginning or end of a nasal sound. The particular muscle controlling that opening responds rather sluggishly, compared to most of the other articulatory organs. When you speak the word *can*, for instance, the velar opening must be open by the time the tongue tip reaches the alveolar ridge to block the airflow there. If the velum is still closed at that time, a *d* sound results, and the word comes out as *cad*. In order to prevent such a slip, the velum begins to open quite early during the *a* sound. To achieve a natural sounding synthesis of this word, it is necessary to adjust the formant frequency and bandwidth values during the latter part of the vowel sound to give it the properties of nasality. The duration of this overlapping of characteristics can be anywhere from a few milliseconds to the entire duration of the vowel itself.

5.2.3. Allophones

Another side of the issue of coarticulation is that of *allophonic variation*. This refers to the variations in the articulatory or acoustic realization of a given class of sounds, depending on the phonetic context. One of the results of coarticulation is that classes of sounds are modified in predictable ways by their neighbors. This modification gives rise to a set of variations on the sounds within each phoneme class. Each of these varieties of the phoneme is known as an *allophone*.

Each of the examples of coarticulation (previous section) can also be viewed as an example of allophonic variation. In the case of the nasalized vowel, the vowel sound is still recognized as a token of the particular vowel phoneme, /ae/ as in *hat* or *cat*, but it is said to be a nasalized allophone of that vowel phoneme. It is interesting to note that the allophonic varieties of a particular phoneme in one language often correspond to different phonemes in a different language. In the example given, the nasalized vowel acceptable in English as an alternative pronunciation would be perceived in French as a different vowel sound altogether, that is, a different phoneme.

As another example, spectral details during the *s* and *sh* sound are different, depending on the following vowel. The identity of the vowel may be reliably perceived, even when all the vowel-sound proper has been cut away and only the fricative noise played for the listener. To see this effect in a clear-cut case, compare the sound of *s* in *seep* with that of *sop*. Try saying each of these words, but stop just before you begin to hear the voice buzz of the vowel sound. The difference in lip positions, and to some extent tongue positions as well, causes a very different frequency response for each of these allophones of *s*.

5.3. A PHONETIC RULE IN ACTION

As we continue to elaborate our model of the sound structure of speech, we need a better way to represent the details of the system of sound patterns, both for our own understanding and for the computer's use in generating speech. An efficient means of stating these patterns has been found in the form of rules which express both a context and a statement of what happens in that context. Both the context and the change to occur are usually most efficiently expressed in terms of phonetic feature values, sometimes using the symbols for the phonemes themselves. To illustrate the style and application of such a rule, we will explore a phenomenon which occurs in English whenever an *s* is followed by a stop, such as in the words *spin* and *stop*. In this context, the stop is produced with a much weaker aspiration period than it would normally have if the stop occurred alone at the beginning of the word, as in the corresponding words *pin* and *top*. To see this effect for yourself, try holding your hand an inch or two away from your mouth and saying each of the words. For *pin* and *top*, you will feel a definite *puff* of air. Notice that there is also a fairly strong puff after the last *p* of *top*. Compare this with the smaller amount of air released during *spin* and *stop*. You may feel some air during *spin*, but probably quite a bit less than for *pin*. A statement of the phonetic pattern evidenced by these simple experiments might be something like the following: "If any aspirated stop consonant occurs after an *s* phoneme, then the stop should be modified so as to be unaspirated."

A rule to express this pattern could be stated as:

$$s \begin{bmatrix} \text{consonant} \\ \text{stop} \\ \text{aspirated} \end{bmatrix} \rightarrow s \begin{bmatrix} \text{consonant} \\ \text{stop} \\ -\text{aspirated} \end{bmatrix}$$

To avoid repeating all the conditions on both sides of this "assignment" statement, especially as the contexts get more complicated, conventions have been adopted for abbreviating the description. The most common representation is probably that defined by Chomsky. The detail which changes is stated first, both as before and after; and then comes a slash (/), followed by a statement of the context, as elaborate as necessary, with a long dash (———) (or sometimes an underscore) indicating where the changed detail fits in the context. As a further shortcut, various conventions have been adopted which group the features into hierarchies so that implied features need not be stated. For instance, all stops are always consonants, so the feature consonant may be omitted. The same rule may then be rewritten:

$$\text{stop} \rightarrow \text{-aspirate} / s \text{———}$$

"A stop becomes unaspirated when following an *s*."

5.4. GENERATING PARAMETERS BY RULE

To describe the action of this rule in a parameter generation scheme, we need to specify some hypothetical parameter patterns and then show how the patterns would differ when this particular context occurs. To begin, we will briefly review some of the properties of a synthesis model to clarify just what parameter values will be needed to drive that synthesizer.

For this purpose, we will assume a mixed-voicing model, which will allow the aspiration phase of a standalone stop to be blended smoothly into the voicing of the following vowel. We will also assume that the burst part of the stop is generated by the same noise-source amplitude control, but with a shift in the settings of the spectral frequency controls. For simplicity, the formant frequency controls will be lumped into one *spectral frequency* value, which we will assume to be high to generate the stop burst pattern, low to reproduce the aspiration phase, and mid-range for the vowel sound. All this considered, the model we are describing might appear as in Figure 5.1.

Given a synthesizer model as described, we can now specify the parameter patterns needed for a normal stop-vowel sequence. Showing only the two amplitude controls and the frequency control mentioned above, a plot of the time functions might be as shown in Figure 5.2.

If we now compare these parameter values to those in Figure 5.3, showing the sequence s-stop-vowel, we see that the noise amplitude is considerably smaller during the aspiration phase of the stop when the stop follows an s. Phonetically, this allophone of s is referred to as an unaspirated stop.

The mechanisms required to generate these patterns may be fairly simple, based on a few underlying phonetic concepts. First, let us reexamine the original idea of a list of formant frequency values for each phonemic unit to be synthesized. If we treat the formant settings for each

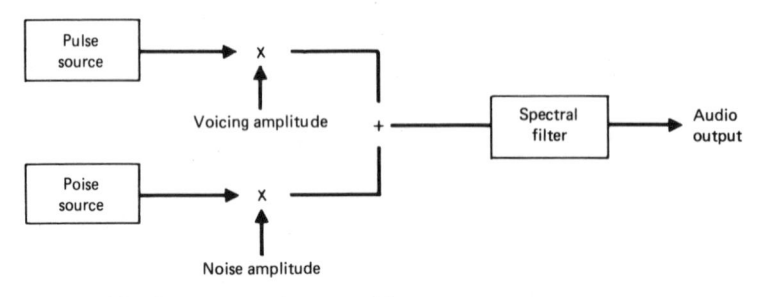

FIG. 5.1. Mixed-voicing synthesis model.

Synthesis by Rule 111

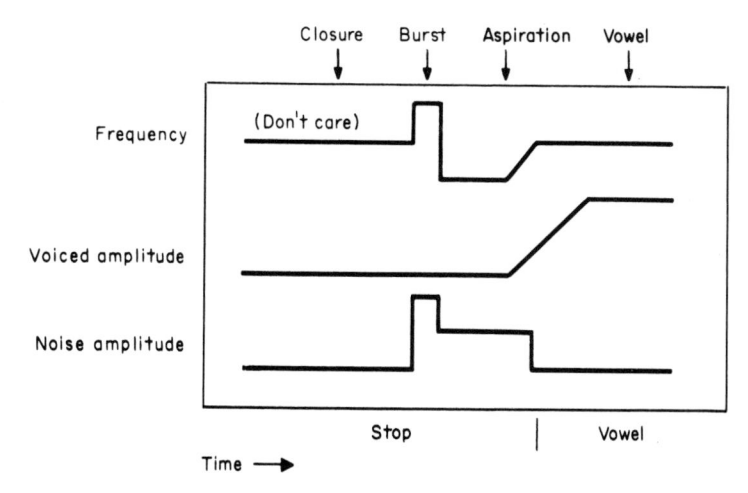

FIG. 5.2. Parameters for a stop-consonant–vowel sequence.

phoneme as a set of ideal target values rather than as explicit frequency settings, we shall see that it provides the basis for a useful model. For the vowels and some of the consonants, reasonable patterns can be constructed by generating arcs curving from one target level to the next. For the stops and a few of the other more complex consonants, we need some extra shape-generator routines which can be called up at the appropriate times.

As far as the aspiration pattern is concerned, we first need to know that

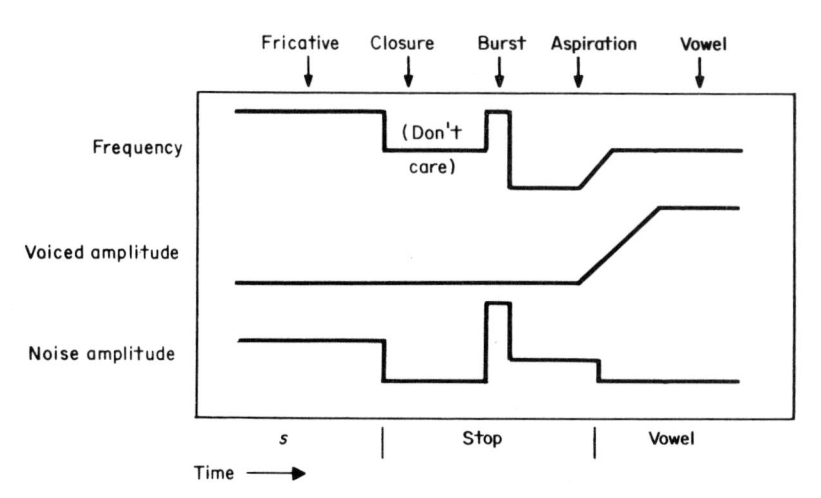

FIG. 5.3. Parameters for *s*-stop-vowel.

an aspiration pattern generator must be called after the burst pulse during any stop. This call can be executed conditionally by testing the stop feature for each phoneme. That aspiration generator can then test the value of the aspiration feature specified for the stop to determine the setting for the noise amplitude control. The normal noise amplitude value is reduced to a lower level if the aspiration feature is turned off. A variety of such conditional calls and feature-dependent parameter levels work together to produce the range of different patterns needed to make intelligible speech.

5.5. DURATION AND INTONATION

Two other patterns which have not been addressed in the above discussions also have to be considered to generate speech signals entirely by rule. These are the sequence of phoneme durations and the overall intonation across the entire phrase or sentence to be spoken. Both of these sentence-level patterns are extremely important in the perceptual effect of the synthetic speech.

If the phoneme durations do not adequately approach those of natural human speech, the result sounds garbled and inhuman. Apparently, the duration pattern contains important cues to the syntactic and semantic structure of the sentence; and if these cues are inappropriate or misleading, the perceptual mechanism is led into a series of misinterpretations of the linguistic structure of the intended utterance. This usually results in the complete loss of intelligibility of the synthetic speech.

The effects of an unnatural intonation pattern are not quite so disastrous in causing misunderstandings but are perhaps worse in the resulting psychological impact. The effect is as if the sentences were spoken with the wrong emphasis, as if the speaker misunderstood the intended meaning or was unable to express that meaning properly. The result is often interpreted as though the speaker had a strong dialect or accent of a foreign language.

Both of these patterns are very difficult to compute properly because of a lack of adequate linguistic models for the underlying mechanisms. For example, the durations used for a particular vowel will vary widely depending on the position of the syllable within the word, the level of stress placed on the word, the position of the word within the phrase or sentence, and several other such factors. Intonation is, in fact, a cover term referring to changes which take place in amplitude settings and phoneme durations as well as in the fundamental frequency, or pitch, contour over the course of the sentence.

Rapid progress can be expected in the next few years, both in the sophistication of computer models for determining the duration and intonation patterns to make synthetic speech sound more natural and in the underlying linguistic theories describing these models. The research needed involves several more or less related fields, including phonetics, psycholinguistics, sociology, computer science, computational linguistics, and artificial intelligence.

5.6. APPLICATIONS FOR SYNTHESIS BY RULE

If you were designing a talking soft-drink machine, it would seem perfectly reasonable to establish the entire range of vocabulary before your design leaves the blueprint stage. The exact words can then be built into the design using the optimum coding technique to achieve the best balance between speech quality and memory costs.

On the other hand, for many applications in a personal computer environment, it is not feasible to make such decisions so far in advance. You might, for example, want to set up a system which speaks words as they arrive over a modem connection. In this case, a more flexible approach is needed. A method is required which can accept a new word not previously considered and synthesize a spoken version of that word. This ability is, of course, one of the major advantages of a system for synthesizing speech by rule. An elementary use of the ability to synthesize new and unique items would be to include some of your friends' names in a new program. Hearing their name come from your machine will invariably bring forth guffaws or squeals of delight.

Two primary characteristics of a rule-synthesis system can be identified. One is that mentioned above, the ability to synthesize new or previously unknown vocabulary items on the spot, without requiring an elaborate analysis process. The other is the dramatic improvement in memory space requirements for speech stored in the form of phonetic symbols. Storing words in this form typically requires from one-tenth to as little as one one-hundredth the amount of space as that needed for storing the synthesizer control parameters themselves.

We can then see that any application which makes use of one or both of these characteristics will be a good candidate for a rule-synthesis system. Interestingly, some applications combine these two characteristics in the sense that the low data rate makes it feasible to bring new materials to the synthesis system in novel ways. An example of this is a book published recently with bar-code strips containing phonetic information for a synthesizer. The synthesizer, of course, contains no built-in vocabulary. If the bar-code strips contained the actual control parameters, they would occupy much of a page for each word instead of the 2- or 3-inch strips actually used, and the concept would not have succeeded.

The simplest games where you fly around in space shooting at various darting objects can be designed adequately with only a few built-in phrases such as *fuel low* and *enemy attack*. However, as the game becomes more complex, the system needs more descriptive power. The real threshold comes when more than one player can interact and introduce new relations and strategies not foreseeable when the game was designed. One possible example of such a game would be a "dungeons and dragons" type game where the player can create new roles and new situations. If the newly created "participants" are then to use speech to talk to the player at the console (or to each other, "overheard" by the player), they will need flexible vocabularies and perhaps even expandable linguistic structures. In this situation, the player sitting in front of a CRT (*cathode-ray tube*) becomes the game designer, and the speech capabilities of the system must be able to serve his or her needs.

Another possible future application of synthetic speech by rule would be the increasing use of speech synthesis devices connected to optical character readers. As the technology develops and such readers become cheap enough for widespread use, a rapid growth in the use of speech synthesis will be seen.

As an even more far-reaching possibility, software for data-base access will be developed to the point where interaction with stored information can take place in a reasonably natural form of English grammar. The turning point here will be the ability of the grammatical controller to construct useful sentences describing the information in the data base. This point is indeed not far in the future. In fact, talking airline travel guides and phone directories are already in use in some research organizations. Such capabilities will find use in the home, in education (talking interactive encyclopedias), and for record keeping of many sorts. Examples of the latter include catalogs for libraries, collectors' items, musical recordings, restaurant lists, shopping guides, physical fitness programs, appointment calendars, etc., etc. In short, as data management systems find their way into the personal computing environment, speech synthesis will be a ready partner each step of the way.

CHAPTER

6

AUDIO FOR SPEECH ANALYSIS

6.1. INTRODUCTION

Despite sophisticated technologies and mathematics, often the most significant errors in speech analysis and synthesis are acoustical in nature. Unlike the VODER's listeners in the 1930s, the public of the 1980s has been educated to expect high-quality audio. Once the novelty of speech itself has worn off, quality less than that of commercial radio and records will be acceptable only in very cheap toys.

Perceived problems with synthetic speech can sometimes be the result of errors in audio design and procedure. Two typical examples of how this may happen are:

1. The amplifier, speaker, enclosure, and environment constitute a system with a significant transfer characteristic (Figure 6.1).

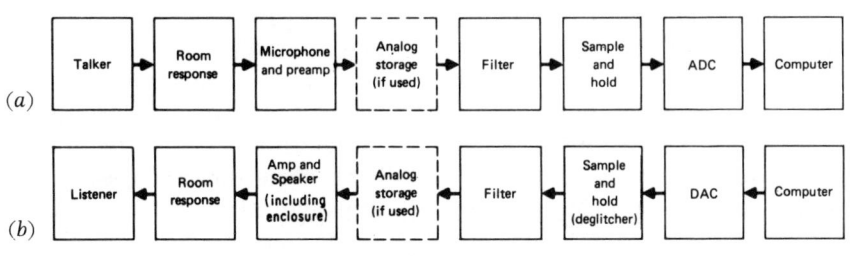

FIG. 6.1. Sound record and playback chains: (*a*) sound recording chain, (*b*) sound v playback chain.

If this is not accounted for, the acoustic speech output may be subject to distortion (acoustic nonlinearity) or muffling (high-frequency loss).
2. The original recordings from which speech parameters are derived should be flawless. It has often been said, "You can't make a silk purse out of a sow's ear." If the audio quality starts off low (noise, distortion, high-frequency loss), the processed speech will in general be no better.

Some will suggest that synthetic speech is so imperfect in comparison to natural speech that such problems will be masked.[1] In practice, the imperfections of the original recording will occur in precisely that manner which will ensure perceptible errors in the resulting synthetic speech.

A relatively simple set of precautions in the audio and acoustic domains will prevent such problems. These are outlined in the next section. The final section introduces techniques for playback and evaluation of synthetic speech.

6.2. ORIGINAL RECORDINGS FOR SPEECH ANALYSIS

6.2.1. Introduction

Vocabularies for commercial speech synthesizers are frequently generated by special laboratories, such as National's in Santa Clara and Berkeley and TI's in Texas. At these facilities, specially trained speech engineers greatly assist in achieving the efficiency and quality of the low bit-rate speech representation. It is a common experience, however, for these industrious souls to receive some dreadful sounding cassettes. Remember, these are engineers, not magicians.

Maxim: Do a professional *audio* job, as well as a professional electronic job. The easiest way to do this is to leave the work to the manufacturers (such as National, TI, and GI), who have been educated through experience in the requirements. This may be unrealistic for many applications, however. Some customers may wish to experiment more extensively than the service centers' time will permit.

If the users wish to record their own speech, they must take certain precautions. Most of these can be taken care of by using a professional recording studio. Be forewarned, however, that some of the requirements of speech analysis for synthesis are different from those of speech for broadcast, film, or records. The user must be aware of the unique considerations involved to avoid generating an inferior product.

---

[1] Fie on these cretins! Their hypothesis suggests a trust in the cosmos that can be easily countered by Murphy's law, "If anything can go wrong, it will."

In the following subsections, I will assume that the reader has some control on each of the variables discussed. This control may come through choice of a professional announcer and/or studio, or perhaps by discussion with the involved parties of an existing studio. You may even achieve control by designing your own recording room.

This last choice offers the greatest flexibility, but at the highest cost. You had better know what you're doing! Using your uncle's garage as a recording booth is not a serious contender. It is a prescription for failure.

6.2.2. Talker considerations

6.2.2.1. Proper enunciation by talker

The best studio and the best electronic equipment in the world can't save a recording of someone who doesn't say the right things in the first place. To listen properly for this, you must remove yourself from your normal manner of listening to speech. In the usual mode, you might hear someone say an entirely different set of phonetic elements from what a clear enunciation would present. Yet you'd understand them so well that you wouldn't notice anything wrong. For example:

        English text: "Did you eat your breakfast."
        Speaker says: "Djou e chur breakfast."

Unless an *entire phrase* is being recorded for analysis and synthesis, you must get *all* desired *phonemes* from the talker for later use. The main rule here is to *listen for the clear utterance of each expected phoneme.*

6.2.2.2. Pitch

The specific analysis technique used will have corresponding limitations with regard to pitch tracking. The intended user must be aware of the range available as well as its ability to track irregular contours. Given this knowledge, you can have the announcer redo sounds that were too low or too high in pitch or too irregular. Without this knowledge, a best bet is to try to enforce slowly varying pitch contours that reside in medium ranges (80–160 Hz for males).

6.2.2.3. Voice quality

"Gravelly" sounding voices, while interesting for Saturday morning cartoons, can violate many standard speech assumptions. Barring specific knowledge to the contrary, use normal smooth-sounding voices.

6.2.2.4. Speaking rate

Make sure that the rate at which the words are spoken will be appropriate for the application. The bit-rate compression will give more impressive figures for slowly spoken speech (bits per second), but the overall bit budget won't be changed much.

6.2.2.5. Choice of words or phrases

Words can never be pieced together as well as phrases themselves. If at all possible, record each entire phrase you intend to use. For example, if we wish a product to say, "The time is six o'clock," "The time is seven o'clock," etc., even though the final storage will be

>The time is _____ o'clock
>>one
>>two
>>three
>>four
>>five
>>six
>>seven
>>eight
>>nine
>>ten
>>eleven
>>twelve

do *not* record it this way! The result will sound unnatural. Instead, record all the full phrases. Then the intonations of each number will be correct for insertion. Record multiple versions of each sound, preferably at different times. Since each technique works better with some speech than with others, this will give the analysis a greater chance of working well.

Insert "dummy" phrases for the announcer to say before and after the desired sequence. This counters the speaker's natural tendency to waste early phrases "warming up" to a consistent quality. Insert a phrase at the end. This allows for the inevitable change of speaking style when the talker knows he is arriving at the end.

If all of these considerations are adhered to, we can be assured that the talker's vocal apparatus is putting out the right stuff.

6.2.3. Room Acoustics

6.2.3.1. Sound isolation

6.2.3.1.1. How much do you need? Probably the most obvious requirement of a speech (or any audio) recording is to keep unwanted sounds out. The extraneous sounds in the preceding cartoon *cannot* be easily "fixed in the lab." So then, how stringent should we be at protecting our recording from subtle noises? It is tempting to say that *no* noise should intrude on our recording. Unfortunately, this is not realistic. The "real world" of engineering has some important limitations. For example:

All electronic equipment generates some noise.

A door that attenuates sound by 60 dB (decibels) is *far* more than twice the expense of a door that attenuates 30 dB. This is not surprising when you realize the 60-dB door leaks one one-thousandth the energy of the 30-dB door.

Fortunately, a reasonable estimate of the isolation required can be computed in the following manner:

1. Estimate the dB in *sound pressure level*, or SPL (referenced to 0.00002 microbar of pressure), the noise level outside the area to be isolated. Think worst case, but don't be absurd. Call this number E (for *external noise*).
2. Estimate the dB signal level of the announcer's voice at the microphone. Thinking worst case, take the lowest number (typically 65–70 dB). Call this number V (for *voice*).
3. Estimate the dB range required to fit in the worst storage-transmission element used. For instance, allow 50 dB for a cassette, 60 dB for a reel-to-reel tape, and 70 dB for a 12-bit ADC. In general, no better

signal-to-noise ratio (SNR) is required at the mike than what comes later. (Although being at least marginally better than the weakest link prevents deterioration of the SNR.) Buzzes and other periodic noises will be more audible than broadband noise of the same total energy, however, so you should essentially eliminate them. Call the *required dynamic range* $SNR_{required}$.

If $L(loss)$ is the required transmission loss in dB,

$$SNR_{achieved} = V - E + L$$

For $SNR_{achieved} \geq SNR_{required}$,

$$L \geq SNR_{required} - (V - E)$$

For example, let the ambient noise level outside be as high as the sound level 6 to 8 inches from a fairly soft-spoken talker. For this situation, the transmission loss must be roughly equal to the system signal-to-noise ratio (50–70 dB for the equipment examples above). Such a high transmission-loss requirement suggests a very expensive construction job.

The preceding analysis has overlooked many significant details, all of which should be examined by a qualified acoustician. For your own rough determinations, though, it will work. As a slight sophistication of this method, let's examine *frequency-dependent* transmission loss.

In general, high-frequency loss is much easier to accomplish than low-frequency loss. The former's wavelength is smaller, so the materials providing attenuation are smaller and consequently cheaper. Even the air itself provides significant absorption at high frequencies. Wideband sounds, such as fan noise or paper rustling, tend to be low-pass filtered by the absorption characteristics of environmental materials. Most of these materials smooth the rough edges of the traveling sound wave. In addition, many natural sound sources, like speech and music, have predominately low-frequency energy. All of this taken together implies

1. The dB requirement computation should be done over at least two different frequency bands.
2. The *low-frequency portion* is attenuated with the greatest difficulty.

What is the "low-frequency portion"? A high-pass system is one which does not significantly pass signals below some corner frequency. If we are recording on a high-pass system, leakage below that point *may* not be significant (although it *can* be if the amplitude is sufficient to excite system nonlinearities). As humans, who are relatively insensitive to very low-frequency sound, we can generally disregard any leakage below our threshold of audibility.

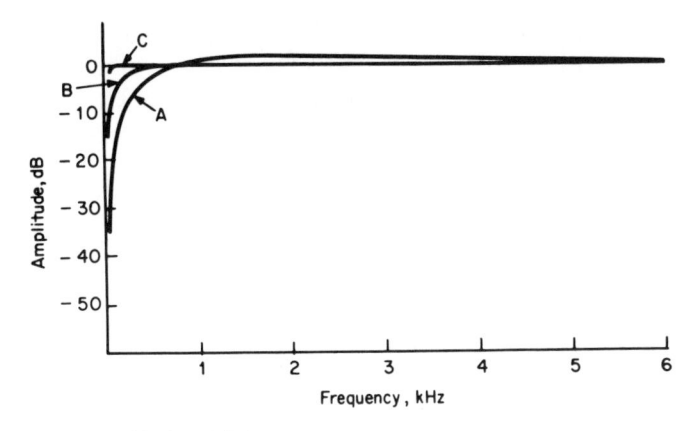

FIG. 6.2. A, B, C weighting curves.

One way of handling these considerations is to use a *frequency-weighting* network for the measurement of these signals and noises. Commonly available on commercial sound meters, these are the A-, B-, and C-weighted SPL scales. A is used most often for these needs. It devalues portions of the sound spectrum according to a rough approximation to human sensitivities at medium loudness. A single calculation using A (dBA) will suffice for most purposes (Figure 6.2).

Unfortunately, some analysis results can be corrupted by high-energy noise even if not audible to the listener. Such noise can cause improper *decisions* or move spectral modeling parameters. While it is true that inaudible noise can be filtered at the input to the speech system, this filtering can sometimes cause its own set of problems. It can degrade the spectral estimate by throwing a steep frequency characteristic into the response to be estimated, thus reducing the number of degrees of freedom left for estimation of the true speech spectrum.

To be safe, the user should calculate a worst-case transmission-loss number and use the C weighting, which is relatively flat.

6.2.3.1.2. How is isolation achieved? Some of the worst public misconceptions concerning acoustics lie in this area. Many think that tossing up some absorbent and/or irregular surfaces (foam, egg cartons, carpet) will reduce the transmission of sound. It will do so, but not by very much. They may improve the quality of sound within the room, as well as reduce the loudness due to *internally* generated sounds, but they will do very little to reduce the leakage from *externally* generated sounds.

Consider sound approaching an "absorbent" barrier, such as fiberglass. Three things can happen. Sound energy can be reflected, absorbed (transmuted to heat), or transmitted (Figure 6.3).

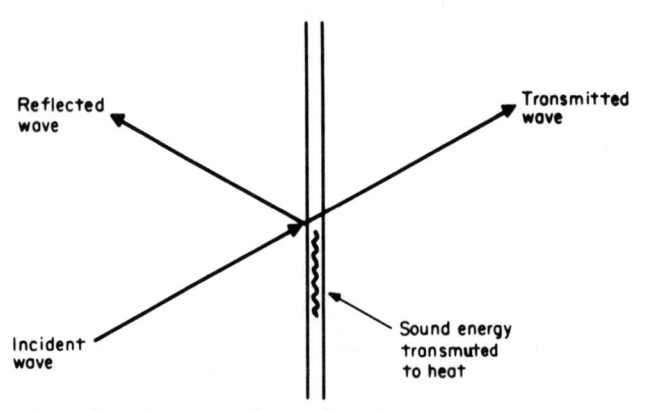

FIG. 6.3. Sound-wave incident on boundary.

In practice, all three occur to some degree. But for sounds of all but the shortest wavelength, very little reflection takes place. For these longer wavelength sounds, the energy level is only reduced a few dB by absorption. This means that a significant portion of the sound energy will fly past, as though nothing were there.

What is needed to stop sound is *lots of molecules*. There is no good substitute for putting a large amount of mass between the areas you wish to isolate (Figure 6.4).

This is another oversimplification, of course. Building a recording room, or checking the qualities of an existing one, is not a simple task. Care must be taken with many of the details (windows, doors, air passage, electrical conduits, etc.) to prevent sound leaks. Absorptive material *does* have a place in sound isolation for improving the efficiency of massive barriers. But the major point is clear:

$$\text{No mass} \rightarrow \text{no transmission loss}$$

Mass for sound isolation can be anything from double-walled construction to sound insulators, such as lead or concrete.

Finally, *all* aspects of the room seal must be considered. A high-attenuation boundary with holes in it is useless. This may seem obvious, but the "holes" are sometimes not readily visible. For instance, the backs of ac power-outlet boxes have knockout holes in them. These can provide a significant sound leakage path if not patched up with sealing compound. The finished room should be carefully inspected to find those many overlooked flaws in the sound barrier.

6.2.3.2. Sound absorption

6.2.3.2.1. Why? Sound-absorptive materials are utilized to reduce noise *within* a room. Such materials possess the capability to *absorb* sound energy, rather than *contain* it. They can be used to absorb energy from *multiple reflections* of a given sound in a room. This reduces the *reverberation*, or sound decay time. Why is this desirable?

1. For the time-domain description, the sound received at the microphone consists partly of sound reflected from room boundaries. If the boundaries are not sufficiently absorptive, sound can still hold considerable energy after many reflections. This has the effect of *smearing out* the sound over time.

   The room's average echo pattern is a reasonable approximation to an *impulse response* for the room as a linear acoustic system. This impulse response smears the original acoustic signal so that it becomes spread out in time when it reaches the microphone (or ear). If this time smear is long enough and loud enough, it can reduce the intelligibility of adjacent phonemes. In general, researchers have found a direct correspondence between the increase of reverberation time and a decrease in the intelligibility of speech.

   For short reverberation times, such as those found in most small rooms, these interphonemic effects are minor. However, *any* smear-

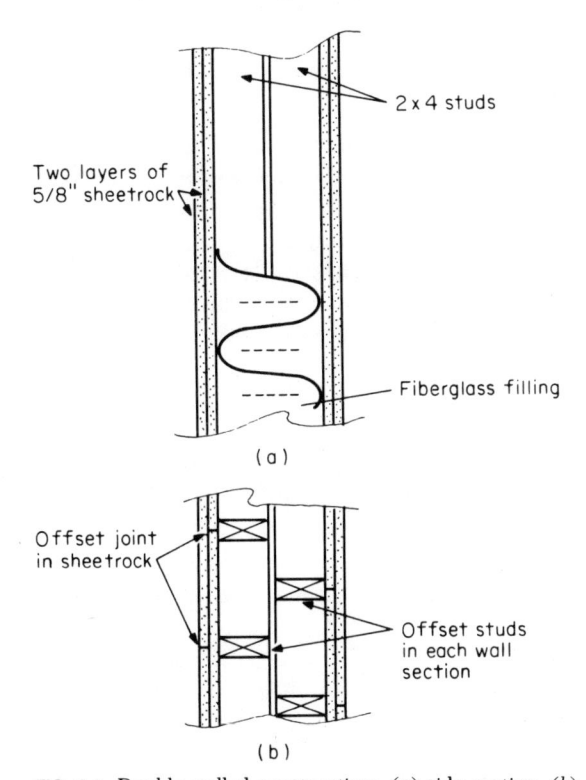

FIG. 6.4. Double-walled construction: (*a*) side section, (*b*) top section.

ing changes the waveform to be analyzed. How serious this is depends on the details of the analysis methods used and may not be obvious. The safest bet is to eliminate as many reflections as possible by making the room boundaries extremely absorbent.

2. For the frequency-domain description, consider the transfer characteristic between the talker's acoustic output and the microphone input.

   For many purposes, this may be approximated by a linear system. In the frequency domain, the room reverberation will have the effect of adding resonances and antiresonances to the speech. Since all low bit-rate speech analysis methods attempt to match the spectrum of the speech, these effects are clearly undesirable.

   Given finite degrees of freedom, any analysis technique will be less accurate at modeling the speech spectrum if it must also model the room spectrum. The clear conclusion, then, is to *deaden the room*. This is desirable *despite* the fact that slightly reverberated speech tends to sound more pleasing to the ear. Fortunately, most stored speech is played back in a reverberant environment, so it sounds acceptable. When low bit-rate synthesizers become more intelligible than they are today, we may see experiments to alter the quality by reverberating the synthesis output.

6.2.3.2.2. How? Making a room nonreflective is in general much easier than making it acoustically isolated. The materials used are lighter and generally much cheaper. A reasonable job may be done with almost anything available that is soft, such as carpeting.

If the budget allows, commercial materials are available which not only do a nice job but also have published absorption ratings. Common choices are fiberglass boards for the walls, porous ceiling panels overhead, and thick carpeting on the floors.

6.2.3.3. Standing waves

Because of their long wavelength (55 feet for a 20-Hz wave), very low-frequency sound waves will generally be relatively unaffected by the absorption techniques described. This is usually not a problem. However, if the room itself *resonates* at one of these low frequencies, then *standing waves* will form. In that case, variations of only a few inches in room position might yield a radically different speech spectrum. Since neither the microphone nor the talker's head is likely to be precisely positioned, this would clearly be a sad state of affairs. To avoid this problem, one should:

1. Use irregular or *diffusive* surfaces to disperse reflections of waves too long to be efficiently absorbed by the materials at hand.

2. Use nonparallel room boundaries, where one inch of splay per foot of boundary is generally considered sufficient.

Some combination of these two methods is usually sufficient for speech laboratory purposes.

6.2.4 Microphone choice and proper use

6.2.4.1. Choice

OK, now you have the talker saying the right things, and the room isn't echoing them back, and you can't hear the trucks outside! The next step is to choose an appropriate microphone. As the basis of this choice, you must be certain that the microphone's electrical output is properly representative of the speech.

Commercial microphones are either omnidirectional (essentially the same response regardless of the direction of the sound source) or directional (most sensitive to sound from certain directions). They are also either dynamic microphones (acting as a generator) or condenser microphones (operating on the electrostatic principle). Other types of microphones (such as carbon or crystal) should be rejected immediately.

Omnidirectional microphones are simply pressure sensors, generally sealed from all sides but one and sensitive to pressure regardless of the direction of the source.

Directional microphones are usually just omnidirectional microphones with extra acoustic paths opened to permit cancellation of sounds originating from the microphone's side and rear.

Directional microphones are useful for isolating a signal from noises in other directions. If recording is done in a quiet room, omnidirectional microphones are generally the better choice. The reasons they are favored are:

1. Because of lower design complexity, "omni mikes" cost less for the same basic capsule.
2. Omni mikes generally have a smoother on-axis frequency response than the corresponding directional version.
3. All but the most expensive directional microphones have a frequency response that varies greatly with source direction (Figure 6.5).
   Thus, as the talker turns his head, both the amplitude *and* the overall speech spectrum change.
4. As the talker moves *toward* a directional microphone, the bass response becomes extremely dependent on position (Figure 6.6). The response at 100 Hz can easily vary 10–20 dB over a few inches of movement. Not so for the omni.

126   Talking Chips

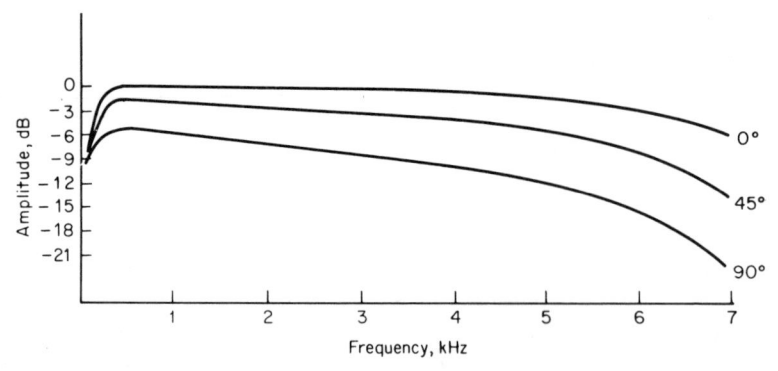

FIG. 6.5. Typical frequency response vs. angle of approach for a directional microphone.

So the case is clear: *if* the background noise level is low enough, omnis are the preferred choice for speech synthesis recordings.

Dynamic microphones are electromotive generators. Sound pressure waves impinging on the microphone's diaphragm cause motion of a conductive coil. These pressure changes are converted to proportional voltages by the change of magnetic flux (from a stationary magnet) across the coil. There is an inherent sluggishness to this process due to the mass of the coil.

In contrast, *condenser microphones* are variable capacitors. The diaphragm motion varies the interplate distance and thus the capacitance between the diaphragm and a back plate. Given a fixed amount of charge, this results in an output voltage variation that is proportional to the pressure changes. Any sluggishness is usually less pronounced due to the lack of a voice coil. This results in a better transient response than that for the dynamic mike. They are generally preferred for accurate recording of sound events, including speech.

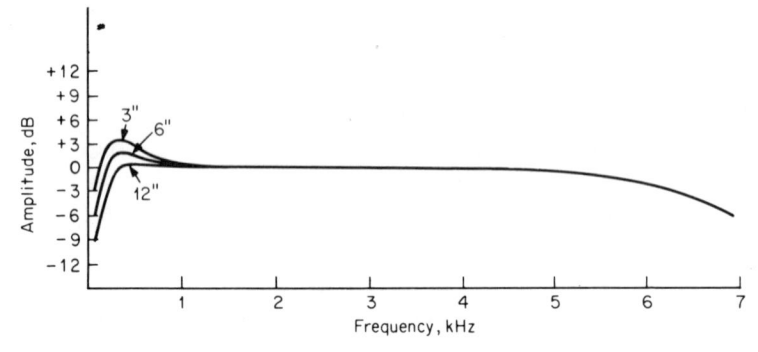

FIG. 6.6. Typical frequency response vs. talker distance for a directional microphone.

There are, however, some rather expensive dynamic microphones that perform quite well. There are also some inexpensive condenser microphones that have very uneven frequency response. Rather than stating a hard-and-fast rule, then, let me conclude with the following rules of thumb:

1. Don't use a cheap microphone.
2. Don't buy a microphone unless you can get a frequency response chart from the manufacturer. Demand one for the *individual* microphone,[2] not just a printed one for the model.
3. Be sure that the response meets your needs. Laboratory-quality speech microphones should be "flat as a board" between 50 Hz and your high-frequency limit. That limit can be between 3.2 kHz and 8 kHz, depending on the analysis technique.
4. Use an omnidirectional mike if feasible in your environment. Make certain the frequency response does not vary appreciably over about a 45-degree range from directly on axis.
5. Get a windscreen. Yes, I know you weren't going to use it in the wind, but believe me, it will help. An internal pop filter (so named for the "pops" sometimes heard in burst sounds) is also a good idea. Both protect the microphone from overload problems due to exhalations during and near speech events.

6.2.4.2. Microphone placement

If you can use a good omni mike with a pop filter, placement will not be excessively critical. Generally engineers place such mikes 4 to 8 inches from a talker and out of the direct path of his airstream. Closer placements increase the effects of nonidealities in the microphone's pop filter and omnidirectionality, while with farther placements, room imperfections and electronic noise are more of a problem.

If you are forced to use a directional microphone because of environmental noise, speaker positioning must be watched quite closely because of the large variations in response.

6.2.5. Analog storage

6.2.5.1. Introduction

The next major consideration in speech recording is the storage medium. Since the analysis is done on a digital computer, digital storage would not degrade the speech at all. Unfortunately, it is frequently inconvenient to use digital media for original sound recording. Most studios are still not

---

[2] Neumann, Schoeps, and AKG are among the manufacturers that routinely do this for their better microphones.

128   Talking Chips

equipped with digital audio recorders, and high-speed computers are not currently in use in the recording industry.[3]

Since the analog tape recorder is by far the most frequently used device for temporary speech storage, I will discuss its proper use exclusively. First, some of the quality considerations, and then some conclusions.

6.2.5.2. Dropouts

Dropouts are sudden reductions in signal level due to an irregularity (such as a protruding iron-oxide nodule) on the magnetic tape surface. All current commercial magnetic tape brands have these irregularities. When occurring on a high-quality reel-to-reel tape, the effect is usually not noticeable. These recordings are done at 7½ ips (*inches per second*) (or 15) on a half or full-track ¼-in tape recorder. For the full track at 15 ips, this means that one period of a 5-kHz sine wave will use up a space 3 mils long. If a surface irregularity causes a 0.3-mil separation of the tape from the head, there will be a momentary loss of 5 dB at 5 kHz. The duration of this condition will also depend on the tape speed. For an irregularity 15 mils long (a typical length), the dropout would last about a millisecond and probably not be heard at all.

On the other hand, consider a cassette recording done at 1⅞ ips. This is one-eighth the speed, so the dropout would last eight times longer (8 milliseconds for this example). The attenuation at 5 kHz would be *40 dB*. Therefore, dropouts on cassettes are far more audible than dropouts on reel-to-reel tapes.

These problems will be utterly unrelieved by tape-deck sophistication, noise reduction, filtering, etc. They are a function of the nonuniformity of the tape itself. The recommended procedure is to use digital recording when possible, analog reel-to-reel when necessary, and cassette machines when in dire need. In the last two cases, listen *extremely* carefully to the recorded tape for *intermittent fluctuation* in high-frequency response.

6.2.5.3. Dynamic range

Cassettes have a smaller dynamic range than reel-to-reel tapes, and both have a smaller range than a 14- or 16-bit digital recording.

With metal tape and noise reduction, cassettes have an acceptable signal-to-noise ratio for speech applications. However, the noise reduction is a nonlinear processing technique and so is not recommended for speech which will be analyzed for synthesis.

Reel-to-reel recordings can be made with sufficient dynamic range to

---

[3] As of this writing, the only exception is Lucasfilm Ltd. in San Rafael, California. The "force" must be with someone.

fit the signal into a 12-bit ADC (commonly used in speech analysis). These recordings must be carefully done to make full use of this dynamic range. The lower noise and distortion properties of tape recording at a speed of 15 ips make this higher speed preferable whenever possible, despite the doubling of tape usage. However, 7½ ips will give good enough results for 12-bit analysis work if the machine is correctly aligned.

6.2.5.4. Print-through

This term refers to the signal leakage from one layer of tape to the next. For recorded tape that is rewound and stored, this phenomenon results in a preecho on the tape. The magnitude of this preecho is dependent on the signal strength, tape thickness, and tape remanence. The effect is carried by unstable iron-oxide domains. Because of this instability, the problem can be reduced by winding and rewinding before play. It can be partially prevented by storing the tape in a played-out ("tails out") condition.

For speech analysis, print-through can have serious consequences.

Therefore, in addition to the above recommendations, one should always:

1. Use thick tape (1.5 mil for reel-to-reel, C45's for cassette).
2. Use tape specifically designed for low print-through.
3. Keep signal levels conservative. That is, don't go for the *maximum* possible level before audible distortion. These high-signal levels will increase print-through, which is more damaging than the random noise of the tape hiss.
4. Keep all tapes at room temperature or below and away from stray magnetic fields (speakers and headphones). These can give you other problems as well, but they will also increase print-through.

6.2.5.5. Alignment

Tape decks are electromechanical devices that must be in precise alignment to perform within specification. While professional recording studios generally keep their reel-to-reels in good shape, they frequently use their cassettes rather informally. These machines are often in a below-spec condition. Consumer tape recorders do not usually come from the factory properly adjusted. Without a professional alignment of such equipment, you may never really know what you are recording. In particular, the bias, equalization, and tape-head-position adjustments are usually only just good enough to ensure satisfactory record and playback. Tapes recorded on one consumer machine may play back poorly on another machine. With a proper alignment to standard test tapes, of course, tapes should be transferable between machines (Figure 6.7).

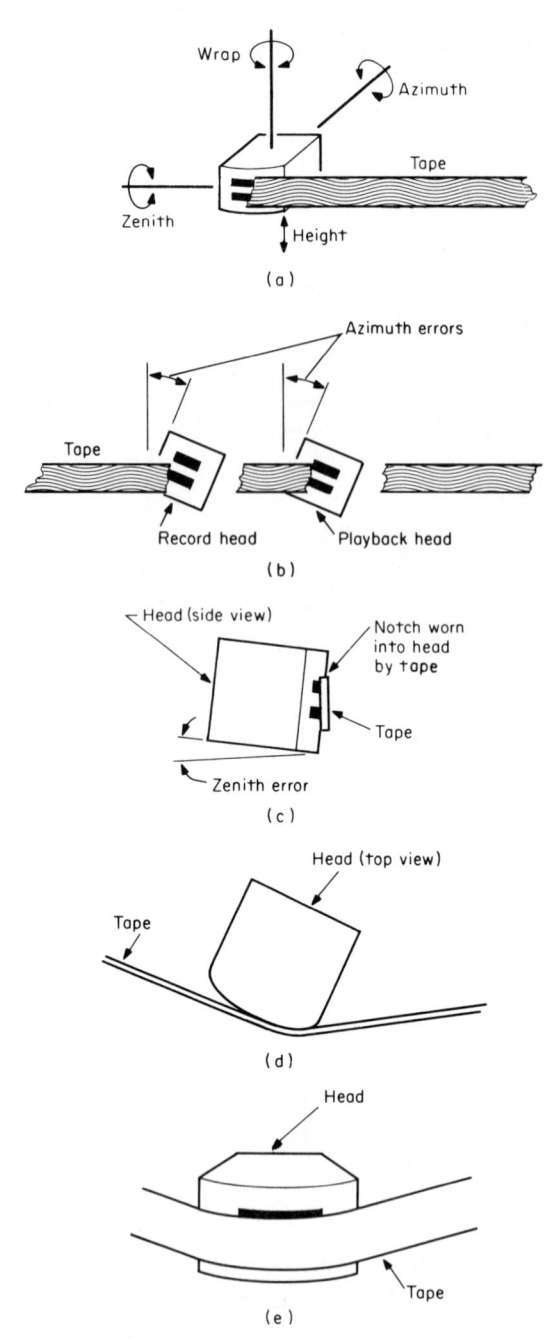

FIG. 6.7. Tape alignment parameters: (*a*) properly mounted head, (*b*) exaggerated azimuth errors, (*c*) exaggerated zenith error, (*d*) wrap error, (*e*) height error.

For example, look at record and playback heads with an exaggerated azimuth error. Since these errors are matched, the misalignment will cause no error in the record and playback frequency response. The same tape played back on a properly adjusted machine (or, worse yet, a machine with a playback head tilted in the opposite direction) will sound "dull" as a result of high-frequency loss. This effect can be quite severe for a small angular error. An azimuth error of ½ degree on a ½ track reel-to-reel at 7½ ips will cause a loss of 7 dB at 7.5 kHz.

Wisdom suggests that you use only professionally aligned machines for professional purposes. While you probably won't do this alignment yourself, you should be aware of the major types of adjustments.

1. *Head azimuth.* As described previously, this refers to the angular deviation from 90 degrees between the head (actually the head gap) and the tape direction. This must be quite precise, so visual inspection and adjustment are insufficient. The recorder's electrical output must be monitored for a calibrated test tape with an azimuth tone on it. The head is adjusted both for maximum signal output (for coarse alignment) and phase matching of the left and right channel (for fine alignment on a multichannel machine). The latter can be done with Lissajous figures on the XY display of an oscilloscope. The playback head is aligned using a test tape, and then the record head is aligned by recording on the kind of tape which will be used while monitoring the playback output.

2. *Head wrap, height, and zenith.* These head adjustments may all be done visually. By coating the head surface with a substance such as blueing compound (don't worry—it comes right off with acetone!) and then running some tape in play mode, you create a "wear pattern" on the head. This will show errors in wrap (the angle of orientation toward the tape), height (which aligns the gap properly with the standard track positions on the tape), and zenith (tilt toward or away from the tape). These can all be adjusted and checked with playback and record response checks. All of these adjustments are coarse compared to the azimuth alignment.

If the machine has been used for a while with improper head alignment, an improper wear pattern will have already been cut into the head. This will make adjustment undesirable. The tape will have essentially worn a groove into the head. The record and playback response will be considerably worse if the tape rides out of the groove or rides in it with uneven pressure. Don't use an older machine that is out of alignment with respect to wrap, zenith, or head height.

3. *Bias and equalization.* These are relatively simple adjustments, providing the manufacturer has made the appropriate trimmers

accessible. As before, adjustments are made to playback parts first, and then the effects of record adjustments are monitored on playback. Record alignment is done with the exact type of recording tape you will be using.

Most of these adjustments are made to optimize the frequency response of the machine. While general audio requires a wider bandwidth than does speech for analysis, the latter requires an extremely flat response within the bandwidth used. This is required because of the spectral matching that all low bit-rate methods use. Extraneous "bumps" in the record and playback frequency response degrade the resulting synthesis. The response should be *very flat* between 50 Hz and 8 kHz.

Many inexpensive recorders don't have easy access to trimmers and/or head positioning adjustments. Some of these even bolt the heads on, permitting no adjustment at all! *Lesson*: Don't use unprofessional equipment for a professional job!

6.2.5.6. *Common irrevocable analog tape errors*

There are five distinct "boo-boos" that can't be easily fixed:

1. *Head bumps.* These are irregularities in the low-frequency response near the frequency corresponding to the half-wavelength equal to the distance between the playback head's pole pieces (Figure 6.8).

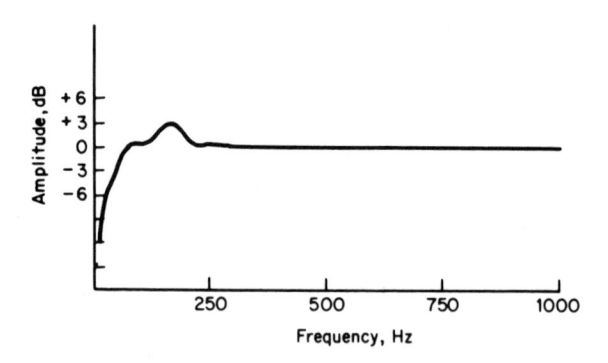

FIG. 6.8. Typical "head bump" for tape recorder.

These are typically variations of several dB below 200 Hz. They can be equalized separately but not without significant phase error. In any event, most recorders do not compensate for this effect.

2. *Phase error.* Unless the tape machine has phase correction, and almost none of them do, it will have a highly nonlinear phase characteristic (Figure 6.9).

Audio for Speech Analysis 133

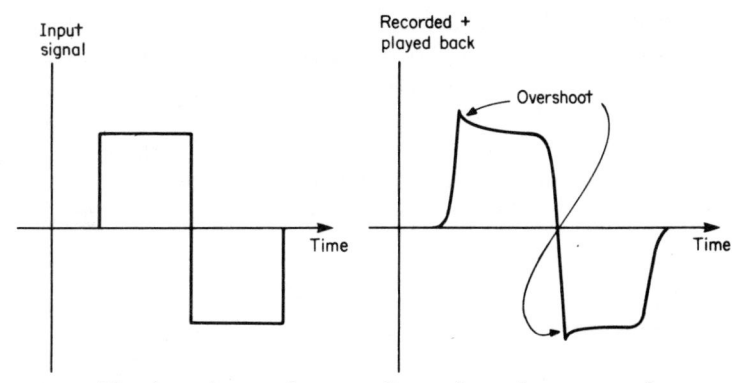

FIG. 6.9. Waveform changes due to nonlinear phase of a tape recorder.

This is important for any analysis technique which relies either on direct waveform measurement (time-domain pitch detector, such as Gold's) or which subjects the speech waveform to major nonlinearities (rectification for channel vocoders or speech recognition feature extractors). The results of such analysis can be degraded by the phase/time delay error of the tape recording process.

3. *Wow and flutter.* These are slow and fast tape-speed variations. In good recorders that are aligned, they are a minor problem. Yet time-base errors can be coarsely quantitized by speech analysis systems. All analog tape machines have this effect to some measurable degree (usually much worse for cassettes). Digital recorders need not, as the output rate is corrected by a crystal-controlled clock, independent of transport variations.

4. *Distortion.* Analog tape recording is fundamentally nonlinear.

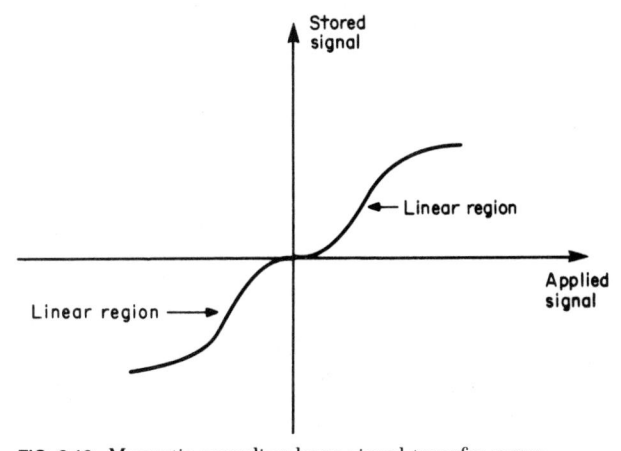

FIG. 6.10. Magnetic recording large-signal transfer curve.

Linearity is approximated by adding a high-frequency "bias" signal which puts the total amplitude in the roughly linear region of the recording transfer curve (Figure 6.10). Peak recording levels usually have several percent harmonic distortion. If this is too large an error for the analysis technique in use, the analog recording will simply be unusable unless high noise levels can be tolerated. Lower signal levels will reduce distortion (and simultaneously reduce print-through).

6.2.5.7. Conclusions

The following is an approximate order of preference for speech storage, based on the considerations of this section:

1. Digital storage on the computer that will do the analysis. This imposes no added degradation over that necessitated by A/D conversion and analysis.
2. Digital storage on an intermediate digital audio recorder. This imposes no degradation given sufficient error correction, but adds a modicum of inconvenience for transfer.
3. A professional analog reel-to-reel tape recorder in good alignment. There is some unavoidable degradation, but quality is sufficient for most analysis techniques.
4. A semiprofessional reel-to-reel recorder in good alignment. This type of machine usually performs very closely to a professional machine.
5. A cassette machine. If of high quality and professionally aligned, this type of machine may be suitable for some types of analysis. It will have worse dropouts, noise, distortion, wow and flutter, and head bumps than a reel-to-reel. Noise reduction will improve the dynamic range at the expense of degrading some types of speech analysis. Risky.
6. Reel-to-reel or cassette recorders either of an inexpensive variety or of unconfirmed alignment status. Forget it!!!

6.2.6. Filtering

Whether analog storage is used or not, the speech signal must eventually be sent to the computer. Before it can be converted to digital form, it must be prefiltered to remove frequency components above the half sampling frequency. This is the *Nyquist* criterion referred to in Chapter 2. In the real world, unfortunately, we do not have ideal filters.[4] So speech analysis considerations must affect the choice of the best filter characteristic.

---

[4] An ideal low-pass filter has unity gain below the half sampling frequency and zero gain above it. Unfortunately, this frequency response can only be instituted by a filter which responds to inputs infinitely far into both the past and the future. This is hard to design, even for clever fellows.

Available filters will usually be from 4th to 8th order. Such filters would ordinarily (for digital storage only) be operated at 80 to 90 percent of the half sampling frequency to permit sufficient attenuation at that frequency. However, such a choice for speech would move a significant spectral characteristic into the region being modeled. For such techniques as LPC, filtering at or near the half sampling frequency is preferred, even though this permits some aliasing distortion. With the Mozer technique, the input sampling rate (25.6 kHz) is so high that filtering can be significantly lower than the half sampling rate without impeding the spectral modeling.

Analog filters can be either all-pole or pole-and-zero (resonance only or resonance and antiresonance). The latter can achieve a greater loss at a particular frequency, but usually at the expense of a worse transient response. In filtering for speech, we are more concerned with attenuation of all frequencies *above* the half sampling frequency. Therefore, pole-only filters are typically sufficient.

The major types of pole-only filters are:

1. *Bessel.* This has the best time-domain response (low overshoot) but the least attenuation for a given filter order (Figure 6.11). A good idea when phase/time response is paramount.

2. *Butterworth.* This has a somewhat worse time response but good attenuation (6 dB per octave per pole) and *maximally smooth* frequency response in the passband (Figure 6.12). A good overall choice.

3. *Chebyshev.* The worst time response of the three. It has ripple in the passband magnitude response, but the best attenuation of the three. This attenuation may be traded off against variations in the size of the ripple (Figure 6.13).

Each of these three filter types corresponds to a choice of component

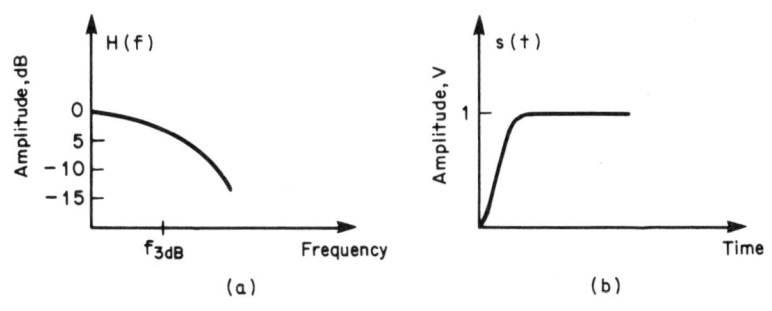

FIG. 6.11. Bessel filter response: (*a*) frequency response, (*b*) step response (response to a waveform which is 0 for time <0 and 1 for time >0).

136   *Talking Chips*

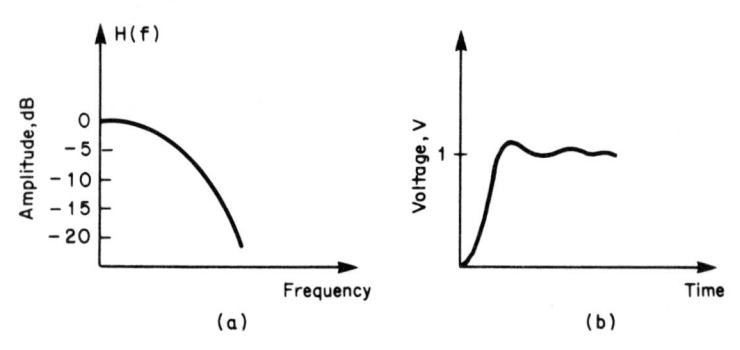

FIG. 6.12. Butterworth filter response: (*a*) frequency response, (*b*) step response.

values for a given order of filter of a particular architecture. Two such implementations for a 4th-order filter are shown in Figure 6.14.

With the proper choices for component values, either of these structures will implement the various filter types.

This discussion has been confined to low-pass filtering for antialiasing the input to a sampled data system. Some of the recording nonidealities may suggest further filtering. For instance, high-pass filtering may be required because of acoustic rumbling sounds from the environment. Care should be taken with such steps, as any spectral modification more extreme than that performed in the analysis software can cause spectral modeling problems.

6.2.7. A/D conversion

The last step in the process of getting natural speech on the computer is the A/D conversion. Many degradations can be introduced by this step.

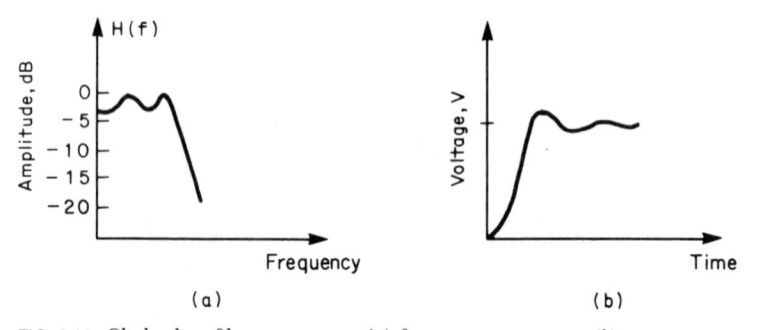

FIG. 6.13. Chebyshev filter response: (*a*) frequency response, (*b*) step response.

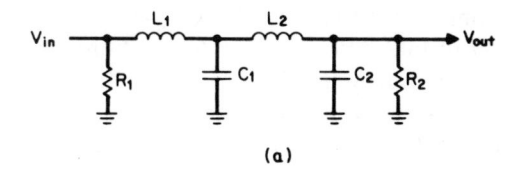

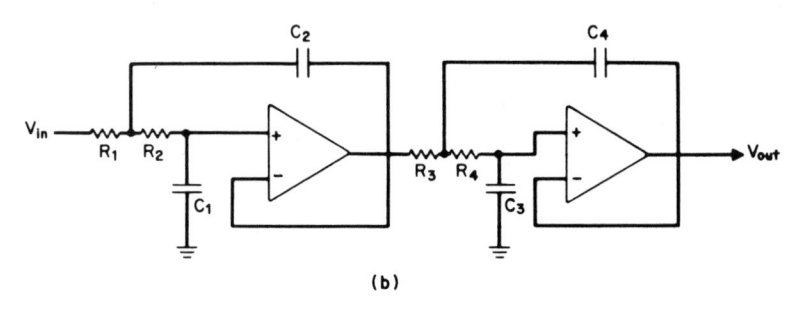

FIG. 6.14. Some filter topologies: (a) passive filter, (b) active filter.

The major requirements for A/D conversion are:

1. *Sufficient dynamic range.* For the wide range of speech analysis types, the safest approach is to use a linear conversion of a sufficient number of bits. The minimal requirement is 12 bits. Conversion systems of up to 16 bits can be fruitfully employed for wide-range speech recording.
2. *Sufficient conversion speed.* Minimally, the converter must produce the correct code within a sampling interval (100 microseconds for 10-kHz speech processing). However, the analog elements must be of sufficiently high slewing capability to avoid generating distortion components for large, rapidly varying signals.
3. *Aperture jitter for sampling.* This is the uncertainty in the sampling timing (Figure 6.15).

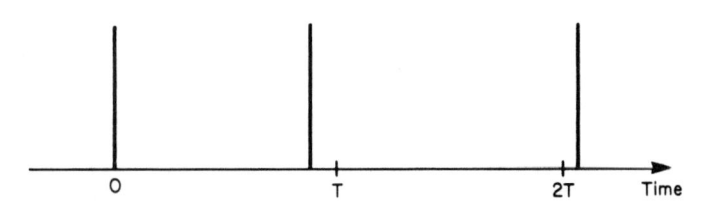

FIG. 6.15. Sampling jitter.

Ideally, it should be held down to $T/2^N$, where T is the sampling period and N is the number of bits. Note that for $N = 12$ bits and $T = 100$ microseconds, this uncertainty is 25 ns, a rather stiff requirement, which many commercial A/D systems do not meet. This requirement can be relaxed somewhat if the aberration is random and not correlated to some signal.

4. *Smooth nonlinearity.* The overall transfer curve can be somewhat "bowed," so long as the distortion products are not sufficiently large to disturb the analysis (Figure 6.16).

   This requirement is really no tougher than that for the other analog components. Harmonic distortion of a few tenths of a percent or less will not degrade the speech over the microphone and preamp distortion.

5. *Differential linearity.* The local behavior of the transfer curve is most significant (Figure 6.17).

   Increases in analog voltage should always produce codes that are at least as high. This should result in a total lack of missing codes between the extremes that the converter provides. This need not be the ideal full range, since that amounts to just an overall gain or volume error.

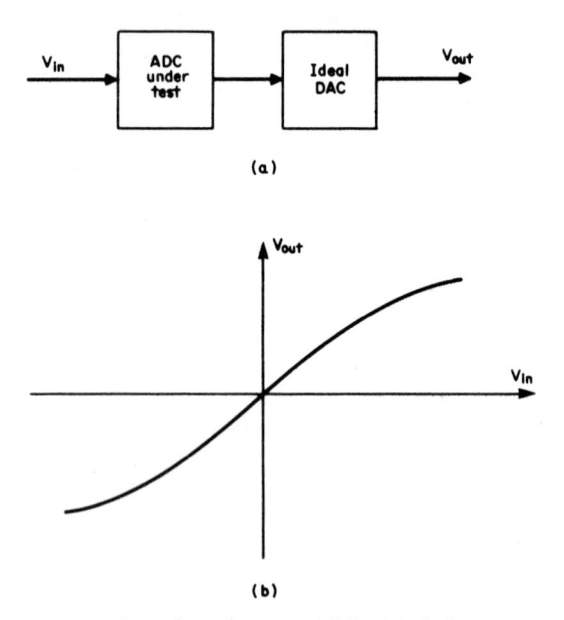

FIG. 6.16. Smooth nonlinearity, ADC: (*a*) ideal test connection, (*b*) "bowed" transfer curve.

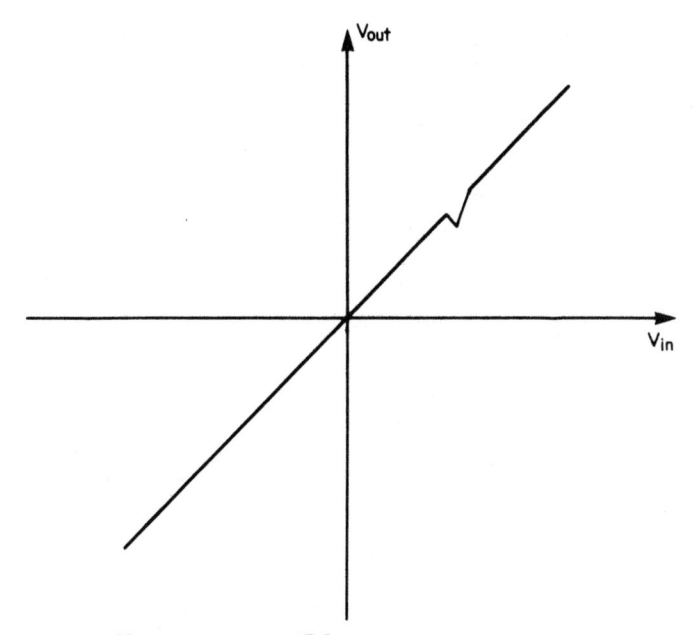

FIG. 6.17. Nonmonotonicity, ADC.

This is a small sampling of A/D requirements for speech analysis. They are somewhat more esoteric than the audio equipment requirements but are more frequently attended to.

6.3. EVALUATION OF SYNTHETIC SPEECH

6.3.1. Introduction

Once you have recorded natural speech and processed it to create synthetic speech, you will undoubtedly wish to evaluate the results. Here, as in the original recordings, there are a number of acoustically oriented considerations which must be followed to ensure the validity of your findings.

6.3.2. Playback equipment

We have seen that the relatively low quality of synthetic speech (with respect to natural speech) does not excuse a sloppy job of speech recording. Similarly, care must be taken in playing back synthetic speech for evaluation. Playback nonidealities can indeed be sufficient to mask or falsely imply speech synthesis problems.

A wide variety of playback systems may be used with little problem. One should never, however, use a low-quality speaker-amplifier just because the final application will also use a low-quality speaker-amplifier, *unless* the speaker under test is *exactly* the same type that will be used. Low-quality audio equipment does not adhere to any particular standard (i.e., it does not always have the same types of degradation). For example, one cheap speaker might have a 10-dB peak at 3 kHz, while another might have a notch at that frequency (Figure 6.18).

On the other hand, good speakers adhere to a reasonable approximation of flat and linear playback. Therefore, they are the next best thing to having the actual end product available.

Any good high-fidelity speaker should work well for speech. If listening in a small-dimensioned room, you should use a small-dimensioned speaker and listen at a close distance. Two good speakers in this category are the KEF 101s and the Rogers BBC monitors.

For careful attention to detail, no speaker will work as well as headphones. Headphones produce a sound signal at your ear with little modification from the environment. Head positioning with respect to the room boundaries is not important. If you are listening for pops, clicks, glitches, pitch errors, etc., this is the method of choice. Headphones do, however, provide an unrealistically direct play of the speech, and some potential clarity problems may not show up.

Listening for assessment of intelligibility and quality should be done via a speaker. That way the sound diffraction about the head will occur as

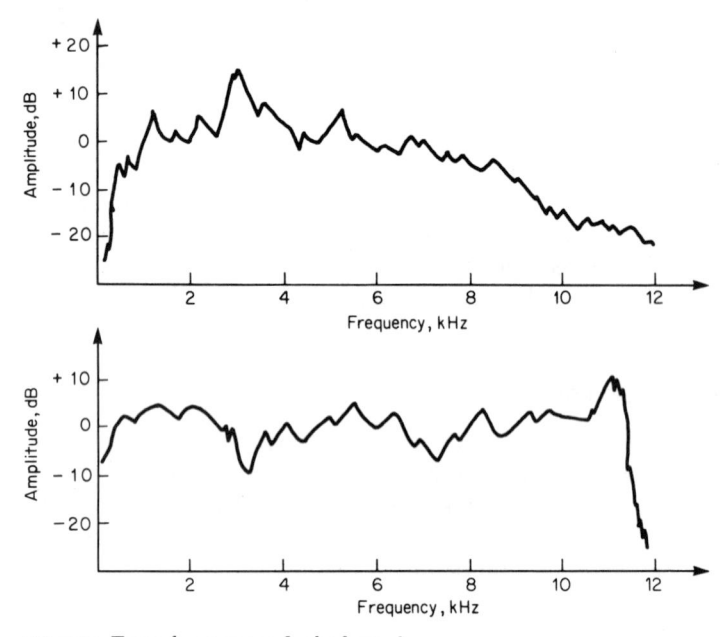

FIG. 6.18. Typical responses for bad speakers.

it does for natural speech communication. Ideally, both speaker and headphone playback should be available.

I will not go into further detail here about other aspects of the playback equipment (D/A, preamps, mixers, tape decks, amplifiers). These considerations do not differ appreciably from those for the recording equipment. Just be sure to use properly matched components (e.g., provide enough power to drive the speaker that has been chosen).

6.3.3. Playback environment

For headphone playback, the environment is obviously secondary (as long as the ambient noise level is low). For speaker playback, the requirements are similar to those for recording rooms. Sound isolation must be almost as good as in a recording room, since there should be no audible sounds except for the speech under evaluation. While normal listening conditions include sounds other than speech, your particular background noise may not model this well. It is better to have the room quiet and add in noise of the desired type (random noise or recorded versions of a particular background, such as office noise).

Although recording rooms should be sufficiently isolated to keep the entire dynamic range intact, listening rooms need only keep out *audible* interference. For instance, a 16-Hz rumble could cause significant error in some speech analysis. This same noise is inaudible to a human and so would not hurt the quality of a listening room. Similarly, a 60-Hz hum could contain enough energy to hurt speech analysis and thus be bad for a recording room but quiet enough for a listening room. Here's a rule of thumb:

> A listening room is good enough for speech playback on speakers if the A-weighted average sound pressure level of the ambient noise is at least 40 dB below that of the average SPL of the speech at 2 feet (a typical listening distance).

Sound absorption requirements can also be relaxed somewhat from that of the calibrated recording room. The main requirement is that the room not add enough resonances or reverberation to slur or obscure speech features. Do not use small closetlike rectangular booths if at all possible. The walls, ceilings, and floors should be generally absorptive and irregular, although this aspect is not as critical for the speech recording application.

6.3.4. The listener

What should we listen for? Once we are assured of a high-quality playback capability, we still must choose what to play and what to listen for. If the playback is synthesis from analyzed speech, phoneme durations and pitch contours should be quite natural. The major practical errors are those which detract from *intelligibility*, or identification, of phonetic elements. There are standardized tests, such as the DRT (*Diagnostic Rhyme Test*), for this purpose, as well as collections of test sentences such as the Haskins Anomalous Sentences, a collection of nonsense sentences. A purely syllabic consonant-confusion test is currently under development by the author and D. Isenberg.

Most speech synthesis users will be judging synthesis and analysis techniques on the basis of specific phrases, usually those which will be used in some application. Clearly, these phrases should serve better for evaluation than any "representative" set of sounds.

How can the listener decide on the "goodness" of his material without a standardized test? This is a difficult question. A good listener can make reasonable decisions if he knows what to listen for. Some suggestions:

1. For low bit-rate speech, listen phonetically. This is, make sure that each individual phoneme is audible. If it is not, make sure that it *was* present in the original natural speech. In particular, check for the bursts (p, t, k, b, d, g) and make sure they are clear in the synthesis. Then listen for abrupt changes in volume, pitch, or phonetic character. *Hint*: Use *sounds* (such as *bah, gah, dah, ahb, ahg,* or any other vowel-consonant or consonant-vowel combinations) rather than

words, so as not to confuse linguistic expectations with what you are actually hearing. Also be sure that the one who is listening does not know beforehand which sound will be played. These simple precautions can prevent a lot of meaningless results for even informal experiments.
2. For medium- and high-rate synthesis, first listen in the above manner to the speech and observe any major problems. Then listen in comparison to the original speech. Over a limited bandwidth at least, they should sound roughly the same. Note the types of sounds for which they do not.

These approaches are no substitute for the controlled testing of a system, but they should get you started.

CHAPTER

7

WHAT'S NEXT?

7.1. INTRODUCTION

Up to now, this book has functioned as an introduction to the status of IC speech synthesis as it is today. Given the remarkable trends of modern technology, I would be remiss if I didn't give some indication of what to expect in the years ahead. Polishing up the old crystal ball, I see . . .

7.2. MAKE YOUR OWN SPEECH

Almost all final parameter sets for production vocabularies are now created at specialized labs. Those labs are primarily run by the IC manufacturers. For the small- and medium-volume customers, the cost per word and the backlog in time are unacceptably long.

What is needed is low-cost word production stations. True, some outside companies have recognized this need and are beginning to perform a similar service. Yet until the true single-user production station is achieved, synthetic speech is stuck, orders of magnitude shy of where it could be. As of this writing, some such systems have been devised. They are a promising start, still lacking in sufficient flexibility for the simple manual parameter modification required to clean up analysis errors. Soon, however, better systems will be available (Figure 7.1).

What are the requirements for such a system?

1. The computational hardware must be sufficiently powerful to perform the speech analysis quickly. Probably 1 to 10 times real time is acceptable for interactive work. Times up to an order of magnitude longer might be tolerated as a trade-off for higher quality results on a batch basis.
2. There must be a high-quality analog I/O subsystem. As indicated in the previous chapter, this means there must be:
    a. At least a 12-bit ADC and DAC
    b. Low-pass filters
    c. A high-quality (low-noise) microphone preamp with a balanced input and phantom powering of an external condenser microphone
    d. Switchable gain and overload indication via peak-reading circuits and LEDs (*light-emitting diodes*)
    e. Low distortion analog signal-handling circuitry capable of feeding a high-quality power amplifier and speaker
    f. A low distortion headphone amplifier

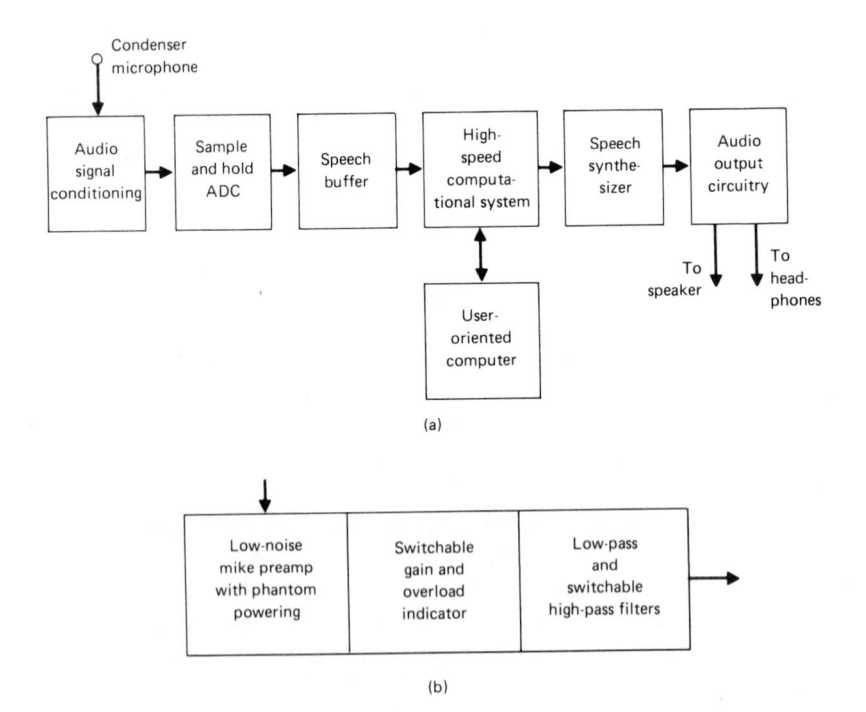

FIG. 7.1. Development system hardware: (*a*) overall system, (*b*) signal-conditioning block.

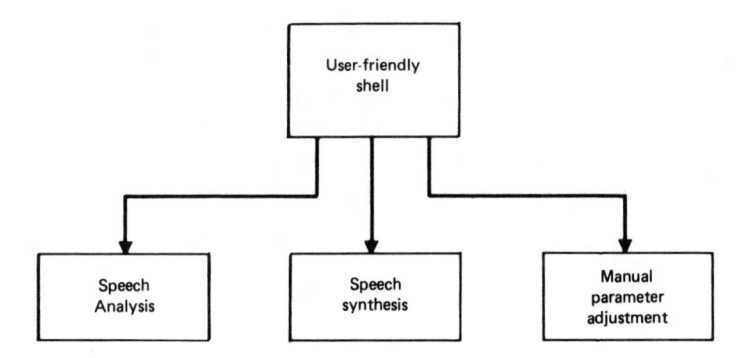

FIG. 7.2. Development system software.

  g. Direct memory access under hardware control to minimize sampling jitter and D/A error (such as would be expected from interrupt-driven sampling)
  h. Sufficient speech buffering to store 5–10 s of digitized speech
3. A convenient user interface. This is primarily a software issue, although the hardware should be based on a general-purpose computer, so that a flexible and mutable user shell could be constructed (Figure 7.2).

A likely candidate for an operating system is UNIX®,[1] although the traditional forms of this system are not intended for real-time tasks such as speech acquisition. With additional buffering hardware, however, such a system could be quite workable.

4. Easy manual adjustment of speech parameters. Numbers must be represented graphically in such a way that errors are usually obvious. Fixes should be done using a convenient input device—such as a light pen, graphics tablet, or "mouse."
5. Quiet operation. The device itself, or at least that portion which remains in the room with the microphone and/or speaker, must be physically quiet.
6. The system should be affordable for medium-volume users. It should be at least as low in cost as a typical microprocessor development system.

This is certainly a large bundle of requirements. Still, many companies have prototypes which are at least part way there. Quality systems should be readily available for the more popular speech ICs by 1984.

[1] UNIX is a trademark of Bell Laboratories.

7.3. RESIDUAL-DRIVEN SYNTHETIC SPEECH

The main emphasis in the first generation of talking chips has been on achieving a low (1–2 kbits/s) bit rate for intelligible speech with low-cost hardware. By providing a huge storage reduction over PCM, this has made semiconductor speech commercially viable. As memory densities take leaps and bounds and chip prices plummet, this low bit-rate requirement can be relaxed in favor of improved speech quality. While consumers may initially accept degraded speech, they can be expected to demand broadcast quality once the novelty wears off. Medium bit-rate speech (4800–16,000 bits/s) should be of increasing interest in the mid- to-late 1980s.

A particularly interesting class of speech algorithms are *residual driven* (Figure 7.3). This nomenclature refers to a time-varying filter driven by a time-varying waveform which is derived from the error in the frequency-domain analysis.

Ideally, an LPC synthesizer driven with the unquantized LPC error signal yields the original speech at the output. Close approximations to this error signal yield correspondingly close approximations to the natural speech at the output of the synthesizer. The coarsest such approximation is given by the use of a single pulse for the filter excitation for each period, which is the standard LPC approach for voiced speech. The quality of synthetic speech can be smoothly varied between these two extremes by changing the excitation accordingly.

In the future, algorithms such as these may become the mainstay of commercial speech production. They have yet to survive trial by fire, however.

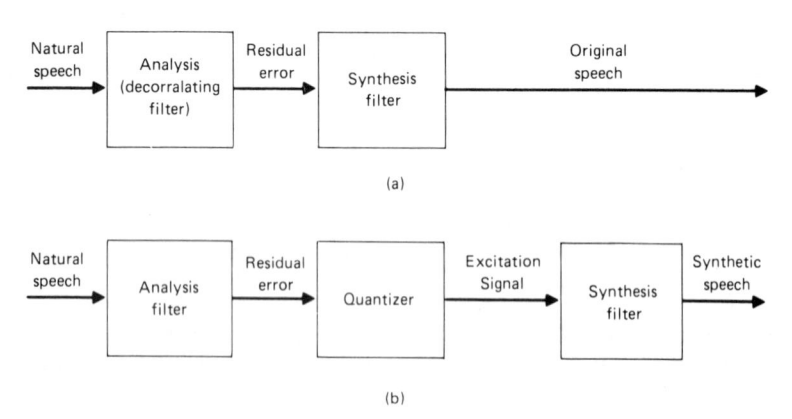

FIG. 7.3. Residual-driven synthetic speech: (*a*) ideal, (*b*) actual.

7.4. MUSIC AND EFFECTS

Current speech chips have an extremely limited capability to produce nonspeech sounds, although special-purpose chips for limited types of sound-effects generation do exist. In the future, as their complexity grows, speech chips can be expected to gain the capability to make a wide variety of sounds. A speech synthesizer may be considered a special-purpose processor for the computation of waveforms. Electronic music production has a similar form.

The two principal approaches to electronic music synthesis are referred to as *additive* and *subtractive*. Additive synthesis produces each note by adding sinusoids (pure tones) at the harmonic frequencies. The proportions of each tone in the mixture determine the overall timbre of the result, much like the stops on an organ. This approach is useful for many steady-state sounds and can be implemented using a small number of parameters. It is a low bit-rate method of music synthesis.

To perform additive synthesis (Figure 7.4), one must:

1. Generate sinusoids.
2. Multiply them by gains.
3. Add them together.

The last two operations are necessary in any digital filtering type of speech synthesizer.

Sinusoidal generation may be done either by trig table lookups, or by calculation. While the latter may seem prohibitively expensive in computational power, sequential values of a sine or cosine function may be easily calculated using *rotational* algorithms. These follow from the observation that

$$\cos(x + dx) = \cos x \cos dx - \sin x \sin dx$$
$$\sin(x + dx) = \sin x \cos dx + \cos x \sin dx$$

Since the increment (dx) is known from the frequency of the sinusoid and the sampling rate, each new point may be computed with four multiplies and two adds. Approximate versions of this algorithm exist, which use half the number of multiplies. Thus, additive musical synthesis can conveniently be done using a digital filtering structure.

Subtractive synthesis refers to the filtering of a harmonic-rich waveform. This is what is done in frequency-domain speech synthesis. Music can be generated in this manner assuming that sufficiently "interesting" waveforms can be used to drive the filters. If future speech ICs can be driven by a residual waveform, they should be capable of being driven by musically rich waveforms. Subtractive musical synthesis will certainly be possible (Figure 7.5).

Subtractive synthesis can be used on time-varying waveshapes for simulation of attacks and decays on instrumental voices. In the case of residual-driven approaches, extremely complex musical forms can be implemented.

Nonmusical sound effects may also be synthesized either by residual or Mozer-type techniques.

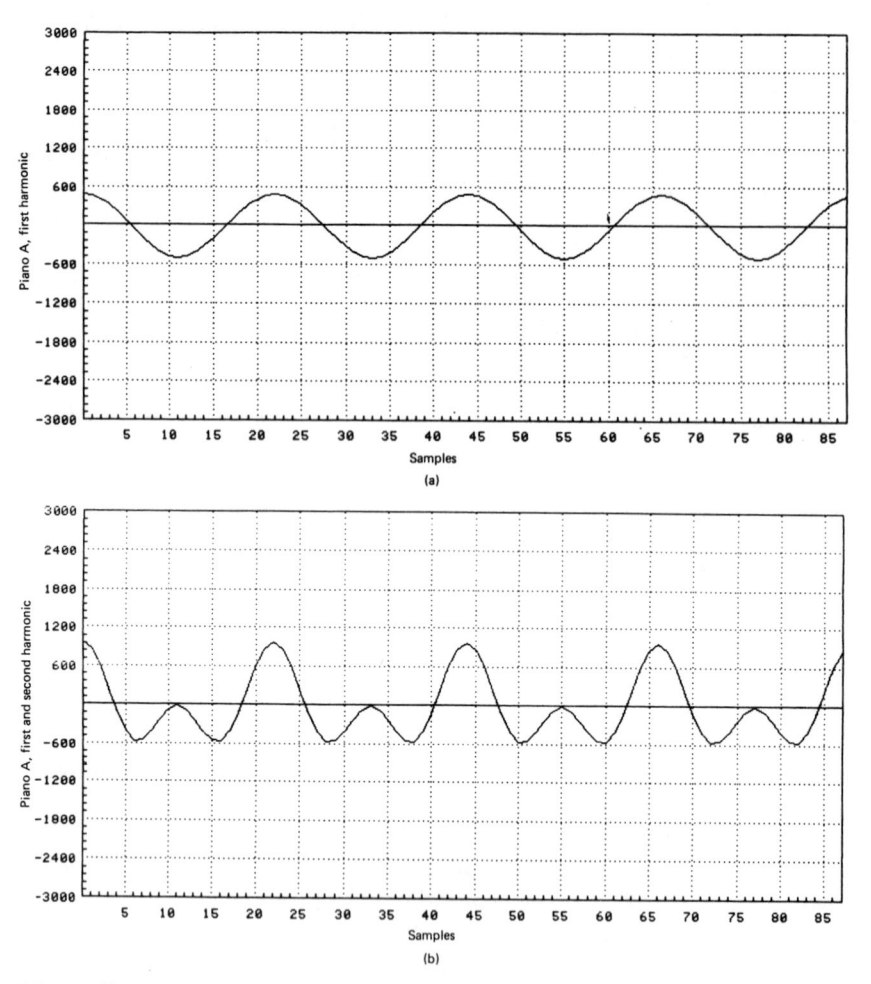

FIG. 7.4. Frequency components of the piano note A (440 cps): (*a*) fundamental (first harmonic), (*b*) fundamental and second harmonic (0° phase), (*c*) fundamental and harmonics 2 to 10 (0° phase), (*d*) fundamental and harmonics 2 to 10 (correct phase), (*e*) the actual piano note.

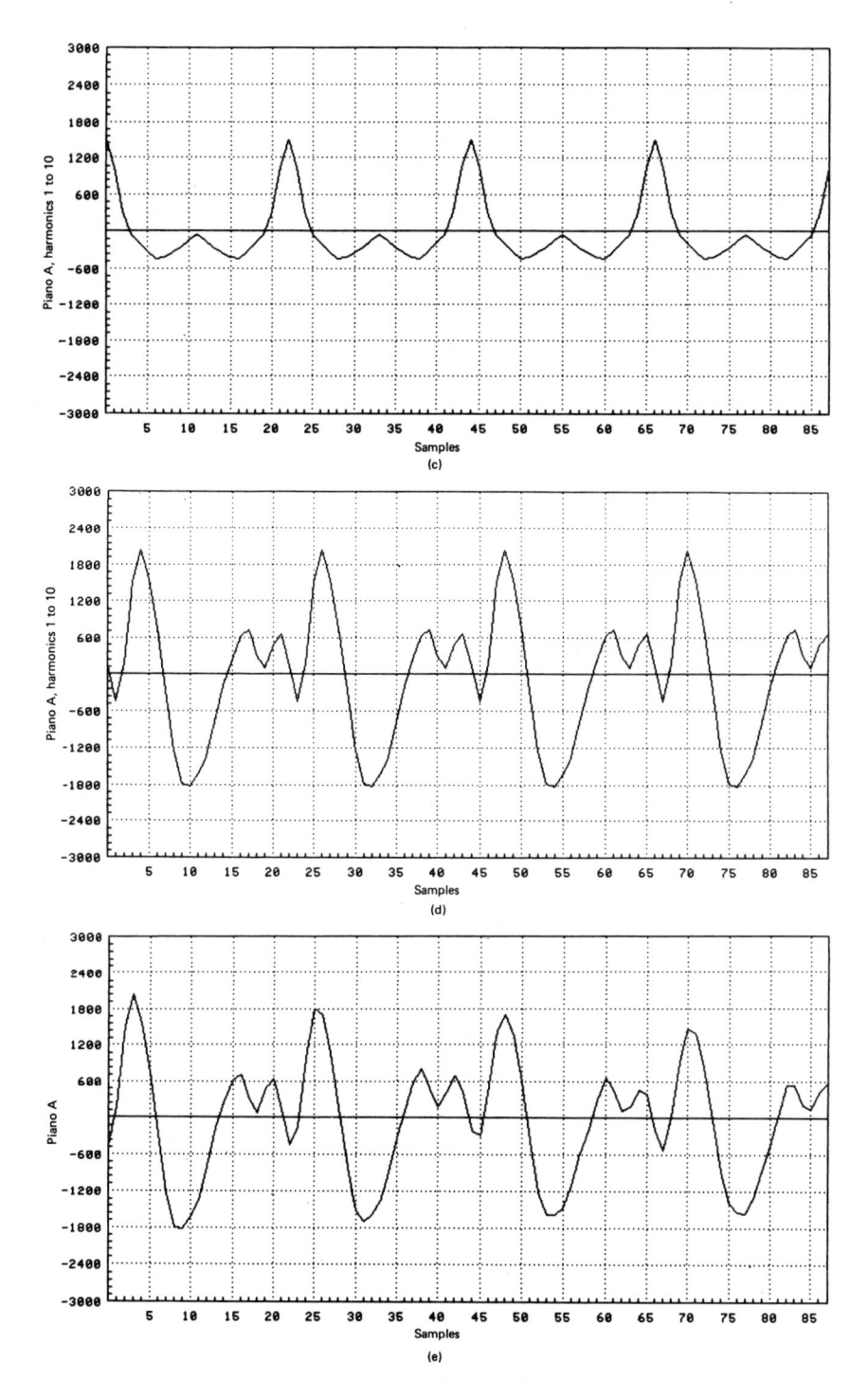

FIG. 7.4. Continued

152   *Talking Chips*

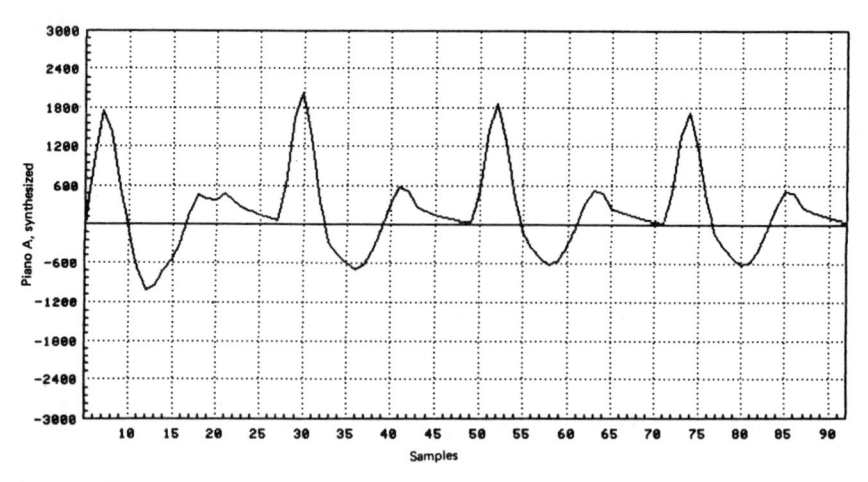

FIG. 7.5. The piano note A (440 Hz) synthesized "subtractively."

7.5. SPEECH RECOGNITION

Recognition is a major topic, worthy of a book in its own right. While this is a book on speech synthesis, I would be remiss in not discussing at least the major considerations of recognition. Synthesis and recognition are closely tied as research topics and applications. With the cars and computers of the late 1980s expected to both speak *and* listen to the driver, speech synthesis is clearly only half of the anticipated communication between man and machine.

In speech analysis for synthesis, parameters are derived from natural speech. These parameters are chosen to be ones which have some correspondence to the more perceptually significant aspects of speech, such as the short-term magnitude spectrum. In speech synthesis, these parameters are used to control a synthesizer which produces speech (Figure 7.6).

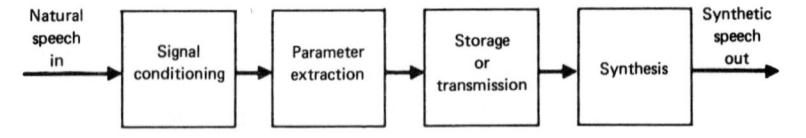

FIG. 7.6. Analysis/synthesis of speech.

In speech recognition, these parameters are compared with other sets of parameters representing words to be identified (Figure 7.7).

Acoustic recognition is based on perceptually significant differences between words. As one would expect, classes of parameters that are good

What's Next? 153

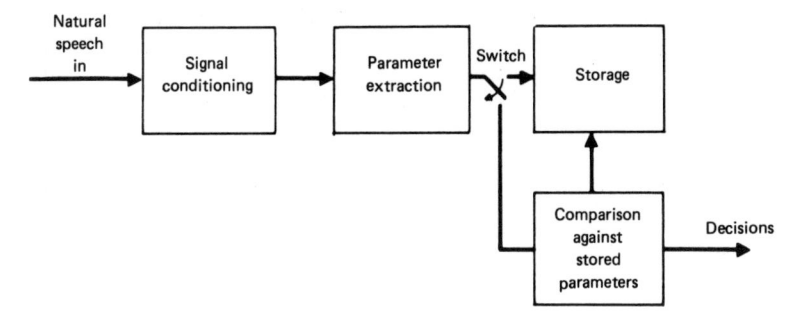

FIG. 7.7. Acoustic recognition of speech. (The switch is UP for training, DOWN for recognition.)

for synthesis are also good for recognition. Typical of such parameters are reflection coefficients, rectified and smoothed bandpass filter outputs, formants, and Fourier transform magnitudes. On the other hand, some features that are critical for proper production of speech, such as pitch, must sometimes be ignored for the identification of words.[2]

Speech recognition carries its own host of problems. We take our own understanding of speech for granted and do not typically notice the complex nature of the process. For instance, we can listen to someone mumbling without missing any of the words. Our brain supplies information missing from the acoustic input on the basis of *syntax* and *semantics*. A general speech recognizer must similarly have an *understanding* of both the grammatical rules of a language and the meanings of the words (Figure 7.8).

In fact, since the meaning of a word varies greatly depending on current social context, the machine would have to have a broad understanding of the world around us.

This complexity is not necessary for the recognition of words by comparison to trained versions, if the acoustic matching is good enough. Unfortunately, because of human speech variability and unpredictable environmental noise, good acoustic matching is a very tough requirement.

Another important speech recognition difficulty is *time registration*. If someone says *hello* as a reference and then says *heelllo* (stretching out the *el* sound, but saying the rest the same), a comparison of corresponding time periods would yield a bad match. The *o* sound would not match the reference *el* in the same time moment.

Researchers have devised an algorithm, called a *dynamic time warp*, to

---

[2] If you say *hello* at two different pitches, it should still be recognized as the same word. On the other hand, pitch perturbations can be used as a cue for consonant voicing.

154   Talking Chips

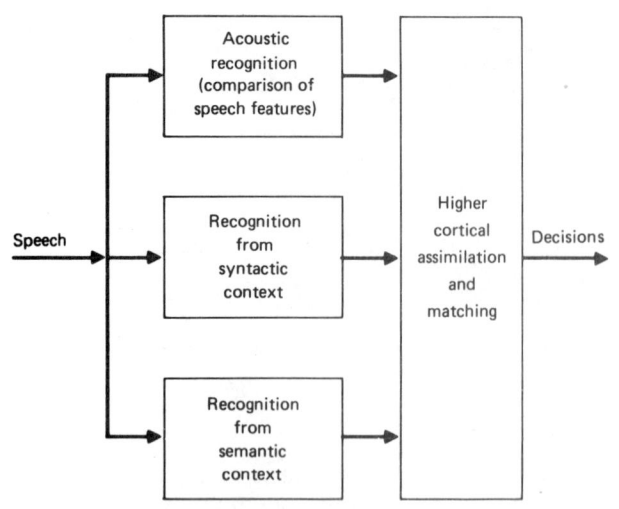

FIG. 7.8. A simple model of speech understanding.

counter the problem. This algorithm warps the time axis of the new sound to give the best match to each reference (Figure 7.9).

Working speech-recognition systems do currently exist. Unfortunately, only the most expensive ones do an acceptable job on connected speech. Still, even discrete word recognition can be a powerful tool for human input to a machine.

Even in a limited system, speech recognition must *work* a very high percentage of the time (such as 98 or 99 percent) to be acceptable to the public. Unfortunately, inexpensive recognizers only work this well in the laboratory. This is why low-cost products incorporating speech recognition have been slow in coming. Currently, the more expensive systems do achieve workable error rates in real-world environments. IC's are certainly becoming dense enough to emulate these systems someday. We can expect that highly accurate, medium-vocabulary, discrete-word-trained speech recognizers will soon be appearing in inexpensive products.

Aside from specific "listening" products (such as televisions, cars, games, door bells, etc.), recognition is primarily interesting as the complement of computer speech in the man-machine interface. With

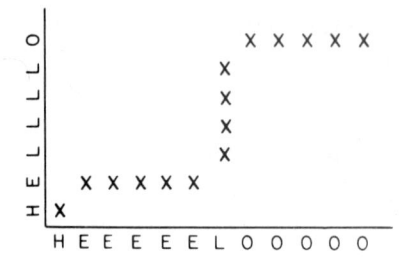

FIG. 7.9. Symbolic representation of time warp.

accurate speech recognition as well as high-quality speech synthesis, we can start using the growing computational power around us in a more natural way. Soon the *Star Trek* style of interaction between us and our computers will be commonplace.

7.6. FINALE

I've shown the rudiments of the new technology of talking (and listening) machines that will soon be all around us. A natural follow-up question might be, When will they have something intelligent to say?

We can view the current group of synthesis/recognition filtering ICs as *integrated signal processing systems*. Indeed, as of this writing, the trend has not yet peaked. Orders of magnitude of improvement can still be expected. Yet fundamental improvements in the symbolic representation of problems, and of knowledge itself, are still necessary. Symbolic knowledge techniques are necessary if the performance of speech systems is to be improved past levels possible with acoustic models alone. We don't hear with our ears exclusively—but also with the "hardware" and "software" of the brain.

This suggests that the next major field for VLSI application may be that of artificial intelligence. The machines with which we converse may someday develop a sophisticated "world view." This expanded perception will greatly assist in their interpretation and understanding of what we say. They may even develop intelligent and original things to talk about (such as how to build an even smarter computer).

APPENDIX A

THE SHORT-TERM SPECTRUM

A.1. INTRODUCTION

The short-term spectrum is generally considered to be the most perceptually significant feature of speech. The purpose of this appendix is to give a minimal mathematical framework for these concepts. Those wishing to read further may want to consult a text on digital processing, such as the excellent one by Rabiner and Schafer (see More Advanced Reading).

A.2. FOURIER ANALYSIS

The "spectrum" of a given signal is the content of that signal at different frequencies. Specifically, this means the amount of pure tones (mathematically described as sine or cosine functions of time) which must be added together to get the analyzed signal. This description is also called Fourier analysis, after the 18th-century French mathematician who discovered this principle. Fourier analysis yields the magnitude and phase of each sinusoidal component and is accomplished by the evaluation of an integral:

$$X(f) = \int_{-\infty}^{\infty} x(t) e^{-j2\pi f t} dt$$

$$= \int_{-\infty}^{\infty} x(t)(\cos 2\pi f t - j \sin 2\pi f t) \, dt$$

$$= \int_{\infty}^{\infty} x(t) \cos 2\pi ft \, dt$$

$$- j \int_{\infty}^{\infty} x(t) \sin 2\pi ft \, dt \qquad \text{(Eq. 1)}$$

This operation is essentially an averaging of the product of the analyzed signal and a sine and cosine of each examined frequency. The property of orthogonality of these trigonometric functions is used here. That is, the integrated value of such a product is zero for all sinusoidal components in the signal except for that portion which is at the multiplier frequency.

For:

$$\cos A \times \cos B = \tfrac{1}{2} [\cos(A + B) + \cos(A - B)]$$

the average value is obviously zero unless $A = B$.

Therefore, all frequency content in the signal except that at the analysis frequency f is averaged out to zero, yielding a value for the signal component at that frequency.

A.3. WINDOWING

Since the limits to the original integral are infinite, the above kind of calculation would require access to the signal over all time. Such a spectrum would smear together all finite-time events. Clearly, such time-varying events are the things that convey information in speech.

Therefore, some measure of the "frequency content" must be given for a small segment of time. "Small" means a length of time over which the spectrum of the signal doesn't change perceptibly. This is roughly 10–30 ms for most speech sounds, because of the inherent sluggishness of our auditory apparatus, and happens to coincide with a similar latency in our mechanisms for production of speech.

What error is introduced by amending the spectral integral to have finite time limits? This error is comparable to that experienced in particle physics when the possible position of a particle is restricted. The uncertainty principle limits the accuracy to which the particle's momentum may be known. In signal processing, the restriction of a signal to a particular time period similarly limits the accuracy with which its spectrum may be known.

The spectral data are smeared by the spectral spread of the observation window. The more we pinpoint the time accuracy of events, the less accurately we can describe the frequency content of these events. As an extreme example, we clearly have no information above the spectrum of a single time point. Thus, the limitations of short-term spectral analysis may either be described as an aspect of the uncertainty principle, or as, "There's no such thing as a free lunch."

In summary, short "windows" (intervals of speech to be analyzed) give good time resolution of the changing features of speech but yield poorly defined frequency information. Longer windows smear events together but yield finely defined frequency information.

"Windowing" of speech may be considered the premultiplication (prior to the analysis) of the infinite-length signal by a function that is nonzero only over a (usually) finite interval. The mathematics of Fourier analysis tells us that the nature of this function determines the inaccuracy (or smearing) of the frequency-domain results. In general (an exception being the windowing of one period of a periodic function) use of a "rectangular" window function, namely

$$w(t) = 1 \quad \text{for speech segment of interest}$$
$$w(t) = 0 \quad \text{elsewhere}$$

causes undesirable "ripples" or erroneous bumps in the observed spectrum.

Smoother functions, such as raised cosines (the Hamming and hanning windows), are generally preferable. These sacrifice some time information at the edge of the window to eliminate the spectral lobe effect caused by using the untreated data segment.

The tricky point is to recognize that the use of a finite sequence of data points, even without explicit multiplication by a window function, is in fact the result of an implicit multiplication by the rectangular window, resulting in the spectral effects described above.

The spectrum of a segment of a signal may be described as

$$X_s(f) = \int_{-\infty}^{\infty} w(t)\, x(t)\, e^{-j 2\pi f t}\, dt$$

$$= \int_{-\infty}^{\infty} w(t)\, x(t)(\cos 2\pi f t - j \sin 2\pi f t)\, dt$$

$$= \int_{-\infty}^{\infty} w(t)\, x(t) \cos 2\pi f t\, dt$$

$$- j \int_{-\infty}^{\infty} w(t)\, w(t) \sin 2\pi f t\, dt \qquad \text{(Eq. 2)}$$

where $X_s(f)$ = spectrum at frequency f
$x(t)$ = time function
$w(t)$ = window

Since $w(t)$ is usually chosen to be zero outside of some interval from t_1 to t_2, we may also express this as

$$X_s(f) = \int_{t_1}^{t_2} w(t)\, x(t) \cos 2\pi f t\, dt$$

$$- j \int_{t_1}^{t_2} w(t)\, x(t) \sin 2\pi f t\, dt \qquad \text{(Eq. 3)}$$

If we were to generate spectral magnitudes for storage as perceptually salient features, we would use a discrete time approximation to Fourier analysis (since we would store a finite amount of frequency amplitudes and would analyze a finite number of speech values). This approximation is a summation, called the DFT (*discrete Fourier transform*), and is expressed as (including the window function):

$$X_s(k) = \sum_{n=0}^{N-1} w(n)\, x(n)\, e^{-j(2\pi n k/N)}$$

$$= \sum_{n=0}^{N-1} w(n)\, x(n) \left(\cos \frac{2\pi n k}{N} - j \sin \frac{2\pi n k}{N} \right)$$

$$= \sum_{n=0}^{N-1} w(n)\, x(n) \cos \frac{2\pi n k}{N}$$

$$- j \sum_{n=0}^{N-1} w(n)\, x(n) \sin \frac{2\pi n k}{N} \qquad \text{(Eq. 4)}$$

where k is the frequency index, n is the time index, N is the number of points in the time sequence, and the scale of frequency is normalized so that a frequency of 2π corresponds to the frequency that the original time waveform is sampled.

The magnitude of this function then gives a measure of the spectral content of each analyzed segment.

APPENDIX B

DISCRETE TIME SIGNAL PROCESSING

B.1. SAMPLED SIGNALS

Signals are functions over time (or space) that represent the variation of some physical quantity. Examples are the variation of body temperature over time, or the variation of light intensity across the scan line in a television picture. This book has been concerned with speech signals, which are time functions representing variations in air pressure or velocity. These are measured with microphones, which convert the acoustic signal to an electrical signal which may be more conveniently processed (Figure B.1).

While some processing is still done on continuous signals such as these (simple filtering, for instance), almost all speech processing is done on *sampled* versions of those signals. These functions preserve only the signal amplitudes at discrete times. Hence the name *discrete time signal processing* for this field (Figures B.2 and B.3).

Whether the sampled signal may take any value in a continuum (as in switched-capacitor processing) or discrete values only (as in digital processing), the mathematics of the sampling process is the same. A simplified discussion can clarify the effects of the sampling operation.

Sampling is equivalent to the multiplication of the original signal by a periodic pulse waveform. For example, take the time signal $x(t)$ in Figure B.1. We may imagine this to be a graph of the amplified output from a microphone a few inches from a talker enunciating a vowel. By *sampling* this waveform every 100 microseconds, for instance, we have essentially

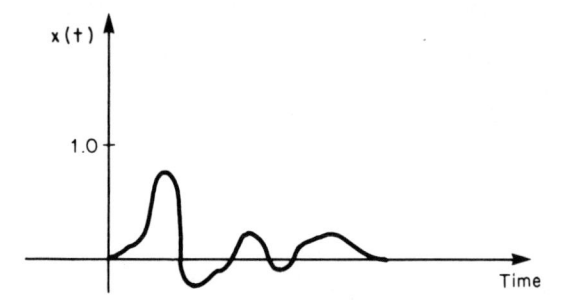

FIG. B.1. A continuous-time waveform.

multiplied $x(t)$ by a periodic sampling waveform, shown in Figure B.2. What is the effect of this sampling?

Of course, the sampled waveform looks quite different. It appears that we have lost all information between sample times. It turns out, however, that it is possible to reconstruct the original continuous signal *if* it is sufficiently band-limited. To explain this, we turn to a *frequency-domain* interpretation.

Suppose that $x(t)$ is a band-limited signal. This means that there is no energy in $x(t)$ at frequencies above some number Fh. Note the fictitious spectrum in Figure B.4.

Now, as in AM (*amplitude modulation*) generation, multiplication of a signal spectrum by a high-frequency carrier yields sum and difference frequencies. This is true because

$$\cos A \times \cos B = 1/2 \cos (A + B) + 1/2 \cos (A - B)$$

Assuming a multiplying signal at $Fc \gg Fh$, we get a spectrum like that in Figure B.5.

A periodic waveform such as our sampling waveform $s(t)$ may be

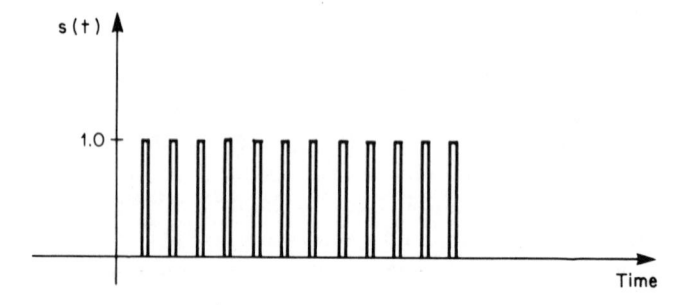

FIG. B.2. Sampling waveform.

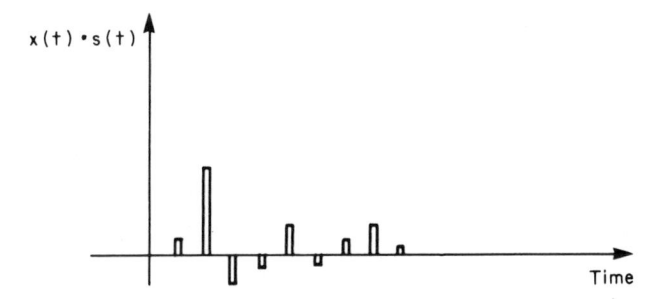

FIG. B.3. Sampled waveform.

expressed as a Fourier summation, that is, a sum of harmonically related cosines with some amplitude and phase. Each one of the cosines in this sampling waveform is multiplied by the message signal to generate sum and difference frequencies. Adding all of these together (including some of the original signal due to the dc content in the sampling signal), we get a total sampled spectrum like that in Figure B.6.

The amplitudes of the heterodyned (transposed in frequency) spectra are shown here as being as high as the original speech amplitude. In actuality, this would only be true for a sampling waveform with "flat" frequency content, such as a train of ideal impulses would have.

These spectral images are called *aliases*. We can readily see from Figure B.6 that $Fc < 2Fh$ would result in an overlap of these images. This effect is called *aliasing distortion*. In general, this degradation is irremediable and must be avoided.

If *Fc is* high enough, that is $Fc > 2Fh$, then the original signal can be recovered *exactly* if we can filter out the higher sum and difference

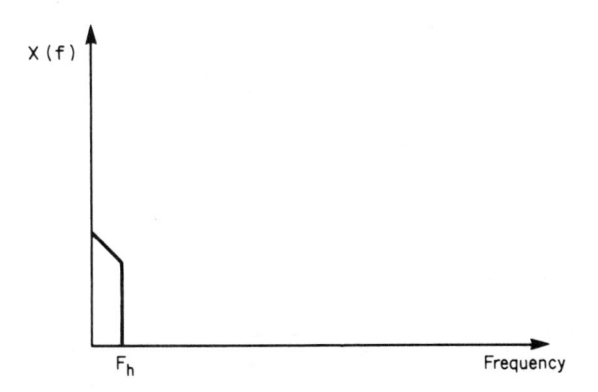

FIG. B.4. Frequency response of continuous waveform.

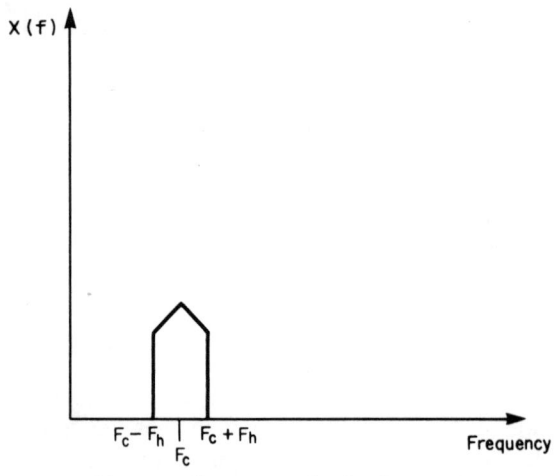

FIG. B.5. Transposed spectrum for fundamental component of $s(t)$.

frequencies. Since the first alias is transposed by the fundamental frequency of the sampling waveform, which is the sampling rate itself, we can state the sampling theorem as:

> A signal which is band-limited to Fh can be exactly reconstructed from samples taken at least as often as $2Fh$, using an ideal low-pass filter.

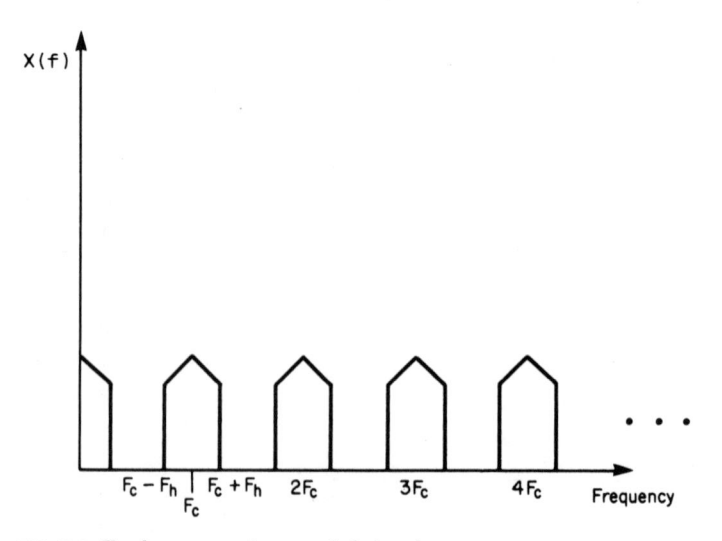

FIG. B.6. Total spectrum for sampled signal.

Of course, ideal low-pass filters are hard to come by,[1] but realizable filters can come amazingly close.

Another even more informal view of this phenomenon is:

If the signal changes slowly enough, and you sample quickly enough, you won't miss anything.

B.2. FILTERING OF DISCRETE TIME SIGNALS

For linear filtering, the output of the system is dependent on the present input and on past inputs (and past outputs if recursive). That is,

$$y(t) = f[x(t - u), y(t - v)]$$

where y = output signal
  x = input signal
  $0 \le u < \infty < v < \infty$
  u,v = time variables indicating memory of system with regard to past inputs and outputs (respectively)

As with a resistor and a capacitor (Figure B.7), a perfect impulse at the input yields

$$y(t) = e^{-t/RC} \quad \text{for } t \ge 0$$

at the output.

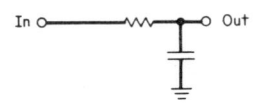

FIG. B.7. RC circuit.

This is a linear system. The output is a superposition of outputs due to the input at each moment in the past. The input at each moment can be approximated as an impulse with size given by the signal amplitude.[2] This means the output of an RC filter like this is a *smeared* version of the input. The output at any time is due partly to the tail of the response to previous portions of the input. In other words, the circuit has memory.

This memory causes sharp, well-defined amplitude changes in the input to be smeared out in time at the output. This kind of hardware acts

---

[1] They require infinite memory and infinite precognition. Certainly a lofty requirement.

[2] Strictly speaking, these impulses have no value outside of a functional operator like an integral. We're not speaking strictly here.

as a *low-pass filter*. That is, its frequency description will reveal that high-frequency signals are attenuated.

It can be shown by sampling theorem arguments that a discrete time implementation of this filter (one which performs the same at sampled moments in time) will perform substantially the same as the continuous time version. This correspondence will not generally be perfect, since the frequency response will usually be nonzero at the half sampling frequency.

If we sampled this response, we would get an output of

$$y(n) = e^{-nT/Rc} \quad \text{for } n \geq 0$$

where T = sampling period.

A discrete time system which had this response to a single nonzero sequence element would be indistinguishable from a continuous time system which was observed at the sample times only.

To get such a response, consider Figure 1.8.

The low-pass filter at the input restricts the bandwidth of the input for sampling theorem considerations. The ADC and DAC are included if the discrete time filter is numerical (digital). Finally, the output low-pass filter removes high-frequency images of the signal spectrum which are a by-product of discrete time implementations.

This complicated arrangement performs filtering comparable to that of a resistor and a capacitor. What a collection of systems just to duplicate those two components! Such a discrete time approach begins to look much more attractive for more complicated filters.

In general, filtering computations are of the form:

$$y(n) = \sum_{k=1}^{N} b_k y(n-k) + \sum_{k=0}^{M} a_k x(n-k)$$

Complicated filtering functions may be flexibly altered with techniques such as these. Thus the interest in the discrete time approach for speech, in which the filter characteristic must be changed many times a second.

APPENDIX C

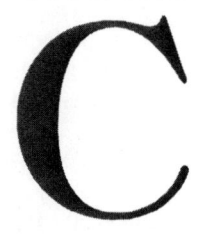

VOCABULARY GENERATION— DIGITALKER® II

C.1. NUTS AND BOLTS

The following is a nuts-and-bolts walk through the process of creating a time-domain vocabulary with the Digitalker® II development system. These procedures are unique to the Mozer process. The techniques of Chapter 6 should, however, be reviewed before attempting to apply them.

1. Classify previously digitized speech segments and mark pitch periods. An automatic process does a first guess at voiced and unvoiced and pitch period for voiced, which is then manually corrected.
2. Normalize speech segments to a convenient length for Mozer analysis (such as 64).
3. Run the automatic phase finder (called "fixer").
4. Examine analysis hard copy for library planning. Consider issues such as rate of change for the sounds and original period lengths.
5. Select unvoiced standard sounds. Usually one *s* will do, but two or three each are required for *t* and *k* (at least one for an initial sound and one for a final sound).
6. Build up a word table with choices for component sounds and period repetitions where possible.
7. Run software to create ROM code to run the synthesizer.

MORE ADVANCED READING

Speech Synthesis; J. Flanagan and L. R. Rabiner, eds.; Dowden, Hutchinson, and Ross; Stroudsburg, Pennsylvania; 1973.
An excellent collection of papers, this book is a compilation of historic work in the research area of speech synthesis.

Speech Analysis, Synthesis and Perception, 2d ed.; J. Flanagan; Springer-Verlag; New York; 1972.
This book is a fairly complete treatment of the science of speech from one of the leading researchers in the field.

Digital Processing of Speech Signals; L. R. Rabiner and R. W. Schafer; Prentice-Hall; Englewood Cliffs, New Jersey; 1978.
This is the only significant text on its topic, and the authors do a superlative job of developing the concepts. A background in engineering mathematics is necessary to appreciate this, however.

Linear Prediction of Speech; J. Markel and A. H. Gray; Springer-Verlag; New York; 1976.
This is the basic reference on LPC for speech researchers.

Theory and Application of Digital Signal Processing; L. R. Rabiner and B. Gold; Prentice-Hall; Englewood Cliffs, New Jersey; 1975.
A basic text and reference on all aspects of DSP (from algorithms to hardware), this book is written in a very clear manner—if you have the background.

Introduction to VLSI Systems; C. Mead and L. Conway; Addison-Wesley; Reading, Massachusetts; 1980.
An excellent introduction to IC design, this book is limited to NMOS designs. It does not go into the technical depth that a circuit-design text would, but it is much more accessible to nonexperts. And it has very pretty pictures.

Intuitive IC Electronics; T. Frederiksen; McGraw-Hill; New York; 1982.
This book provides a very clear introduction to the operating principles of IC electronics.

Audio Cyclopedia; H. M. Tremaine; Howard W. Sams; Indianapolis, Indiana; 1959.
This tome is widely accepted as the definitive reference on all things audio. At the present time, some parts of it are dated (especially the specific electronic circuits described), but the bulk of the entries are as good as ever.

GLOSSARY OF TERMS AND ABBREVIATIONS

A/D analog to digital.
ADC analog to digital converter.
ADPCM adaptive DPCM (step size dependent on signal history).
AI artificial intelligence.
algorithm a method for the solution of a problem, as prescribed by a finite sequence of steps.
alias a copy of a signal spectrum, transposed to a different frequency by the sampling process.
analog any signal representation which ranges over a continuum of values.
antialiasing filter the low-pass filter which restricts the signal bandwidth to less than half of the sampling frequency, thus permitting unique discrete time representation.
articulators elements of the vocal apparatus which determine the principal phonetic features. Main examples are the tongue, jaw, soft palate, hard palate, and teeth.
aspiration noiselike sound caused by turbulence at the glottis (vocal cord opening).
band center the frequency of the peak of a resonant filter.
bandwidth the range between frequencies for which a filter response is 3 dB down from the peak.
barrel shifter a register which can shift by multiple bits in a single cycle.
binary search a search technique which divides the possibilities in half with each step.

Booth Recoding an algorithm for multiplication of multiple bits at a time (usually 2).
CAD computer-aided design. In general, this refers to IC design.
cepstrum the inverse Fourier transform of the log spectrum.
CMOS complementary metal-oxide semiconductor: a process using pairs of n-type and p-type MOS transistors, for which ideally no current flows except during state transitions.
D/A digital to analog.
DAC digital to analog converter.
deemphasis low-pass filtering of synthetic speech to compensate for preemphasis of analysis.
derivative rate of change of a function.
derivative, partial rate of change of a multivariable function with respect to one of the variables.
die a processed chip of silicon.
digital any signal representation which ranges over a finite number of values.
domain, iron-oxide roughly a quadrillion molecules, forming a bar magnet about one-sixtieth the size of the head of a pin.
double-poly an IC fabrication process which has two levels of polycrystalline silicon.
DPCM differential PCM. Most commonly DPCM refers to the PCM encoding of the difference between adjacent samples.
EPROM erasable programmable read-only memory (usually programmable electrically, erasable with ultraviolet light).
EXCLUSIVE-OR a logic function which is true only if the two inputs differ.
filter a system which discriminates between portions of an input signal. In the case of a linear filter, it attenuates and delays the signal depending on the frequency of the component.
filter, bandpass a filter which primarily passes frequency content in some band.
filter, high-pass a filter which primarily passes signals above some frequency.
filter, low-pass a filter which primarily passes signals below some frequency.
formant a resonance of the vocal tract, characterized by its band center.
fricative a speech sound originating (at least in part) from friction and turbulence in the vocal tract. Some examples are f, v, s, and z.
Hamming a raised cosine window with end-point amplitude of 0.08. It is specified by $w(n) = 0.54 - 0.46 \times \cos[2\pi n/(N - 1]$ for n between 0 and $N - 1$.
hanning a raised cosine window with end-point amplitude of 0. It is specified by $w(n) = 0.5 - .5 \times \cos[2\pi n/(N - 1)]$ for n between 0 and $N - 1$.
hardware the physical mechanisms that implement an algorithm.
heuristic rule of thumb.
IC integrated circuit (on a monolithic piece of semiconductor material).
impulse response response of a linear and time-invariant system to a perfect impulse.
kbit 1000 bits.
kbyte kilobyte or 1024 bytes.
kHz kilohertz or 1000 cycles per second.

layout geometric specification of actual devices to be integrated, in the form of drawings or graphics.
lifter a filter in the cepstral domain, filtering the log spectrum as a waveform.
limit comparisons comparisons of an analog signal with some threshold value.
Lissajous figures patterns observed when an oscilloscope in XY mode is driven by two related signals.
LPC linear predictive coding.
LSI large-scale integration (smaller than VLSI, bigger than MSI). Usually LSI refers to an entire function on a chip, such as a 16 × 16 multiplier.
magnitude (spectrum) square root of the energy at each frequency.
main memory computer memory that communicates directly with the CPU.
metal gate the controlling electrode, made of aluminum, in the integrated MOSFETs.
microbar a unit of pressure. The threshold of human hearing is about 0.0002 microbars. One million microbars (one bar) is atmospheric pressure.
microcode a stored program which directly implements control for each CPU instruction.
mils thousandths of an inch.
MSI medium-scale integration (smaller than LSI, bigger than SSI). Usually MSI refers to a register level of implementation on a chip, such as a counter.
n-micron process n usually refers to the channel length of a minimum-sized transistor on a fabrication process.
NMOS N-channel metal-oxide semiconductor. The transistor current is carried by electrons.
overshoot the extent to which the output of a system rises above the final value for a step input.
PARCOR coefficients partial correlation coefficients. The same as reflection coefficients.
PCM pulse-code modulation: digitization of a sampled signal using a simple (usually linear) quantization rule.
periodic repetitive waveform.
phase the delay in degrees for each input frequency.
phone a speech sound.
phoneme a type of speech sound which is treated linguistically as a single entity despite variations.
pipeline a hardware assembly line. The data is processed by each of a number of elements in turn, so that the hardware is (ideally) all being used at any given moment.
pitch the frequency of repetition of a periodic speech signal, corresponding to the frequency of vibration of the vocal cords.
PLA programmable logic array: a regular structure of ANDs and ORs with mask-programmable connections to make arbitrary outputs as sum of ANDed signals.
PMOS P-channel metal-oxide semiconductor. The transistor current is carried by holes (deficit of electrons).
pole the root of the denominator of a linear system function. It arises from feedback in the system and causes peaks in frequency response.

preemphasis   high-pass filtering of natural speech to flatten spectrum for analysis.

process   the steps for the fabrication of integrated circuits on silicon wafers.

PWM   pulse-width modulation. The signal is represented by the duration of the output pulse.

quantize   to approximate by the nearest of a finite collection of values.

radix   the number base for a system or technique. Decimal is radix 10.

RAM   literally random-access memory. But RAM also means that it may be written as well as read by the CPU.

reflection coefficient   parcor coefficient: the coefficients of a lattice filter, which correspond to the reflected volume velocity of the speech waveform at discontinuities in the nonuniform tube model of the vocal tract.

remanence   the amount of magnetic induction left after the removal of an applied magnetic force.

residual   the error between natural speech and the synthetic speech produced by LPC analysis and synthesis. Can also be derived from inverse filtering the natural speech with the LPC parameters.

resonator   a filter which exhibits a single peak in its frequency response. This peak is due to two complex conjugate poles.

ROM   read-only memory.

sampling theorem   any band-limited signal may be perfectly reconstructed from samples of that signal taken at a rate at least twice as high as the highest frequency in the signal.

scaling   in IC terms, refers to the effects of size reduction on device characteristics. In signal processing, scaling refers to shifting the numerical range to avoid overflow or underflow.

silicon gate   use of silicon for the controlling electrode in the integrated MOSFETs.

silicon real estate   IC area.

software   the instructions that run on hardware to implement algorithms.

sound pressure level   the intensity in dB over the threshold of audibility, roughly 0.0002 microbars.

spectrum   the frequency content of a signal.

SSI   small-scale integration. Generally consists of a few logic gates at most.

stable system   classically, a system which has a bounded output for any bounded input. Since all systems which use finite numerical ranges have a bounded output, they are all strictly stable. A more useful definition for such systems is that they are stable if bounded inputs do not result in oscillatory or latched outputs.

standard cell   a CAD representation of an often duplicated block such as RAM or an ALU cell.

successive approximation   a binary search approach to A/D conversion.

transversal filter   a tapped delay line.

TTL   transistor-transistor logic.

uncertainty principle   in general, a rule of interspatial mapping which restricts the resolution in one domain given a certain amount of accuracy in a reciprocal

Glossary of Terms and Abbreviations 173

domain. This has applications in particle physics (momentum vs. position of a particle) and signal processing (frequency vs. time).

unvoiced speech which results from fricative (noiselike) excitation of the vocal tract.

vector a list of numbers, called the components of the vector. The geometric interpretation is of a point in a space dimensioned by the number of components, with each component being the position of the point with respect to one of the dimensions.

VLSI very large-scale integration. There are no firm boundaries between LSI and VLSI, but generally VLSI refers to complete systems (such as a mainframe-complexity CPU, or a complete speech recognizer) on a single chip.

voiced speech which results from vocal (pulselike) excitation of the vocal tract.

wafer a circular slice of single-crystal silicon which is processed to fabricate IC's.

white noise a random signal in which there is no correlation between the signal at any time and the same signal at any other time.

widget singular of widgets.

window a function which is multiplied by a signal segment to reduce end effects in spectral analysis. See Hamming, hanning, Appendix A.

yield the number of good die per wafer, greatly affected by die size and number of critical masking and processing steps.

zero the root of the numerator of a linear system function. Arises from feedforward in the system, causes valleys in frequency response. Also commonly used to describe the sum of negotiable currency actually received from the guy who told you, "The check's in the mail."

INDEX

Acoustics:
    sound absorption, 122–124
    sound isolation, 119–122
    for speech playback, 141
    for speech recordings, 119–125
    standing wave patterns, 124–125
    of vocal tract, 12–16
A/D (*see* Analog-to-digital conversion)
ADC (*see* Analog-to-digital conversion)
Aliasing, 163
Allophones, 26, 108
Analog signal processors, 46–53
Analog-to-digital conversion (A/D; ADC):
    audio requirements for, 136–139
    definition of, 18
    by successive approximation, 52
Analysis (*see* Linear predictive coding, for speech analysis; Mozer speech techniques, analysis)
Antialiasing filters, 134–136
Applications of talking chips, 2–4, 113–114
Articulators, 13

Bessel filter, 135
Bit-rate chart, 8
Bits, 8
Butterworth filter, 135, 136

CAD (computer-aided design), 53–55
Charge-transfer devices (CTDs), 46–48
Chebyshev filter, 135, 136
Chomsky, N., 105–106
Classification of speech sounds, 99–103
    (*See also* Phonetic features)
Coarticulation, 107–108

Codecs, 49–52
    (*See also* Analog-to-digital conversion; Digital-to-analog conversion)
Computer-aided design (CAD), 53–55
Computer architectures, 39–43

DAC (digital-to-analog conversion), 18
Delta modulation, 23
    adaptive, 23–24
Development system for vocabulary generation:
    hardware, 146
    software, 147
Differential pulse-code modulation (DPCM), 22
Digital signal processors (DSPs):
    examples of: Bell DSP, 62–63
    Intel 2920, 60–62
    Texas Instruments TMS320 DSP, 63–65
    types of: general-purpose, 39–44
    special-purpose, 44–45
Digital-to-analog conversion (DAC), 18
Digitalker®:
    the chip, 65–68
    vocabulary generation process, 167
Direct form LPC filters, 28–29
Discrete Fourier transform (DFT), 160
Discrete time signal processing, 161–166
DPCM (differential pulse-code modulation), 22
DSPs (*see* Digital signal processors)
Dudley, Homer, 2

Filter-bank analyzer, 91
Filtering, discrete time, 165–166

175

Index

Filters:
  antialiasing, 134–136
  switched-capacitor, 46–49
Formant synthesizers, 27–28
Formants:
  band centers and bandwidths of, 27
  definition of, 13
  estimation of, 90–92
Fourier analysis, 157–158
"Frankenstein complex," 4
Fricative (see Unvoiced speech)

Gold-Rabiner pitch detector, 103

Harvard computer architecture, 41–43
Hearing:
  model of, 11–12
  (See also Speech synthesis evaluation)

Integrator, switched-capacitor, 48

Lattice LPC filters, 29
Linear predictive coding (LPC):
  for speech analysis, 93–94
  for speech synthesis, 28–31
    direct form filters, 28–29
    lattice filters, 29
Loudspeakers for synthesis playback, 139–141
LPC (see Linear predictive coding)

Microphones:
  directional characteristics of, 125–126
  operational types of, 126
  proper placement of, 127
Mozer speech techniques:
  analysis, 94–99
  synthesis, 24–25
Mu, 17
Mu law, 20
Music synthesis, 149–151

Nyquist rate, 38

Ohm's law of acoustics, 12
  (See also Phase deafness)

PARCOR coefficients (see Reflection coefficients)
Pattern recognition, 101–102
PCM (see Pulse-code modulation)
Phase deafness, 95–96
Phonemes, 26
Phonetic duration and intonation, 112–113
Phonetic features, 106–107
Pipelining, 41, 77
Pitch, physiological definition of, 12
Pitch tracking, 99–103
  (See also Gold-Rabiner pitch detector)
Pulse-code modulation (PCM), 20–21
  differential (DPCM), 22

Quantization, 19–20

Radiation characteristic, 14
Reflection coefficients, 29
Resonances:
  in rooms, 124
  in vocal tract, 13–16, 27
  (See also Formants)
Rules (see Synthesis by rule)

Sampling theorem, 37–38, 164
Short-term spectrum, 11, 157–160
Signal processing (see Analog signal processors; Digital signal processors)
Signals, 9, 161
  digital, 38
  discrete-time, 161–165
Silicon compiler, 53–54
  MACPITTS, 54
Silicon "real estate," 45, 59
Sound, definition of, 9
Sound pressure level, 119
Spectrogram, 102
Spectrum, short-term, 11, 157–160
Speech production model:
  enhanced, 32–33
  simplified, 12–13
Speech recognition, 152–155
Speech recordings for analysis:
  A/D conversion in, 136–139
  filters in, 134–136
  microphones in, 125–127
  room acoustics in, 119–125
  talker considerations in, 117–119
  tape recorders in, 127–134

Index

Speech sounds, classification of, 99–103
   (*See also* Phonetic features)
Speech spectrum estimation, 89–99
   cepstral liftering for, 91–92
   filter-bank analyzer for, 91
   formant tracking for, 90–92
   linear prediction for, 93–94
   Mozer DFT approach to, 94–99
   peak picking for, 91
Speech synthesis, residual-driven, 148
Speech synthesis evaluation, 139–143
Stop consonants:
   types of, 106
   use of, in speech synthesis evaluation, 142
   (*See also* Phonemes)
Successive approximation A/D technique, 52
Switched-capacitor filters, 46–49
Switched-capacitor synthesizers, 52–53, 84–87
Synthesis by rule, 105–114
Synthesizers:
   dedicated analog: AMI, 84
      Votrax, 85–87
   dedicated digital: GI IC, 82–83
      GI system, 79–82
      Hitachi, 83–84
      National's Digitalker®, 65–68
      National's Microtalker, 70–73
      Sanyo, 83
      Sharp, 68–70
      Speak and Spell (IC), 75–78
      Speak and Spell (product), 73–75
      Telesensory Systems, 83

Tape recording, 127–134
   alignment, 129–132
   dropouts, 128

Tape recording (*Cont.*):
   dynamic range, 128–129
   irrevocable errors, 132–134
   print-through, 129
Text-to-speech systems, 10–11
   (*See also* Synthesis by rule)
Toasters, talking, 3

Unvoiced speech, 13
   (*See also* Phonetic features)

Vocabulary generation development system:
   hardware, 146
   software, 147
Vocal tract as an organ pipe, 13–14
Vocoder:
   Berkeley implementation, 55–56
   channel, 92
VODER, 1–2
Voiced fricatives, 32
Voiced speech, 12
   (*See also* Phonetic features)
Voiced-unvoiced determination (*see* Classification of speech sounds)
Von Neumann computer architecture, 40–41

Waveform, 9
Waveform coding, 18
Waveform prediction, 21–23
Widget, 44
Windowing, 158–160

Yield, 59

ABOUT THE AUTHOR

Nelson Morgan began his speech career at age 10 by recording the evening news and editing the reports to his liking. He still claims the ability to fabricate any desired message given a few minutes of taped speech and a razor blade.

After extensive work as an audio engineer, Morgan returned to school to get his Ph.D. from UC-Berkeley. He received the usual honors (Phi Beta Kappa[1], Eta Kappa Nu, etc.), and has several patents granted or pending, all in the area of discrete-time signal processing hardware. More recently, he has worked in the areas of artificial reverberation, coding and evaluation of synthetic speech, signal processing architectures, and pattern recognition as applied to speech analysis. He currently heads up National Semiconductor's speech synthesis research and development effort.

He admits to having written most of this book (although he bids us not forget IC designer-extraordinaire Jake Buurma, who wrote almost all of chapter 3, and speech-by-rule impresario Lloyd Rice, who contributed chapter 5).

---

[1] Morgan is currently under investigation for revealing the secret handshake to noninitiates. No charges have as yet been filed.